The Moral Case for Profit Maximization

Capitalist Thought: Studies in Philosophy, Politics, and Economics

Series Editor: Edward W. Younkins, Wheeling Jesuit University

Mission Statement

This book series is devoted to studying the foundations of capitalism from a number of academic disciplines including, but not limited to, philosophy, political science, economics, law, literature, and history. Recognizing the expansion of the boundaries of economics, this series particularly welcomes proposals for monographs and edited collections that focus on topics from transdisciplinary, interdisciplinary, and multidisciplinary perspectives. Lexington Books will consider a wide range of conceptual, empirical, and methodological submissions, Works in this series will tend to synthesize and integrate knowledge and to build bridges within and between disciplines. They will be of vital concern to academicians, business people, and others in the debate about the proper role of capitalism, business, and business people in economic society.

Advisory Board

Books in Series

Water Capitalism: The Case for Privatizing Oceans, Rivers, Lakes, and Aquifers, by Walter E. Block and Peter Lothian Nelson

Capitalism and Commerce in Imaginative Literature: Perspectives on Business from Novels and Plays, edited by Edward W. Younkins

Pride and Profit: The Intersection of Jane Austen and Adam Smith, by Cecil E. Bohanon and Michelle Albert Vachris

The Seen, the Unseen, and the Unrealized: How Regulations Affect Our Everyday Lives, by Per L. Bylund

Global Economics: A Holistic Approach, by Clifford F. Thies

On the Private and Public Virtues of an Honorable Entrepreneur: Preventing a Separation of the Honorable and the Useful, by Felix R. Livingston

Perspectives on Ayn Rand's Contributions to Economic and Business Thought, by Edward W. Younkins

The Dialectics of Liberty: Exploring the Context of Human Freedom, by Roger E. Bissell, Chris Matthew Sciabarra, and Edward W. Younkins

Markets against Modernity: Ecological Irrationality, Public and Private, by Ryan H. Murphy

The Moral Case for Profit Maximization, by Robert White

The Moral Case for Profit Maximization

Robert White

LEXINGTON BOOKS
Lanham • Boulder • New York • London

Published by Lexington Books
An imprint of The Rowman & Littlefield Publishing Group, Inc.
4501 Forbes Boulevard, Suite 200, Lanham, Maryland 20706
www.rowman.com

6 Tinworth Street, London SE11 5AL, United Kingdom

British Library Cataloguing in Publication Information Available

Library of Congress Cataloging-in-Publication Data

Names: White, Robert, 1973- author.
Title: The moral case for profit maximization / Robert White.
Description: Lanham : Lexington Books, [2020] | Series: Capitalist thought: studies in philosophy, politics, and economics | Includes bibliographical references and index. | Summary: "The Moral Case for Profit Maximization considers the moral status of profit maximization, arguing that profit maximization is moral when businessmen seek to maximize profit by forming values and cultivating the virtues"-- Provided by publisher.
Identifiers: LCCN 2020001262 (print) | LCCN 2020001263 (ebook) | ISBN 9781498542630 (cloth) | ISBN 9781498542654 (pbk) ISBN 9781498542647 (epub)
Subjects: LCSH: Profit--Moral and ethical aspects. | Profit--Philosophy. | Business ethics.
Classification: LCC HB601 .W47 2020 (print) | LCC HB601 (ebook) | DDC 174/.4--dc23
LC record available at https://lccn.loc.gov/2020001262
LC ebook record available at https://lccn.loc.gov/2020001263

To Stefan, my son

Contents

Introduction

It is a Sunday morning in a remote New Zealand town. A teenager wakes to rain pounding the roof. He decides to spend the day reading a novel. He opens the Kindle Store on his laptop and reviews Amazon's recommendations, which are tailored to his interests. He comes across a novel that looks interesting, clicks "Buy Now," and flips open his Kindle Paperwhite. The Kindle connects to Amazon in the United States, and a few seconds later, the novel is downloaded, ready to read.

This teenager bought a Kindle because he judged it to be of value. Without a Kindle, a book from the United States would take at least a week to arrive. The local bookstore does not stock many novels. He enjoys reading novels on electronic paper because the ink mimics regular books. He likes being able to choose from a catalog of over six million titles.

Amazon finds the Kindle profitable because other people make similar value judgments. An academic judges the Kindle to be of value because he can carry his research library to conferences, giving him ready access to his tools of trade. A soon-to-be mother judges the Kindle to be of value because she can download books on infant care. A sports coach judges the Kindle to be of value because she can download books on the latest coaching techniques.

The Kindle's profitability is how Amazon knows that its customers judge the Kindle to be of value. If Amazon's customers did not value the Kindle, it would make a loss.

These value judgments are not subjective. Books are of objective value because they give us access to the thoughts of other people across time and space. Aristotle's books bring us into contact with his thinking, even though he died over two thousand years ago. Accessing books through a Kindle is an objective value because electronic books are portable and can be downloaded from anywhere there is an internet connection.

Consider the thinking required to create the Kindle. The Kindle is a technological achievement. Scientists needed to create minuscule capsules containing black dye that can be forced to the top or bottom of the capsule through the application of positive or negative charges. The Kindle is also a value achievement. Amazon's executives had to conceive of how electronic paper can benefit their customers. Moreover, Amazon's executives needed to conceive of the ecosystem needed for electronic paper to be of value. Without the Kindle Store, electronic paper would be nothing more than a technological curiosity.

An innovator must cultivate a virtuous character to discover the physical principles that make an electrophoretic display possible and to conceive of how such a display can serve human life. Among other traits, innovators need to cultivate a commitment to the absolutism of the facts of reality.

This book argues that profit maximization is moral when businessmen seek to create goods or services that are of objective value.

DOING GOOD WHILE DOING WELL

Proponents of corporate social responsibility (CSR) claim that "businessmen can do good while doing well."[1] CSR's proponents cite the examples below as instances of businessmen "doing good." As you read this list, consider the examples that are *not* cited.

- Avon does good when it donates a percentage of sales from its "pink ribbon" products to the Avon Foundation, which funds breast cancer research.[2]
- Pampers did good when it joined the "Back to Sleep" campaign to encourage parents to put infants on their backs to sleep.[3]
- Ben & Jerry's did good when it created a campaign to raise awareness of the threat posed by global warming.[4]
- General Motors did good when it provided vans to transport presenters for Mothers Against Drunk Driving (MADD) programs.[5]
- Coca-Cola did good when it worked with its bottlers in Africa to battle AIDS by offering workers free condoms.[6]
- Hasbro does good by allowing its workers to take four hours a month of paid time off to do community service.[7]
- Timberland does good when it expects its salespeople and executives to take part in service projects, such as building affordable housing or a computer room for a school.[8]

- Cisco's former CEO, John Morgridge, did good when he matched employee gifts to local food banks.[9]

The goods or services that these businesses produce are not mentioned as examples of these businesses doing good. The assumption is that producing goods and services is "doing well" not "doing good." Had CSR's proponents regarded profit maximization as good, then among these examples would have been Avon's cosmetics, Pampers's disposable diapers, Ben & Jerry's ice cream, General Motors's cars, Coca-Cola's beverages, Hasbro's toys and games, Timberland's outdoor clothing, and Cisco's networking services.

Business ethics is unusual in the field of professional ethics in that it does not regard its own profession as ethical. Business ethicists do not accept the bromide that business ethics is an oxymoron. They claim that businessmen can be ethical. However, being ethical, for business ethicists, typically means expecting businessmen to engage in non-business activities. They assume that there is no ethics in the pursuit of profit as such.

Courses on medical ethics instruct students on how to be ethical in the practice of medicine. These courses do not tell students that to be ethical doctors they need to raise awareness of global warming, build affordable housing, or match employee gifts to food banks. Proponents of medical social responsibility do not assure students that they can do good while practicing medicine. Medical ethics is about ethics *in* medicine because medical ethicists recognize that practicing medicine is "doing good."

Business ethicists do not generally recognize that maximizing profit is "doing good." Consequently, business ethicists have been concerned with persuading students that there are things more important than profit. This approach to business ethics is wrong. Business ethics should be like medical ethics in that business students need to learn how to maximize profit ethically. To do so, business ethicists need to appreciate the relationship between profit, value, and virtue, which is the subject of this book.

AN ANTI-PROFIT CULTURE

Popular culture is littered with attacks on profit. The standard cultural evaluation of profit maximization was immortalized in the character of Gordon Gekko from the movie *Wall Street*. Gekko is the movie's villain. He tells shareholders, in an oft-quoted scene, "Greed . . . is good. Greed is right. Greed works. Greed clarifies, cuts through, and captures the essence of the evolutionary spirit. . . . Greed for life, for money, for love, knowledge—has marked the upward surge of mankind."[10]

The American Film Institute named Gekko number twenty-four on its top fifty movie villains of all time. Why? Did Gekko commit mass murder? No.

He did not kill anyone. Did Gekko rob banks? No. He did not steal anything. Did Gekko run a Ponzi scheme? No. He did not con anyone. Gekko is one of the top-ranked villains in movie history because he made a speech defending greed for profit.

The Wolf of Wall Street dramatizes the true story of Jordan Belfort, a financier turned scam artist.[11] Belfort establishes a stock brokerage firm that runs a pump and dump scam, after being fired from a legitimate firm. Belfort's brokers purchase cheap stock, talk up the price, and then dump the stock at a price significantly higher than the stock's actual value. Belfort and his brokers get significant returns while investors lose their life savings. Belfort's financial successes lead him to embrace animalistic pleasures such as drugs and mindless sex. Belfort's lifestyle is presented as that of a profit-maximizing businessman.[12]

Star Trek's producers created a fictional culture based on the morality of profit maximization. The Ferengi are an alien species devoted to the pursuit of profit. Devout Ferengi make pilgrimages to their holy site, Earth's Wall Street.[13] Ferengi would admire someone prepared to sell his or her mother because so doing would demonstrate his or her commitment to profit maximization above all else.[14]

Newspapers announce bank profits in a tone appropriate to a burglary report. Barry Soper asserts, in an op-ed for the New Zealand Herald, that New Zealanders "have themselves to blame for *obscene* bank profits" (emphasis mine). He writes: "The eye-watering profits sucked out of Kiwi households every year are obscene and this year's no exception." He recommends that New Zealanders bank with Kiwibank because it makes significantly less profit than other banks.[15] An article in the same newspaper about a report damning the life insurance industry's culture opens with the following headline: "Companies choose profit over people."[16]

There was a time, not so long ago, when politicians would have been ashamed to be associated with socialism. Today, a new generation of politicians stand as proud opponents of profit, wearing their anti-capitalism on their shirt sleeves. Alexandria Ocasio-Cortez is a member of the United States House of Representatives and a member of the Democratic Socialists of America. She has called for a 70 percent marginal tax rate for incomes above $10 million. While campaigning for the House, Ocasio-Cortez criticized the United States of America for being a hypercapitalist country in which people seek "profit at any cost."[17]

Jacinda Ardern is the prime minister of New Zealand and a former president of the International Union of Socialist Youth. She declared capitalism "a blatant failure" shortly after her party's election.[18]

There is an urgent need to understand the moral status of profit maximization because an anti-profit culture feeds anti-profit politicians, who wield the political power to cripple the profit-maximizing businessmen who have raised our standard of living to unprecedented levels.

OUTLINE

You will be able to answer the following questions by the conclusion of this book: What is profit? What is the difference between "profit," "surplus," and "loot"? What conditions must profit meet to be moral? What is objective value? What virtues characterize a life of production? What is the historical evidence for the relationship between profit, value, and virtue? Can profit maximization be defended on economic grounds alone? Should businessmen be socially responsible?

Chapter 1 locates the debate over the morality of profit maximization. It identifies the issues that any argument for or against the morality of profit maximization must address. This chapter demonstrates that a moral case for profit maximization must address the value status of goods and services and the virtues of businessmen.

Chapter 2 explains why profit maximization is moral. It argues that profit maximization is moral when businessmen seek to profit from conceptualizing objective values. This chapter explains what an objective value is, the relationship between values and virtues, the relationship between profit and objective values, and why businessmen should seek to *maximize* profit. This chapter also identifies the conditions under which profit maximization is immoral.

Traditionally, profit maximization is defended on the grounds that it incentivizes the production of goods and services. In this view, businessmen do not need to be virtuous to maximize profit, so long as they deliver the goods. This book challenges the traditional defenses of profit maximization by focusing on the role of the mind in the production of goods and services.

This book is not the first to recognize the relationship between profit and virtue. Jaana Woiceshyn has written an insightful book demonstrating how virtue redounds to the bottom line.[19] Though this book concurs with most of Woiceshyn's conclusions, she does not identify what it is about profit that requires businessmen to be virtuous. This book argues that businessmen must be virtuous to maximize profit because the virtues are needed to conceptualize objective value.

Chapters 3 and 4 provide historical evidence for the morality of profit maximization. Chapter 3 provides evidence for the role of value judgments in the creation of the wheel, the refrigerator, and the shipping container. Chapter 4 provides evidence for the role of the virtues in the biographies of three superlative businessmen—J. P. Morgan, John D. Rockefeller, and Thomas

Edison. Chapter 4 also provides evidence, from the biography of Louis Pasteur, that the virtues are needed to create value across all fields.

Chapter 5 considers common confusions about profit maximization in light of the foregoing argument. This chapter argues that profit maximization does *not* require businessmen to set aside non-profit considerations, to prioritize profit above other values, or to extend a "market mentality" to every area of human life. Moreover, this chapter argues that the moral case for profit maximization does not imply that businessmen are necessarily moral or that everyone has a duty to maximize profit.

Chapter 6 considers the shortcomings of Elaine Sternberg's and Milton Friedman's classic defenses of profit maximization. This chapter also explains why profit maximization cannot be defended on economic grounds alone.

Chapter 7 identifies a fundamental and irresolvable flaw in CSR, namely that CSR is an invalid concept. CSR's proponents think that businessmen who choose social responsibility over profit maximization take the moral high road. They are wrong. Business ethics proper is to be found in understanding businessmen's role in creating objective value.

PROFIT MAXIMIZATION IN THE CONCRETE

People generally recognize the contribution that particular goods and services make to their life. People do not, generally, grasp the identity between the morality of these contributions and the morality of profit maximization. People grasp profit maximization's morality in the *concrete* but not in the *abstract.*

Consider the "double thank-you" moments in your life.[20] You purchase a milk bottle from a grocery store. The shopkeeper thanks you as you hand over the money. You thank the shopkeeper as he hands over the milk. You thank each other because you both benefit. These double thank-you moments can be observed throughout the economic system.

There is no such *thing* as profit. Profit is not something that we can see or touch. "Profit" conceptualizes specific facts of reality at a high level of abstraction. We can recognize profit all around us only after we grasp the facts that profit conceptualizes.

Causality is also something that we cannot see or touch. We need first to understand that causality conceptualizes the fact that things act in accordance with their natures before we will see causality in an infant dropping a spoon from his highchair, in a dog chasing after a ball, in the stock market crashing, and in a student passing her final exams.

Once we understand the moral basis of profit, we will see the evidence for the morality of profit maximization everywhere. The evidence is to be found in the morality of a mother purchasing pizza for her family's dinner, a young man purchasing a rose for his lover, a brilliant philosopher sitting in a movie theater watching *Whiplash*, a young girl's parents purchasing a soccer ball for her birthday, a family purchasing a world cruise, a young man purchasing sunglasses, and a middle-aged woman purchasing a raincoat.

We do not establish the morality of these things and then, as a separate task, establish the morality of profit maximization. The morality of profit maximization *is* the morality of these things grasped in the abstract.

THE ONE IN THE MANY

The moral case for profit maximization is made by seeking to grasp the *one in the many*. Leonard Peikoff argues, in *The DIM Hypothesis*, that the brilliance of the Classical Greeks consists of their conceiving a new method of cognition. Previous peoples saw a multitude of objects. The Classical Greeks were the first in recorded history to ask what these objects have in common. The Classical Greeks conceived of *integration* (or *synthesis*).[21]

We observe, all around us, the particular contributions that particular goods and services make to the lives of particular individuals. Pointing out the benefits of a haircut, a microwave oven, or Google Maps would not strike most people as controversial. Profit maximization is controversial because people do not recognize profit maximization as the *integration* (or *synthesis*) of these benefits.

RECOGNIZING BUSINESSMEN

This book is a "thank-you" note to the businessmen who have contributed to my life and the lives of the people for whom I care. I am not a businessman. I am a modestly paid academic. Going into business does not appeal to me. I did not write this book as an impartial observer, however. I am partial to the businessmen who contribute to my life. I wrote a book defending profit maximization for the deeply personal reason that I want to protect the freedom of profit-maximizing businessmen to continue making my world a glorious place to live.

You might not think that businessmen need to be thanked. You would be wrong. In Ayn Rand's *Atlas Shrugged*, a successful businesswoman is told that if she were to meet the great men of history in heaven, there is something she would want to hear from them, but did not realize she needed. She would want them to say, "Well done."[22] Successful businessmen do not suffer *material* deprivation; they suffer *moral* deprivation. A person who has done good needs his work to be recognized by others, otherwise he feels invisible to the world. One of this book's goals is to bring to light the unrecognized and unacknowledged good that businessmen do.

BUSINESS STUDENTS

This book was written for people who have an interest in understanding the relationship between ethics and profit. This need is especially urgent among business students. The lack of professional idealism among business students is frightening. Business students are implicitly taught that there is no ethics in profit maximization. Consequently, students who care about ethics are suspicious of profit, and students who care about profit are suspicious of ethics. Generations of students are taught that ethics impedes the goal of profit maximization. The fault lies with business programs that focus on the technical skills needed to succeed in business while implying that these skills serve a morally suspect end.[23] This book provides students with the education that their business programs are missing. I hope that students who care about ethics and students who care about profit will come to appreciate the need to integrate the two.

This book will also be of interest to businessmen who would like to understand their profession better. Successful businessmen typically understand their profession in the concrete. They do not necessarily understand the moral significance of their achievements, however. I hope that businessmen who read this book will gain a greater appreciation of the work to which they have devoted their lives.

Traditional business ethicists are unlikely to sympathize with this book. Sadly, too many see profit maximization as the enemy. For evidence, observe the vicious reaction to Friedman's mild defense of profit maximization, discussed in chapter 6. Ethicists suspicious of profit do not appreciate the relationship between profit, value, and virtue. I hope that traditional business ethicists will be open to this possibility by the conclusion of this book, even if they disagree with my specific arguments.

MY STUDENTS

I taught a course on business ethics at the American University in Bulgaria for almost ten years. This course was required as part of the business administration major, the most popular major at the university. Students had to write two essays and meet with me twice for each essay. Over these ten years, I estimate that I taught around two thousand students, read around four thousand essays, and held around eight thousand one-on-one meetings with students in which we discussed the morality of profit maximization. These meetings were the genesis of this book. Though this book does not replicate the content of my business ethics course, former students will recognize many of the examples.

In fall 2018, I taught a course titled "The Nature and Morality of Profit Maximization." The textbook was an early draft of this book. Students had to submit critical questions about each chapter before class, and the final assessment was an essay critiquing one of the chapters. A well-written book does not need commentary from the author to explain its meaning. The feedback from these students helped me to understand which arguments were unclear to someone who did not share my context of knowledge.

ACKNOWLEDGMENTS

I want to thank A. M. Endres from the University of Auckland for his enduring support of my work over the years, and my wife and son, Yuliya and Stefan, for enriching my life.

Lastly, I want to thank Edward W. Younkins for creating the Capitalist Thought series and for suggesting to me that I should propose a book.

NOTES

1. Variants of this statement appear throughout the CSR literature. See, for example, Archie B. Carroll et al., *Corporate Responsibility: The American Experience* (Cambridge: Cambridge University Press, 2012), 297; Andrew Crane et al., "Conclusion," in *The Oxford Handbook of Corporate Social Responsibility*, ed. Andrew Crane et al. (Oxford: Oxford University Press, 2009), 570; J. J. Asongu, *Strategic Corporate Social Responsibility in Practice* (Lawrenceville, GA: Greenview Publishing Company, 2007), 111; Mary Ann Leeper, "Social Commitment and Entrepreneurship," in *Women in Business: The Changing Face of Leadership*, ed. Patricia Werhane et al. (Westport, CT: Praeger Publishers, 2007), 99; Brian Nicholson, Ron Babin, and Mary C. Lacity, "Introduction," in *Socially Responsible Outsourcing: Global Sourcing with Social Impact*, ed. Brian Nicholson, Ron Babin, and Mary C. Lacity (London: Palgrave Macmillan UK, 2016), 4–5.
2. Philip Kotler and Nancy Lee, *Corporate Social Responsibility: Doing the Most Good for Your Company and Your Cause* (Hoboken, NJ: John Wiley & Sons, 2005), 89–91.
3. Ibid., 121–22.
4. Ibid., 55–56.
5. Ibid., 161–62.
6. Ibid., 214.
7. Marc Benioff and Karen Southwick, *Compassionate Capitalism: How Corporations Can Make Doing Good an Integral Part of Doing Well* (Franklin Lakes, NJ: Career Press, 2004), 10.
8. Ibid., 26.
9. Ibid., 29.
10. Oliver Stone and Stanley Weiser, *Wall Street* (American Entertainment Partners, 1987), 1 hour, 18 min.
11. Terence Winter, *The Wolf of Wall Street* (Red Granite Pictures, 2013).
12. I prefer the locution "business-*man*" to "business-*person*." The well-meaning attempt to achieve gender neutrality in writing often does more to obscure the fact that we are talking about individuals than to avoid gender bias. Historically, the word "man" denoted the thinking animal, not a male human being. Women are thinking animals. Women, therefore, are also

men. As Jerry Kirkpatrick explains, the danger with replacing "man" with supposedly gender-neutral alternatives is that we excise the concept of the rational animal from the English language. Jerry Kirkpatrick, *In Defense of Advertising: Arguments from Reason, Ethical Egoism, and Laissez-Faire Capitalism* (Claremont, CA: TLJ Books, 2007), 17–18. Women *are* business-*men*, and my observations about businessmen apply to all human beings, regardless of gender, race, or nationality.

13. Mark E. Lasbury, *The Realization of Star Trek Technologies: The Science, Not Fiction, Behind Brain Implants, Plasma Shields, Quantum Computing, and More* (Switzerland: Springer 2017), 67–68.

14. John Vornholt, *Antimatter* (New York: Pocket Books, 1994), 19.

15. Barry Soper, "Kiwis Have Themselves to Blame for Obscene Bank Profits," *New Zealand Herald* (6 November 2018).

16. Jamie Gray, "Insurance Company Boards Must Act Now to Fix Culture and Conduct, FMA Boss Says," *New Zealand Herald* (29 January 2019). The headline about companies choosing profit over people appeared on the front page of the website linking to the article.

17. See Ocasio-Cortez's interview on *Firing Line with Margaret Hoover*, https://youtu.be/AjH9FAXkPSo. The United States of America, like almost every other country in the world today, is a mixed economy.

18. Chris Baynes, "New Zealand's New Prime Minister Calls Capitalism a 'Blatant Failure,'" *Independent* (21 October 2017). Economics refutes the unfounded assertions of Ocasio-Cortez and Ardern. See George Reisman, *Capitalism: A Treatise on Economics* (Ottawa, IL: Jameson Books, 1998); Thomas Sowell, *Basic Economics: A Common Sense Guide to the Economy*, 4th ed. (New York: Basic Books, 2011); Brian P. Simpson, *Markets Don't Fail!* (Lanham, MD: Lexington Books, 2005).

19. Jaana Woiceshyn, *How to Be Profitable and Moral: A Rational Egoist Approach to Business* (Lanham, MD: Hamilton Books, 2012).

20. John Stossel coined the phrase "double thank-you" to describe the mutual benefits of economic trade. John Stossel, *No, They Can't: Why Government Fails—But Individuals Succeed* (New York: Threshold Editions, 2012), 53.

21. Leonard Peikoff, *The DIM Hypothesis: Why the Lights of the West Are Going Out* (New York: New American Library, 2012), 3–4.

22. Ayn Rand, *Atlas Shrugged* (New York: Signet, 1992), 679.

23. John A. Allison, "Foreword," in *Perspectives on Ayn Rand's Contributions to Economic and Business Thought*, ed. Edward W. Younkins (Lanham, MD: Lexington Books, 2018), xiii.

Chapter One

The Questions of Profit Maximization

This chapter identifies the questions that a case for the morality of profit maximization must answer. It does not make a moral case for profit maximization. Instead, it is concerned with a prior issue, namely the questions that such a case must address.

This chapter argues that the debate over the morality of profit maximization must address the value of *what* businessmen produce and the virtue of *how* they produce it. This chapter shall proceed by identifying the facts that give rise to the concept of "profit" through an analysis of its antecedent concepts. In particular, this chapter shall analyze the concepts of *goods*, *services*, *creation*, *value*, *money*, and *price*.

This chapter also considers the distinction between defending the morality of *profit* and the morality of profit *maximization* and explains why contemporary business ethics is not concerned with the *what* and *how* questions.

CONCEPTUALIZING PROFIT

To understand the questions that the morality of profit maximization raises, we must first know what businessmen maximize when they maximize profit.

In accounting, "profit" refers to the excess of revenues over expenses. A boy opens a lemonade stand on the lawn outside of his parents' house. Neighbors purchase the boy's lemonade, and, at the day's end, his revenues total $200. The boy's expenses (the lemons, the sugar, the water, a jug in which to store the lemonade, paper cups, plywood for the stand, and so on) total $65. The difference is an excess of $135. This excess is the boy's *profit*.

The word "profit" is regularly thrown around with little regard to the facts that the concept signifies. As a consequence, "profit" is often used to classify activities essentially different from a boy selling lemonade. Greenpeace and the Red Cross are sometimes cited as examples of profit-maximizing businesses, even though they are *non-profit* organizations. Enron and WorldCom are also sometimes cited as examples of profit-maximizing businesses, even though their profits were a chimerical fraud.[1]

In *The Godfather Trilogy*, Mafioso refer to themselves as businessmen. In the first *Godfather* movie, Virgil "The Turk" Sollozzo, a narcotics peddler, says, "I don't like violence. . . . I'm a businessman. Blood is a big expense."[2] Similarly, in the second movie, Michael Corleone asserts, "All our people are businessmen; their loyalty is based on that."[3] Mafioso see themselves as businessmen who sell protection services, provide arbitration between criminals, and enforce contracts.

"Profit" is thus used to denote the excess *produced* by a boy selling lemonade to his neighbors, the excess *obtained* by non-profit organizations, the excess *obtained* by fraudsters, and the excess *obtained* by a crime syndicate. As the children's television series *Sesame Street* used to lyricize, one of these things is not like the others.

Accountants recognize that "excess" is a broader concept than "profit." In accounting, different language is used to describe the accounts of businesses and non-profits. When preparing a business's accounts, the excess is called *profit*. When preparing a non-profit's accounts, the excess is called *surplus*.[4] This difference is not semantic. The shift in language acknowledges that "profit" and "surplus" conceptualize different facts of reality.

PROFIT IS A HIGH-LEVEL CONCEPT

To understand how "profit" can be so widely used yet not well understood, one must first understand the difference between first-level and high-level concepts.[5] A first-level concept is a conceptualization of that which we can directly see or touch. "Chair" is a first-level concept, because we can see and touch chairs. If a non-English speaker were to ask, "What is a 'chair'?" you could point to a chair and say, "By 'chair' I mean *this*." One cannot similarly see or touch the units of high-level concepts. High-level concepts are conceptualizations of first-level concepts. The difference between first-level and high-level concepts is the distance from direct perception. "Furniture" is a high-level concept. One cannot see or touch furniture; one can see or touch chairs, tables, stools, beds, wardrobes, and so forth. Concepts such as "justice," "love," and "gravity" are much higher up the conceptual chain. One can observe an apple falling from a tree. Conceptual knowledge is needed to identify that the falling apple is an instance of the law of gravity. Seeing an apple fall is insufficient. For centuries, people saw apples falling from trees. It took a person with Isaac Newton's knowledge to see gravity at work in the fall of an apple.

We induce *first*-level concepts from the direct observation of reality when we are children. We do not typically induce *high*-level concepts from the direct observation of reality. Instead, we borrow our high-level concepts from other people. Tragically, we are not usually taught to grasp the facts that initially give rise to high-level concepts, so the concepts become disconnected from the facts that ground them.[6]

We would think it strange for a person to use the word "chair" to refer to chairs, tables, stools, beds, wardrobes, and other types of furniture. Nevertheless, people regularly misuse high-level concepts in this way. We think a loose use of the word "chair" odd because our concept "chair" is thoroughly integrated with its existential referents. We do not think the similar misuse of high-level concepts odd, because these concepts float in our mind, sometimes referring to *this*, and other times to *that*.

Consider the misuse of "capitalism" as one example. Used precisely, the concept "capitalism" signifies *laissez-faire* capitalism, the complete separation of state and economics. "Capitalism" does not denote a mixed economy, which is a mixture of capitalism and statism. Many people, nevertheless, think of the United States of America as a capitalist country, even though, in economic terms, the United States today is significantly less free than countries that the same people would never dream of labeling capitalist, such as Canada and the Netherlands.[7] The United States is capitalist in certain respects and statist in other respects. Taken as a whole, the United States is a mixed economy. When "capitalism" is used to denote mixed economies, we empty the concept of meaning.

We encounter instances of profit every day. We might be businessmen. We might work for businessmen. We might purchase goods and services from businessmen. We might read about businessmen in the newspaper, or hear about businessmen on television. These instances do not impress the nature of profit on our minds. "Profit" is a conceptualization of specific facts of reality, and we need to engage in mental work to grasp the facts that the concept of "profit" conceptualizes.

"Profit" denotes specific facts of reality. When discussing profit maximization's morality, we need to ensure that we are discussing the morality of *profit* maximization and not the morality of maximizing something else.

ECONOMIC GOODS

High-level concepts presuppose lower-level concepts. To understand what profit is, we must first understand the lower-level concepts upon which the concept of "profit" depends. Let us begin with the concepts of *goods* and *services*.

A *good* is an entity, a thing that one can see or touch.[8] There are *economic* goods and *free* goods. A free good is a beneficial thing that does not require human effort to be of benefit, such as air and sunlight. An economic good is a beneficial thing that requires human effort to be of benefit.[9] "Profit" is concerned with economic goods. "Goods," from now on, shall refer to *economic goods* unless the context indicates otherwise. Economic goods include paperclips, milk cartons, swimming pools, vitamin tablets, nail clippers, the shirt on your back, an infant's pacifier, and all of the things one can purchase from Amazon or Walmart. Economic goods also include things that we do not consume ourselves, but which go into making the goods we consume or providing the services we purchase, such as a barber's chair, the sign outside the local cinema, the leaves in one's tea bag, or the incubator a pediatrician uses to sustain a premature baby's life.

Goods are not found in nature. We take raw materials and turn them into goods. Petroleum is a good, today. Petroleum was not a good before the second half of the nineteenth century, because people then did not know how to place petroleum in the service of human life.[10] Moreover, we need to extract petroleum from the earth, process it, and, in the case of gasoline, transport it to gas stations across the globe before petroleum can acquire the status of a good. Petroleum untouched by the hand of man is not a good.

Businessmen produce goods by rearranging that which already exists to bring into existence something new. Specific components constitute a laptop—a central processing unit, a solid-state drive, random access memory, a screen, external ports, a video card, a motherboard, a keyboard, a cooling fan, a soundboard, a wireless network card, a battery, and a web camera. Initially, these components exist as entities in their own right, physically separate from each other. There is no laptop at this point. The manufacturer takes these separate entities and, through the manufacturing process, brings them together to form a new entity, the completed laptop. Physically separate entities are now parts of a single entity, an entity that did not previously exist. The same process applies to each of the laptop's constituents, with each constituent being ultimately reducible to the raw materials from which it originally came.

Producing economic goods consists in bringing new entities into existence. Even so-called natural resources must be produced. Resources are natural in the sense that they come from nature, not in the sense that they exist as *resources* in nature.[11] Human effort is required to take what we find in nature and turn them into resources. The fruit from the tree has to be plucked, the fruit picker selecting between fruit that is ripe and fruit that has gone off. The fruit has to be washed, boxed, and transported to grocery stores. Trees have to be harvested, converted into logs, and transported to building sites, where they will become part of someone's home, or to paper mills, where they will be pulped and turned into the paper that becomes books, newspapers, diaries, and greeting cards.

Strictly speaking, all economic goods come from nature. A computer housed in a plastic box is no less natural than a timber house. Though we do not find computers growing in forests, a computer's ultimate constituents come from nature. Sand is the ultimate constituent of a computer's central processing unit, for instance. The difference is the extent to which human beings had to act on what we find in nature to turn the "natural resource" into the goods sold by retail stores.

SERVICES

A *service* is an activity; it is something that human beings *do*.[12] In providing a service, businessmen create value. In some cases, the value of a service is in its contribution to the production of economic goods. A retailer retails goods. A cleaner cleans goods. A freight operator transports goods. A financier provides the finances for the production and distribution of goods. A marketer markets goods.[13] In other cases, the service is itself of benefit to human beings. A physician provides medicine for your sore throat. The hairdresser trims and styles your hair. The comedian makes you laugh.

Services make a substantial contribution to our lives. We shop at supermarkets and in malls. We eat dinner at restaurants. We seek advice from a lawyer. We read the newspaper delivered to our door. Our son receives tutoring in mathematics. We catch an Uber home after a late night partying with friends. We stay in a hotel while on holiday. We store our possessions in a storage unit when shifting houses.

The provision of services is no less creative than the production of goods. When a businessman produces a good, he or she brings a new entity into existence. When a businessman provides a service, he or she brings about a new state of affairs. For a hairdresser, the customer's hair was long and untidy; now, it is short and tidy. For a retailer, the goods were in various manufacturing plants in Korea and Taiwan; now, they are located in a single store in downtown New York. For a repairman, the washing machine was broken; now, it is repaired. For a courier, the parcel was here; now, it is there. For a stockbroker, the money was in my savings account; now, it is invested in a range of companies. For an airline, my family and I were in Blagoevgrad, Bulgaria; now, we are in Dunedin, New Zealand.

CREATION

"Profit" also presupposes the concept of *creation*. Producing goods and services is a creative activity, no different from the creative activities that we observe in other areas of life. A father cooks dinner for his wife and son. The meal did not exist. Physically separate ingredients existed. The father brings these ingredients together in the mixing bowl, thereby bringing the meal into existence.

A night of snow blocks the entrance to your garage. You shovel the snow. The curb outside your garage was covered in snow; now it is not. You have changed the state of affairs.

The difference between these creative activities and a businessman's is that businessmen sell the product. A father would turn himself into a businessman if he sold his cooking. You would become a businessman if you were to charge your neighbors for shoveling their snow.

All productive work is creative. There are differences in *degree*, however. Some businessmen are creative in the sense that they *reproduce* an entity, or *copy* someone else's actions. These businessmen are creative in the sense that they bring into existence new entities or change the state of affairs. Their creativity is limited, however, because they are imitating others' work.

The businessman who is *first* in his or her field—the first person to bring an entity into existence or to bring about a new state of affairs—exhibits the highest degree of creativity. Netflix was the first company to think of charging a subscription fee for streaming videos. Other streaming services merely reproduced Netflix's achievement.

These businessmen are the fountainheads of production. They might invent a new good (think, iPod), a new manufacturing process (think, on-demand publishing), or a new service (think, the App Store). Consider Henry Ford and his use of the assembly line to mass-produce cars. Ford did not invent the car. He did not invent the assembly line. His creativity consisted of grasping that an assembly line could be used to mass-produce cars. Ford's insight enabled him to reduce production costs significantly, thereby rendering cars affordable to average income earners. All the car manufacturers who followed are beneficiaries of Ford's insight, as is every manufacturer who grasped the assembly line's implications for his or her products.

Look around. Everything you see exists because of the person who first thought of it. People once thought it impossible for a man to fly. Samuel Pierpont Langley, the third Secretary of the Smithsonian Institute, and founder of the Smithsonian Astrophysical Observatory received grants from the War Department and from the Smithsonian to develop a piloted airplane he dubbed the "Aerodrome." Tests failed spectacularly. Experts ruled heavier-than-air flying machines impossible.[14] Then along came two brothers from Dayton, Ohio—bicycle shop owners Wilber and Oliver Wright—who showed us the way. In teaching humanity how to fly, the Wright brothers paved the way for every aircraft manufactured after them.

The word "creation" conjures up images of goods and services that existed only in science-fiction a few years earlier, like delivery drones and driverless cars. We should also pay attention to seemingly insignificant goods that have existed since before we were born. We usually take the existence of such goods for granted and treat them as though they had always existed, when they did not exist for most of human history. Someone had to create them. Consider the humble paperclip. Paper was once held together by making incisions in the upper left-hand corner of the page and threading ribbon through. Today, people use paperclips. Do not underestimate the feat of creativity involved. The clip has to be elastic enough to wrap around multiple sheets of paper, and, yet, there must be enough torsion between the twisting wires to keep the paper in place. The clip cannot generate too much friction, or the paper will tear. Several attempts were made to invent a paperclip before the invention of the one with which we are familiar today.[15]

VALUE JUDGMENTS

"Profit" also presupposes the concept of *value*. Goods and services are sold when customers judge that the good or service will further their lives. This judgment is a *value judgment*.

You enter a supermarket. You select groceries from a range of goods. The range you select from is determined by the goods that you judge will be of benefit. You purchase washing powder because you judge that your life is better when you socialize with friends in clean clothes. You do not purchase from the range of goods that you judge to be irrelevant to your life. A single man would not usually consider purchasing a feminine sanitary product, for instance, because this product would not further his life.

A "value" is "that which one acts to gain and/or keep."[16] (The next chapter explains this definition.) One of the ways we act to gain goods and services is by producing goods and services ourselves. A hairdresser acts to gain a car by cutting hair. A mechanic acts to gain a book by servicing cars. A musician acts to gain a dress by conducting an orchestra. A professor acts to gain toys for her children by teaching history classes.

We have to take specific actions to gain specific goods and services. To purchase a house, we must save a deposit. Once we have a deposit, we have to find a house to purchase, perhaps by searching online listings, speaking with real estate agents, and visiting open homes. Once we have chosen a house, we must arrange for a bank loan.

To take the actions needed to gain a good or service, we must be first intellectually convinced that the good or service is worth acting to gain.

Reality does not compel us to purchase houses. We could have chosen to spend our time differently. Instead of visiting open homes, we could have taken a stroll in the park. The judgments that stand behind our actions are *value judgments*.

When we make a value judgment, we are judging the contribution that a good or service will make to our life. There are competing theories of value. One school holds that value is an attribute of an object, like the color of someone's eyes. A different school holds that value judgments express subjective preferences.[17] Regardless of which school is correct, customers typically evaluate the value of a good or service in terms of its contribution to their life. People do not usually purchase washing powder because they intuit that the powder possesses the intrinsic attribute of value, or because they have an inexplicable and irreducible preference for such powder. People usually purchase washing powder to sanitize their clothes.

Customers who judge that a good or service will further their life do not expect the good or service to further their life and *only* their life. We often purchase goods and services for other people. We do not purchase goods and services indiscriminately, however. We purchase goods and services for people who are important to us.

You purchase a present for a *friend's* wedding, not for a stranger's. You hire a piano teacher for *your* daughter, not for your neighbor's daughter. You purchase groceries for a dinner party that you are hosting for your *friends*, not for your enemies. These purchases further your life because they further the lives of people about whom you care.

Customers need not know that they are making value judgments. A shopper who puts washing powder in his trolley has made a value judgment. He does not have to identify the type of judgment he has made for his judgment to be a judgment of value. The job of philosophers is to observe people making purchasing decisions and conclude that this multitude is united by the fact that they are value judgments.

Businessmen recognize the role of value judgments. A businessman contemplating whether to produce a good or service makes a value judgment of his own. He must judge whether potential customers will want to purchase his good or service. He knows that his goods or services will only sell if customers recognize their value.

Business programs teach students the importance of the *value proposition*.[18] Marketers recognize that businessmen need to be able to articulate the value of their good or service to their potential customers. Customers hand over hard-earned wealth. They will not do so unless they are intellectually convinced that the good or service will be of value to them.

Advertisements are one of the mechanisms through which businessmen communicate the value of their goods or services to potential customers. Consider a video advertisement for Apple's AirPods. One scene uses computer graphics to demonstrate how a pair of beam-forming microphones reduce background noise when users speak on the phone. In so doing, the advertisement demonstrates how Apple's customers can benefit from purchasing AirPods.

Businessmen do not necessarily produce goods and services in response to customers' preexisting values. Businessmen can educate customers about the new possibilities that their goods and services create. Apple built its success on creating products that people did not know they needed. As Steve Jobs explains, "Our job is to figure out what [customers are] going to want before they do."[19] When Apple introduced the iPad in 2010, newspapers gleefully predicted the end of Apple's heretofore unprecedented success.[20] Two years later, Apple would become the most valuable company in the world. Apple did not create the iPad because its customers judged that an iPad would be of value. Apple's customers had not heard of an iPad. Instead, Apple recognized what the newspapers did not, that the iPad opens up possibilities of which its customers had not previously thought.

Apple is not the first company to be several steps ahead of its customers. Before the Model T, the public did not grasp how a car could further their lives. Henry Ford reportedly quipped that if you had asked people at the time what they wanted, they would not have said a *car*, but a *faster horse*.[21]

Progress occurs when businessmen project new goods and services that they expect customers will judge to be of value. Sometimes this expectation is misguided. Indiegogo, Kickstarter, and Amazon Launchpad provide forums through which incipient businessmen can develop a market for new products. Some of these products will be successful. Many will not be. The businessman who produces a failed product misjudged his or her product's value.

Such misjudgments are not the prerogative of startups. Multinational corporations can misjudge the value of new products. In 2006, Microsoft launched Zune to compete against Apple's iPod. Microsoft believed that customers would judge Zune to be of value. It was mistaken, and five years later, Microsoft discontinued the product.[22]

Customers judge the value of a good or service and the place of that good or service on their *hierarchy of values*. You judge a cappuccino to be of value. You enjoy the feel of the froth against your lips and need a caffeine shot in the morning to kickstart your day. You also judge owning your own home to be of value. You value the cappuccino *and* the house. Still, you may decide to forgo the value of the cappuccino to save a deposit for a house because you judge the house to be of *higher value*.

You select your groceries based on your hierarchy of values. You cannot purchase all the goods you value because your money is limited, whether you are on minimum wage or are a multimillionaire. You must decide which goods you value *more*. Do you purchase washing powder or a new dinner set? Since you are out of washing powder, you may decide to purchase washing powder this week and hold off on purchasing the dinner set until the following week. You have judged the washing powder to be a higher value at this time.

Our time preferences inform our hierarchy of values. We can value a good higher at a future time than we value the same good in the present. When we forgo a cappuccino to save for our retirement, we are, in effect, deciding that drinking a cappuccino twenty years from now is more important to us than drinking a cappuccino now.

Businessmen make a profit when revenues exceed expenses. To do so, a sufficient number of individuals must judge the good or service to be of value. The aggregate demand for a good or service is the social expression of the judgments that each of us makes when we purchase a good or service.

Consider the competition between VHS and Betamax for home video recording in the early 1980s. VHS won out over Betamax because more individuals decided that VHS was a value in their lives. An individual decided that the extended recording time of VHS recorders was of higher value in the context of his life than the superior picture quality of Betamax recorders. Given a choice between recording an entire movie off broadcast television or recording part of a movie with superior picture quality, this individual preferred to record the entire movie. Millions of other individuals made the same decision. The sum of these judgments is the demand for VHS recorders.[23]

A company's profitability shifts with individuals' evaluations. In the early years of microcomputing, documents produced on one computer could only be opened by someone who owned the same model. A document created on a Commodore 64 could only be opened by someone who owned the same computer. Microsoft abolished this limitation by licensing MS-DOS to multiple manufacturers. MS-DOS's compatibility was a boon for businesses who wanted to share documents. Consequently, computers running Microsoft's operating systems were preferred to Apple's computers, even though the latter were technically superior.

This evaluation shifted in the early 2000s. Customers judged Apple's computers superior to computers running Microsoft's operating systems when they wanted to shift between multiple devices, moving back and forth between phones, portable media players, computers, televisions, and tablets. Apple's integrated, locked-down approach, which had been its Achilles's heel in the early years of microcomputing, provided users with a seamless experience across multiple devices, making its devices of superior value in the new era of digital computing.[24]

Some economists prefer to talk of *preference satisfaction* instead of *value judgments*. Customers reveal their preferences through their purchasing decisions. These preferences are preferences of *value*. When a customer prefers washing powder to a dinner set, his preference expresses his judgment of the relative value of the two goods. The problem with preference talk is that it drops the context which gave rise to the preference and treats the preference as though it were *sui generis*. A customer does not just happen to prefer washing powder to a dinner set. The customer's preference is grounded in his judgment about which makes a greater contribution to his life.

A sale is not dependent on the veracity of a customer's value judgment. Value judgments can be mistaken. A young woman judges cigarettes to be of value because smoking will help her lose weight. She fails to take into account the health risks that come with ingesting the poisons in nicotine. The purchase of the cigarettes did not further this woman's life, so the cigarettes were not really of value. This woman purchased the cigarettes based on a mistaken value judgment.

Within the aggregate demand for a good or service, there will always be mistakes of value. A good or service of genuine value to one person may not be of genuine value to another. An ice-cream cake may be of genuine value to an otherwise healthy person celebrating his or her birthday. An ice-cream cake may not be of genuine value to an obese man suffering from type two diabetes.

An accountant does not have to inquire into the veracity of customers' value judgments when calculating a businessman's profits. Accounting principles apply to the sale of goods and services, whether or not the sale arose from well-grounded value judgments.

MONEY AS A MEDIUM OF EXCHANGE

Customers purchase goods and services with *money*. A customer exchanges goods or services for the businessman's goods or services. Money is the medium through which this exchange takes place. Perceptually, it looks as though a customer purchases goods or services with pieces of paper. A customer, in fact, purchases goods or services with goods or services. A computer manufacturer purchases a meal with a fraction of a laptop; a hairdresser with three haircuts; a cleaner with two days of cleaning.[25]

A businessman and a customer are not different classes of people. A single person can be a businessman *and* a customer. A person is a *businessman* when he produces goods or services, and a *customer* when he spends the goods or services that he has produced.

A person does not need to be a businessman to be productive. Employees of businessmen also produce wealth. An employee helps a businessman produce goods and services. When an employee spends his wages, he is spending *part* of the goods or services that he helped create.

Customers depend on the production of goods and services for their spending power. When a person purchases goods or services, he is spending goods or services; if not the goods or services he has produced, then the goods or services someone else produced. A customer may be a businessman, an employee of a businessman, a family member of a businessman or his employees, or a beneficiary of the taxes imposed on a businessman and his employees. When a businessman's son spends his allowance, he is spending the goods or services that his mother produced.

A poor person who believes that he or she would be better off in a barter society because it does not use money misunderstands money's function. A money economy is not different from a barter economy in terms of the exchange of goods and services but the range of possible exchanges.

A money economy overcomes a practical limitation inherent in a barter economy, namely that the seller may not want what the buyer has to offer. Computers could not exist in a barter economy even if people had the technological know-how, because a computer manufacturer could not purchase anything with a computer. Could he or she purchase a meal? A meal is the equivalent of a fraction of a laptop. Such exchanges are not physically possible.

Exchanges in a money economy are complex, obscuring the fact that goods and services are being exchanged for goods and services. Such exchanges can be grasped perceptually in a barter economy because we can observe the exchange. We cannot similarly observe a fraction of a laptop being exchanged for a meal in a money economy, because this exchange takes place through many intermediary exchanges. We must grasp the nature of this trade conceptually.

MONEY IS NOT WEALTH

Wealth is goods—physical objects that serve human ends.[26] The value of money consists in our ability to purchase goods and services. For evidence, observe that the wealth of an economy can increase without a corresponding increase in the amount of money. Similarly, there can be an increase in the amount of money without a corresponding increase in wealth.[27] When Benjamin Franklin observed that a penny saved is a penny earned, he was writing at a time when the wealth of an economy increased faster than the money supply, so the spending power of a penny increased over time.[28]

Average income earners today are wealthier than King Henry VIII of England, who inherited £1,250,000 from his father (roughly, £375 million today).[29] King Henry VIII could not spend a single penny of his wealth on an iPhone, a Toyota Lexus, a ticket to the latest Hollywood blockbuster, a Netflix subscription, an air conditioner, a refrigerator, electric lights, an airplane ticket, or fertility treatment for his wives. A person living today, who could only afford the goods and services King Henry VIII had access to, would be classified as living below the poverty line. King Henry VIII had more *money* than average income earners today. Average income earners have more *wealth*.

When arts and humanities professors recklessly condemn businessmen in their classes, they condemn the very people who give value to their salaries.[30] Without the businessmen who stand behind Amazon, Starbucks, Toyota, Walmart, and all of the other companies that have transformed our lives, there would be nothing for these professors to buy. Absent the production of goods and services, the money in your wallet is just numbers printed on green-colored paper.

A trade is a win-win. In a trade of goods, each party gains wealth. A trade consists of changing the form of the wealth that each already possesses. A trade of goods is an exchange of wealth for wealth. A businessman produces computers. Through the medium of money, this businessman exchanges a computer for a car. He no longer owns the computer. His wealth, however, has not diminished, because he now owns the car. The form of his wealth has changed. He held his wealth in the form of a computer. Now he holds his wealth in the form of a car. He agrees to the exchange because wealth in the form of a car is more valuable to him than wealth in the form of a computer.

Businessmen produce their wealth. Customers do not bestow wealth on businessmen as a reward for a job well done. Customers make a trade possible because other people need to produce goods for a trade to take place. Customers do not hand over wealth in exchange for goods. Goods are exchanged for goods—wealth for wealth.

This exchange of wealth may be missed because the wealth that the businessman receives from his customers is concentrated in the hands of a single person or entity. In contrast, the wealth that his customers receive from him is dispersed among hundreds, or in some cases billions, of people. Bill Gates's wealth is visible because a single number represents his wealth—his net worth. The wealth Microsoft's customers obtained from trading with Microsoft is dispersed across the planet, in the homes and offices of billions of individuals. Microsoft's customers did not make Bill Gates wealthy. Gates made himself wealthy through the production of the MS-DOS and Windows operating systems and the Office productivity suites. Gates's wealth is these operating systems and productivity suites given monetary form.

Services are not wealth. Wealth changes form when there is an exchange of goods for goods, not an exchange of goods for services. Services contribute to the production of wealth and also redound to the promotion of human life in other ways.[31] When a customer hands over money in exchange for a service, he or she has less wealth. Customers voluntarily forgo some of their wealth in exchange for a service because they judge the service to be more valuable to them than maintaining their wealth. Forgoing this wealth furthers the customer's life.

THE PRICE SYSTEM

Economists have long recognized that the price system is a mechanism for the efficient allocation of resources.[32] Not widely recognized is that the price system enables businessmen to allocate resources efficiently because the price system transmits to businessmen information about individual value judgments.[33] As an increasing number of individuals judge a good or service to be of value, the price of the good or service increases, sending a signal for businessmen to enter the market and satisfy this demand. The price system is the mechanism through which businessmen learn what individuals judge to be of value, knowledge of which they otherwise would not have access.

Consider Uber's much misunderstood and, therefore, much criticized use of surge pricing. Uber's value does not consist of an Uber being cheaper than a regular taxi. Uber's value consists in its use of a pricing mechanism that responds to customer demand. The price of an Uber ride signals the value judgments of its customers. During peak times, the price surges, sometimes significantly, because customers judge the trip worth the higher price during these times. The price surge provides a positive incentive for Uber drivers to get off their couches or beds and onto the roads, thereby ensuring that there is always an Uber available when needed. Contrast Uber with regular taxi services, where there can be a long wait at peak times. Try catching a yellow cab in New York City on New Year's Eve.[34]

F. A. Hayek argues that economic planning is impossible under socialism because no person or group of persons can possess the knowledge needed to coordinate an economic system. The free market's beauty is that each one of us engages in economic planning, and the price system coordinates our economic plan with everyone else's. Socialism sabotages economic planning by destroying the price signals that make such planning possible.[35]

Hayek mistakenly believes that a price system is needed because human reason is limited. The need for a price system is not based on the limitations of reason, however, but on the fact that a valuer must make value judgments himself (an issue that we explore in the next chapter). A central planner cannot make value judgments on behalf of his or her subjects. The price system helps businessmen to improve the human standard of living by transmitting the value judgments of billions of individuals across the marketplace so that businessmen can identify which goods and services it is profitable to produce.

PROFIT MEASURES VALUE CREATION

Money has a conceptual function. Money enables us to exchange goods and services for goods and services. Money also enables us to represent complex relationships in the form of numbers. Money makes profit possible in the sense that money makes it possible for us to conceptualize profit. Without money, we could not express in numerical terms the costs of production, the revenues from sales, and the difference between the two.

Profit is the monetary measure of the value that a businessman creates. A computer manufacturer's profit represents the difference between the value of the components *qua* components and the value of the components *qua* parts of a laptop. A cleaner's profit represents the difference between the value of a messy room and the value of a clean room.

Profit does not measure the creation of *wealth*. Profit measures the creation of *value*. In the case of goods, the value consists of the creation of wealth. In the case of services, the value consists of bringing about a new state of affairs.

Profit does not measure the creation of all values. Profit measures the value created by goods and services. Profit cannot measure the sentimental value of a family photo album or the love of a father for his son. Profit measures values that can be produced and traded. Many vital values are outside an economic system's scope.

PROFIT IS NOT SURPLUS

"Profit" is misused when its use contradicts the facts that it conceptualizes. Non-profit organizations do not make a profit. This statement is tautological. Still, the surpluses of non-profit organizations are often treated as equivalent to businessmen's profits. "Surplus" and "profit" are not different words for the same thing. We do not just happen to switch words when talking about non-profit organizations. Different words are used to classify the excesses of businesses and non-profit organizations because "profit" and "surplus" conceptualize different facts.

"Surplus" does not have the same conceptual antecedents as "profit." Among other things, "surplus" presupposes the concept of *gift*. "Gift" is not an antecedent of "profit," like "goods" and "services."

A father gifts his son a generous allowance of $100 a week. The son spends his allowance on various goods and services, such as a shirt, a movie, and takeaways. At the end of the week, the son finds that he did not spend all of his allowance. The son studies accounting at high school, so he decides to make a list. In one column, he lists the allowance from his father. In the next column, he lists the goods and services he bought with this allowance. He finds that he has $20 left. This remainder is the son's *surplus*.

This surplus is not the son's profit because the surplus is not grounded in the same facts as profit. The father produced goods or services and gifted this spending power to his son. The son spent some of his father's money, but not all of it. The leftover money signifies the wealth that the son did *not* spend. This money does not signify the value that the father created through the production of goods or services.

Non-profits are in the same position as this boy. They are spending goods and services created by other people. Non-profits are non-profits because the facts that give rise to the concept of profit do not apply to such organizations. These organizations do not sell goods and services; they rely on the goods and services produced by other people for their spending power.

Mother Teresa's Missionaries of Charity purports to help the sick and poor on the streets of Calcutta, India. The Missionaries of Charity receives millions of dollars in donations from around the world, thanks to Mother Teresa's celebrity status. Since the Missionaries of Charity is an organization of Catholic nuns, they have taken a vow of poverty, so much of this money is not spent.[36] Glancing at their ledgers, you would find that they have a large surplus, representing the difference between the money received and the money spent. Not a dime is profit. When a businessman enters a shop and purchases new clothes, he is spending wealth that he produced. When a nun from the Missionaries of Charity enters a shop and purchases new clothes for the Calcutta poor, she is spending wealth produced by the Missionaries' donors. The surplus sitting in the Missionaries' bank account does not signify wealth created by the nuns but wealth gifted to them.

We should expect businessmen to maximize profit because profit signifies the creation of value. We should not similarly expect non-profit organizations to maximize surpluses. On the contrary, we should want non-profit organizations to *minimize* their surpluses because a high surplus signifies that they are not using donors' money for its intended purpose. Businessmen are profit *maximizers*. Non-profits are surplus *minimizers*.

The fundamental difference between a *for*-profit and a *non*-profit organization is that the former creates goods and services, and the latter spends the goods and services that other people created. Greenpeace and the Center for Industrial Progress are advocacy organizations. Greenpeace is a *non*-profit. The Center for Industrial Progress is a *for*-profit. Greenpeace is a non-profit because it relies on donations from people who support its ideas. The Center for Industrial Progress is a for-profit because it sells a service, teaching companies in the fossil fuel industry how to morally defend themselves.

Non-profit organizations do not trade wealth with their donors or beneficiaries.[37] The Missionaries of Charity does not provide its donors with a service in exchange for their donation and does not expect anything from the

Calcutta poor in exchange for having helped them. The donors are, in effect, gifting their money to the Calcutta poor, with the Missionaries of Charity acting as an intermediary. This relationship represents a division of labor. The donors have money with which they wish to help the world's poor. The Missionaries of Charity has an organization established in Calcutta that purports to get the money to where it is most needed.[38]

Some non-profits have larger bank balances than some businesses. Not a single cent on this balance sheet is profit. Profit is expressed in monetary terms. Not everything expressed in monetary terms is profit, however. Profit is not money. One cannot point to a number at the bottom of a ledger and say, "*This* is profit." Profit is not defined by the *quantity* of money, but by what the money *signifies*.

GOVERNMENT SUBSIDIES

Businessmen who receive government subsidies may have a surplus on their profit and loss statement but do not necessarily make a profit. A subsidy is when the government takes wealth produced by one or more people and redistributes this wealth to a businessman who did not create it. The calculation of profit cannot include subsidies. When businessmen do, they misrepresent the value created. Unfortunately, Elon Musk and Tesla are guilty of such a misrepresentation. Tesla relies on California's carbon tax credit to create the illusion of profit on its balance sheet.[39] Tesla's profit is an illusion because Tesla is spending more wealth than it has created.

PROFIT IS NOT LOOT

"Theft" is an antecedent of *loot*, not *profit*. Imagine two bins full of money, like Uncle Scrooge's money bin in *Duck Tales*. Perceptually, these bins are fundamentally similar. One bin, however, is filled with loot from bank robberies, and the other with profits made by a businessman who invented a new type of motor. Though the money in each bin is identical, there is a fundamental difference in what the money measures. The money in the first bin measures the amount of wealth the robber has taken from other people. The money in the second bin measures the value created by the businessman.

Some confidence tricksters pretend to be businessmen. Bernard Madoff and his Ponzi scheme is a notorious example. Just as Frank Abagnale dressing up in a pilot's uniform, in the movie *Catch Me If You Can*, did not make him a pilot, so a confidence trickster dressing up in a suit and tie does not make him a businessman.

From 1821 to 1837, General Gregor MacGregor sold government bonds and land certificates to British and French investors in the fictional Central

American territory of Poyais, which he claimed to rule as cazique.[40] The bonds and land certificates were worthless. MacGregor was not a profit-maximizing businessman. He was pretending to be one. MacGregor did not make a profit. He alleviated his victims of their wealth. He did not create a single cent of the wealth he acquired from his victims. MacGregor's revenue may have exceeded his expenses. This excess, however, represents MacGregor's *loot*, not his *profit*.

Most people understand the difference between a customer and a shoplifter. The former *pays* for the goods. The latter *takes* them. This difference is essential. A shoplifter is not a different type of customer from regular customers. He is not a customer at all. He *pretends* to be one. The difference is the same as between a genuine businessman and a confidence trickster who passes himself off as a businessman. A genuine businessman creates value. He does not loot wealth.

WORKER EXPLOITATION

Capitalism's critics allege that profit measures the *exploitation of workers*, not the value created by the production of goods and services. They claim that profit is a deduction from workers' wages. They assume that when an individual works for himself, he makes *wages*. Profit, in this view, arises when a person is employed to produce goods and services for someone else. The truth is the exact opposite. An individual who works for himself makes a *profit*, and it is when he works for someone else that there is such a thing as *wages*.[41]

A businessman does not take goods or services from his workers. A businessman produces goods or services, and his workers assist him. Apple does not take iPhones from its assembly line workers. Microsoft does not take operating systems from its customer service operators. Fisher & Paykel does not take refrigerators from its cleaners.

On the contrary, employment opens the opportunity for workers to earn a living without having to be businessmen. A person might have good reasons for not wanting to run a business. He or she might not want to risk his or her savings, may not want to invest the time, or may not have a commercially viable idea. The nature of reality is such that each one of us needs to produce to survive. Employment means that someone with limited ability can earn a living by helping a businessman produce goods or services, even if only by cleaning the floor.

For evidence of who depends on whom, observe that the assembly line owners in Apple's factories did not come up with the idea for the iPhone. Without the mind of Steve Jobs, there would be nothing for these workers to assemble. Similarly, it is not the cleaner sweeping the floors of Thomas

Edison's laboratory that made the incandescent light bulb possible. Edison's discovery of the incandescent light bulb made this cleaner's job possible.

PROFIT IS NOT A COST IMPOSED ON CUSTOMERS

Capitalism's critics sometimes allege that profit is a cost a businessman imposes on his customers. The profit-*maximizing* businessman, therefore, must want to increase the price of his goods or services as much as possible. Without profit, these critics allege, goods and services would be significantly cheaper.[42] This criticism sometimes takes the following form: A MacBook Pro's components cost significantly less than the price Apple charges its customers.

Let us set aside the other production costs, and the costs of research and development, which this criticism evades. A MacBook Pro is more expensive than the sum of its parts because a MacBook Pro is of significantly greater value to its owners than the value of its components *qua* components. You can do things with the former which you cannot do with the latter, such as check your Facebook page, purchase clothes, and Skype with family and friends. The difference in price reflects the difference in value.

What about retail stores, which allegedly "merely" shift goods from one location to another? This objection grossly underestimates the value to customers of having a range of goods available in a single, nearby location. Instead of shopping for a washing machine in Korea or Taiwan, and having the manufacturer ship the machine to my home, several thousand miles away, I can take a thirty-minute drive to Walmart and have the machine delivered to my home that afternoon. Furthermore, local retail stores perform intellectual work by using their expertise to select the brands that they are willing to put their name behind and provide their customers with after-sales support, which a foreign manufacturer may be unwilling or unable to do.

THE CONDITIONS OF PROFIT'S MORALITY

We can now identify the conditions that profit must meet to be moral. A businessman must produce goods or services that are of genuine value (the "*what* condition") and must do so virtuously (the "*how* condition"). The morality of profit maximization is concerned with *what* businessmen produce and *how* they produce it.

The *what* condition arises from the fact that profit measures the value of goods and services, as judged by a businessman's customers. Profit, to be moral, must measure the creation of morally legitimate values. The *how* condition arises from the fact that businessmen create goods and services. Profit, to be moral, must also result from virtuous actions.

These are related conditions. The first condition concerns *moral values*; the second, *moral virtues*. Virtues identify the actions that one must take to gain and/or keep values, for the reasons explained in the next chapter. We should not be surprised, therefore, to find a connection between the virtues of a businessman and the value of the goods and services that he or she produces.

A virtuous businessman who knowingly produces illegitimate goods or services is difficult to conceive. A virtuous businessman may produce a good or service that he or she mistakenly believes to be of genuine value. A virtuous businessman would not act to deceive his or her customers. One would not expect a virtuous businessman to peddle the services of a psychic surgeon, for instance, because an honest businessman does not commit fraud.

Still, these conditions cannot be reduced to a single condition. Though a virtuous businessman would not deliberately produce goods or services of dubious value, businessmen of dubious character seem to have produced legitimate values. Most of us have worked for a boss who is a jerk or knows someone who has.

Given these conditions, any discussion of profit's morality must confront two questions: *Do businessmen produce goods and services that are of legitimate value? Do businessmen produce these goods and services virtuously?*

Any debate over the morality of profit must address these questions. Paul L. Poirot defends profit maximization because he believes that businessmen self-sacrificially serve others through producing goods and services.[43] Poirot's argument is flawed. Still, it is on topic because one of the questions that a defense of profit maximization must address is the virtues of businessmen.

Naomi Klein opposes profit maximization. Among other arguments, Klein questions the value of goods, claiming that we purchase goods because of the brand not because we independently judge the good to be of value. We might purchase a jacket because it has the Gap or J. Crew label printed on the front, not because it is functionally better than any other jacket.[44] Klein's argument is flawed. Nevertheless, her argument is on topic because an argument against profit maximization must address the value of goods and services (or the lack thereof).

The moral status of profit has fluctuated, historically, based on how intellectuals answered these questions. Profit was regarded as inherently immoral during the medieval period because there was no way for businessmen to produce goods or services virtuously by the moral standards of the time. A pious man should have his sight on the next life, not on improving people's lot in this one. David Vogel explains that, at this time, a moral businessman would have been like a socially responsible drug dealer, a contradiction in terms.[45]

The moral reputation of profit improved in nineteenth-century America because thinkers noted the correlation between personal virtues, such as frugality, industry, and reliability, and business success. Horatio Alger's novels and Benjamin Franklin's homilies popularized this correlation.[46]

To know whether profit is moral and under what conditions, we must answer the above questions. Profit might never be moral. Profit might be moral under some conditions and immoral under other conditions. Profit might be moral so long as it is not excessive. Profit might be inherently moral regardless of the conditions or amount. We shall see in the forthcoming chapters.

PROFIT MAXIMIZATION

This book makes a moral case for profit *maximization*, not for *profit*. Profit can be moral even if profit *maximization* is not. Robert N. Anthony argues, for instance, that the pursuit of profit is moral when businessmen aim at a *satisfactory* profit. He believes that the pursuit of profit is not moral when businessmen seek to *maximize* profit.[47]

Businessmen must make a profit to stay in business. Few people find such profits objectionable. Profit maximization is thought objectionable because critics believe that the logic of profit maximization leads businessmen to treat profit as more important than other values, such as the well-being of workers.[48] If the owner of a profitable mill calculates that he can increase profit by mothballing the factory and offshoring jobs, then profit maximization seems to require him to do so, in disregard of the effect on local workers and their families.

BUSINESS ETHICS

The above questions are not part of contemporary debates in business ethics. Though profit is central to business, the moral status of profit is not central to business ethics as an academic discipline.

Business ethics is a relatively new discipline. Talk about the ethics of business can be found as far back as the Classical Greeks.[49] Business ethics books, conferences, journals, and university courses did not emerge until the late 1970s. Norman E. Bowie dates the birth of business ethics as an academic discipline to the first conference on business ethics, held in November 1974 at the University of Kansas.[50]

Business ethics as an academic discipline was a response to the perception of incessant corporate irresponsibility. Rachel Carson's *Silent Spring* told us that corporations poison our food.[51] Ralph Nader's *Unsafe at Any Speed* told us that corporations deliberately make unsafe cars that risk the lives of our loved ones.[52] Mike Muller's *The Baby Killer* told us that corporations kill third-world babies.[53]

The source of corporate malfeasance was thought to be something peculiar to the corporate form, namely that a corporation is an artificial entity without a body to kick or a soul to be damned.[54]

We expect Mr. Godsey, our neighborhood grocer, to behave ethically. He is a businessman. He is also a member of our community. We went to school together. We attended his wedding. Our kids play with his. He delivers groceries to our house when we are sick and extends credit when we forget our wallet.

Corporations are not like Mr. Godsey. Corporations are not community members. We did not attend Amazon's wedding (corporations do not fall in love and marry). Our kids do not play with Amazon's (corporations do not procreate). Amazon does not care whether we are sick or forget our wallet (corporations do not sympathize). As Frank Easterbrook and Daniel Fishel explain, "Corporations can no more be said to have moral obligations than does a building, an organization chart, or a contract."[55]

The moral status of profit maximization is not the *raison d'être* of business ethics. Its *raison d'être* is the problem of how to subject an artificial entity to the expectations of morality. The traditional solution to this problem is to point out that the state breathes legal life into corporations and so can impose moral obligations as a condition of its existence.[56] Business ethics is sometimes incorporated into business law courses because the law is thought to define corporations' minimum moral obligations.[57]

For contemporary business ethicists, debate over the morality of profit maximization arises within the context of debate over corporate responsibility. The "profit maximization" view is interpreted to hold that the state cannot impose moral obligations on corporations. To be for profit maximization is interpreted as being against business ethics. Milton Friedman is held up by business ethicists as the primary opponent of corporate social responsibility because he is thought to defend this position.[58] (Chapter 6 discusses Friedman's argument.)

The above questions hark back to nineteenth-century discussions of the relationship between profit and character and do not directly address modern concerns about the responsibilities of corporations. Nevertheless, the issues raised in this book should be of interest to contemporary business ethicists. In showing that the questions of profit's morality raise substantive ethical issues, this book demonstrates why the central debate in business ethics must shift away from the responsibilities of corporations to the value of goods and services and the character of businessmen.[59]

PROFIT MAXIMIZATION'S MORALITY

Profit measures the value created by businessmen through the production of goods and services. The moral case for profit maximization must, therefore, address the value of *what* businessmen produce and the virtue of *how* they produce it. The next three chapters address these issues.

NOTES

1. Students in my business ethics classes routinely made these mistakes. These were intelligent students who had studied accounting and business law.
2. Francis Ford Coppola and Mario Puzo, *The Godfather* (Paramount Pictures, 1972), 51 min., 54 sec.
3. Francis Ford Coppola and Mario Puzo, *The Godfather Part II* (Paramount Pictures, 1974), 40 min., 13 sec.
4. Esther Lodewyckx, "Non-Profit Organizations," in *Financial Accounting: Fresh Perspectives*, ed. Roelien Theron (Cape Town: Pearson Education South Africa, 2007), 427.
5. For a discussion of first-level and higher-level concepts, see Ayn Rand, *Introduction to Objectivist Epistemology*, ed. Harry Binswanger and Leonard Peikoff, expanded second ed. (New York: Meridian, 1990), 204–17; Leonard Peikoff, *Objectivism: The Philosophy of Ayn Rand* (New York: Meridian, 1993), 91–92 and 129–41; Harry Binswanger, *How We Know: Epistemology on an Objectivist Foundation* (New York: TOF Publications, 2014), 137–51; Allan Gotthelf, "Ayn Rand's Theory of Concepts: Rethinking Abstraction and Essence," in *Concepts and Their Role in Knowledge: Reflections on Objectivist Epistemology*, ed. Allan Gotthelf and James G. Lennox (Pittsburgh: University of Pittsburgh Press, 2013).
6. For a discussion of "floating abstractions," see Peikoff, *Objectivism*, 96; Binswanger, *How We Know*, 151 and 214; Gregory Salmieri, "Conceptualization and Justification," in *Concepts and Their Role in Knowledge: Reflections on Objectivist Epistemology*, ed. Allan Gotthelf and James G. Lennox (Pittsburgh: University of Pittsburgh Press, 2013), 71.
7. According to the 2018 edition of the Index of Economic Freedom, published by the Heritage Foundation, the United States of America is ranked eighteenth in the world. Canada is ranked ninth, and the Netherlands seventeenth. The top-ranked countries are Hong Kong, Singapore, New Zealand, Australia, and Ireland. I would do an exercise in my business ethics classes in which I asked students to identify the top five countries on the economic freedom index. Semester after semester, without fail, students ranked the United States of America first for economic freedom. The actual top five countries were never listed. Of course, the index is a ranking of *relative* freedom. The top-ranked countries are *less* regulated than other countries but still suffer from extensive economic regulations that violate the rights of their citizens and undermine their standard of living.
8. M. Northrup Buechner, *Objective Economics: How Ayn Rand's Philosophy Changes Everything About Economics* (Lanham, MD: University Press of America, 2011), 45.
9. George Reisman, *Capitalism: A Treatise on Economics* (Ottawa, IL: Jameson Books, 1998), 39.
10. Ibid., 40.
11. We benefit from untouched trees converting carbon dioxide into the oxygen that we breathe. This biological function does not make trees a natural *resource*, however. A "resource" is a thing that *we* use as a means to an end. We do not use trees to convert carbon dioxide into oxygen. Trees perform this function independent of us and would continue to do so if the human race were to disappear from the planet. For a tree to be a *resource*, we must make use of the tree, and so doing involves discovering the various uses to which we can put trees.
12. Buechner, *Objective Economics*, 45–47.
13. Reisman, *Capitalism*, 41.

14. David McCullough, *The Wright Brothers: The Dramatic Story Behind the Legend* (London: Simon & Schuster, 2015), 99–101. McCullough's biography demonstrates that the Wright brothers possessed the same virtues possessed by J. P. Morgan, John D. Rockefeller, Thomas Edison, and Louis Pasteur, who we discuss in chapter 4.

15. For a history of the paper clip, see James Ward, *The Perfection of the Paper Clip: Curious Tales of Invention, Accidental Genius, and Stationery Obsession* (New York: Touchstone, 2014), 3–10.

16. Ayn Rand, "The Objectivist Ethics," in *The Virtue of Selfishness: A New Concept of Egoism* (New York: Signet, 1964), 16. Cf. Peikoff, *Objectivism*, 208; Tara Smith, *Viable Values: A Study of Life as the Root and Reward of Morality* (Lanham, MD: Rowman & Littlefield Publishers, 2000), 84.

17. For an explanation of these competing theories, see Peikoff, *Objectivism*, 245–47.

18. Larry B. Chonko and Eli Jones, "Sales Force Agility, Strategic Thinking, and Value Propositions," in *The Oxford Handbook of Strategic Sales and Sales Management*, ed. David W. Cravens, Kenneth Le Meunier-FitzHugh, and Nigel F. Piercy (Oxford: Oxford University Press, 2012), 519.

19. Walter Isaacson, *Steve Jobs* (London: Little, Brown, 2011), 567.

20. Ibid., 494–95. Cf. Carrie-Ann Biondi, "Counter-Culture Capitalist," in *Steve Jobs and Philosophy: For Those Who Think Different*, ed. Shawn E. Klein (Chicago: Open Court, 2015), 23–24.

21. David Long, *Henry Ford: Industrialist* (New York: Cavendish Square Publishing, 2016), 12.

22. For a discussion of failed products created by major companies, see Salvador Jimenez Murguía, *Epic Fails: The Edsel, the Mullet, and Other Icons of Unpopular Culture* (Lanham, MD: Rowman & Littlefield Publishers, 2018). Chapter 17 of Murguía's book discusses Zune.

23. Matt Haig, *Brand Failures: The Truth About the 100 Biggest Branding Mistakes of All Time* (London: Kogan Page, 2005), 25; Brian P. Simpson, *Markets Don't Fail!* (Lanham, MD: Lexington Books, 2005), 50.

24. Isaacson, *Steve Jobs*, 513–14 and 33–34.

25. For a discussion of the origins and evolution of money, see Reisman, *Capitalism*, 506–10.

26. Ibid., 39.

27. Ibid.

28. Paul C. Pasles, *Benjamin Franklin's Numbers: An Unsung Mathematical Odyssey* (Princeton: Princeton University Press, 2008), 67.

29. Alison Weir, *Henry VIII: The King and His Court* (New York: Ballantine Books, 2008), 16.

30. For a discussion of the contempt of Western intellectuals for capitalism, see Alan S. Kahan, *Mind vs. Money: The War between Intellectuals and Capitalism* (New Brunswick, NJ: Transaction Publishers, 2010). Rand argues that capitalism gave rise to businessmen and professional intellectuals. Ayn Rand, *For the New Intellectual: The Philosophy of Ayn Rand* (New York: Signet, 1961), 25.

31. Reisman, *Capitalism*, 40–41.

32. For a discussion of the role of the price system in economic coordination, see Yaron Brook and Don Watkins, *Free Market Revolution: How Ayn Rand's Ideas Can End Big Government* (New York: Palgrave Macmillan, 2012), 142–46; Reisman, *Capitalism*, 172–218; Simpson, *Markets Don't Fail!*, 11–12.

33. Robert Tarr, "Economic Theory and Conceptions of Value: Rand and Austrians versus the Mainstream," in *Foundations of a Free Society: Reflections on Ayn Rand's Political Philosophy*, ed. Gregory Salmieri and Robert Mayhew (Pittsburgh: University of Pittsburgh Press, 2019), 367.

34. For a discussion of how Uber has improved people's lives, see Yaron Brook and Don Watkins, *Equal Is Unfair: America's Misguided Fight Against Income Inequality* (New York: St. Martin's Press, 2016), 101–102.

35. F. A. Hayek, "The Pretence of Knowledge," *The American Economic Review* 79, no. 6 (December 1989).

36. Christopher Hitchens, *The Missionary Position: Mother Teresa in Theory and Practice* (London: Verso, 1995), 46–48.

37. Non-profit organizations offer value to their donors. An advocacy organization is saying, in effect, gift money to us, and we will advocate for *your* ideas on your behalf.

38. Questions have been raised about whether the Missionaries of Charity channels donors' money to where it is most needed. If these accusations are true, then the Missionaries of Charity is defrauding its donors. See Hitchens, *The Missionary Position*, 46–48.

39. Jason Mattera, *Crapitalism: Liberals Who Make Millions Swiping Your Tax Dollars* (New York: Threshold Editions, 2014), 237.

40. Paul M. Franklin and Nancy Mikula, *Backroads of Florida: Your Guide to Great Day Trips and Weekend Getaways* (Minneapolis: Voyageur Press, 2009), 83. For details of MacGregor's other exploits in Florida, see Gene M. Burnett, *Florida's Past: People and Events that Shaped the State*, vol. 2 (Sarasota, FL: Pineapple Press, 1988), 73–76.

41. Adam Smith committed this mistake when he claimed that the price paid to a stonecutter is his wages. This price is the stonecutter's *sales revenue*. For a discussion of Smith's mistake, see Reisman, *Capitalism*, 480.

42. Dylan Ratigan, *Greedy Bastards: How We Can Stop Corporate Communists, Banksters, and Other Vampires from Sucking America Dry* (New York: Simon & Schuster, 2012), 168.

43. Paul L. Poirot, "He Gains Most Who Serves Best," *The Freeman* 25, no. 5 (May 1975).

44. Naomi Klein, *No Logo: No Space, No Choice, No Jobs*, 10th anniversary ed. (New York: Picador, 2010).

45. David Vogel, "The Ethical Roots of Business Ethics," *Business Ethics Quarterly* 1, no. 1 (January 1991): 103.

46. Ibid., 104. Cf. Max Weber, "The Spirit of Capitalism," in *Economic Morality: Ancient to Modern Readings*, ed. Henry C. Clark and Eric Allison (Lanham, MD: Lexington Books, 2015).

47. Robert N. Anthony, "The Trouble with Profit Maximization," *Harvard Business Review* 38, no. 6 (1960): 128.

48. For a discussion of why profit maximization is thought objectionable, see Robert White, "Profit Maximization Does Not Necessitate Profit Prioritization," *The Journal of Ayn Rand Studies* 17, no. 2 (December 2017): 202–204.

49. See Part One of Henry C. Clark and Eric Allison, eds., *Economic Morality: Ancient to Modern Readings* (Lanham, MD: Lexington Books, 2015).

50. Norman E. Bowie, "Business Ethics," in *New Directions in Ethics: The Challenge of Applied Ethics*, ed. Joseph P. DeMarco and Richard M. Fox (New York: Routledge & Kegan Paul, 1986), 158.

51. Rachel Carson, *Silent Spring*, 40th anniversary ed. (New York: Mariner Books, 2002).

52. Ralph Nader, *Unsafe at Any Speed: The Designed-in Dangers of the American Automobile* (New York: Grossman, 1972).

53. Mike Muller, *The Baby Killer: A War on Want Investigation into the Promotion and Sale of Powdered Baby Milks in the Third World* (London: War on Want, 1974).

54. Edward Thurlow, Lord Chancellor of England, once observed that corporations could not have a conscience because they have "no soul to be damned" and "no body to be kicked." Quoted in John C. Coffee, "'No Soul to Damn: No Body to Kick': An Unscandalized Inquiry into the Problem of Corporate Punishment," *Michigan Law Review* 79, no. 3 (1981): 386. Cf. Robert White, "Corporations Are People Too: An Argument for Corporate Moral Personhood," *The Journal of Ayn Rand Studies* 14, no. 2 (December 2014): 99–100; Joel Bakan, *The Corporation: The Pathological Pursuit of Profit and Power* (New York: Free Press, 2004), 79.

55. Quoted in Bakan, *The Corporation*, 79.

56. Keith Davis, "The Case for and Against Business Assumption of Social Responsibilities," *The Academy of Management Journal* 16, no. 2 (June 1973): 314. Cf. Ralph Nader, "The Case for Federal Chartering," in *Corporate Power in America*, ed. Ralph Nader and Mark J. Green (New York: Grossman Publishers, 1973), 80; Bakan, *The Corporation*, 158.

57. Kenneth W. Clarkson, Roger LeRoy Miller, and Frank B. Cross, *Business Law: Text and Cases*, 13th ed. (Stamford, CT: Cengage Learning, 2014), 97.

58. Milton Friedman, "The Social Responsibility of Business Is to Increase Its Profits," in *Economic Morality: Ancient to Modern Readings*, ed. Henry C. Clark and Eric Allison (Lanham, MD: Lexington Books, 2015).

59. For contemporary discussion of the relationship between virtue and business, see Jaana Woiceshyn, *How to Be Profitable and Moral: A Rational Egoist Approach to Business* (Lanham, MD: Hamilton Books, 2012); Jaana Woiceshyn, "Lessons from 'Good Minds': How CEOs Use Intuition, Analysis and Guiding Principles to Make Strategic Decisions," *Long Range Planning* 42, no. 3 (2009); Edwin A. Locke and Jaana Woiceshyn, "Why Businessmen Should Be Honest: The Argument from Rational Egoism," *Journal of Organizational Behavior* 16, no. 5 (September 1995); Shelley A. Kirkpatrick, "Lead through Vision and Values," in *Handbook of Principles of Organizational Behavior*, ed. Edwin A. Locke (West Sussex: John Wiley & Sons, 2009); Edwin A. Locke, "The Traits of Business Heroes in *Atlas Shrugged*," in *Perspectives on Ayn Rand's Contributions to Economic and Business Thought*, ed. Edward W. Younkins (Lanham, MD: Lexington Books, 2018); Christine Swanton, "Virtues of Productivity versus Technicist Rationality," in *Economics and the Virtues: Building a New Moral Foundation*, ed. Jennifer Baker and Mark D. White (Oxford: Oxford University Press, 2016).

Chapter Two

Why Profit Maximization Is Moral

This chapter explains how profit maximization meets the *what* and *how* conditions. In the first chapter, we saw that profit maximization is moral when businessmen produce goods or services that are of genuine value (the "*what* condition") and do so virtuously (the "*how* condition"). Profit maximization meets the *what* condition because profit is a businessman's reward for producing goods or services that are of objective value. Profit maximization meets the *how* condition because businessmen must cultivate a virtuous character to produce goods or services that are of objective value.

The fundamental questions in ethics are: *What is value? What is virtue?* and *Who should be the primary beneficiary of our moral actions?* To determine whether profit maximization can meet the *what* and *how* conditions, we must first answer these questions. After doing so, we shall consider why businessmen should *maximize* profit, the moral status of profit in a regulated economy, and the theory of value that dominates contemporary business ethics.

AYN RAND'S ETHICS

We shall focus on Ayn Rand's answers to the fundamental questions in ethics. I am convinced that Rand's approach is correct, and there is no better reason for considering a thinker's views on a subject. Resolving the many debates in ethics over these questions is outside the scope of this book. This chapter alone is unlikely to persuade skeptical readers of the truth of Rand's answers. Instead, the aim of this chapter is to demonstrate that Rand makes a substantial contribution to the debate over the morality of profit maximization and, therefore, her work needs to be taken seriously even by those who disagree with her.

Rand is already part of the business ethics literature. Unfortunately, this literature often grossly misrepresents her philosophy. Rand's critics sometimes present her views as though she believes that greed is good. One book even implies that Rand would approve of businessmen killing third-world infants to maximize profit.[1] More often, critics reduce Rand to the role of a novelist who popularized the ideas of free-market economists, such as Adam Smith and F. A. Hayek, implying that Rand had nothing original to say.[2] Critics rarely mention Rand's theory of value or her account of the virtues.

RAND'S THEORY OF VALUE

Rand defines "value" as "that which one acts to gain and/or keep."[3] Rand's definition does not indicate what one should act to gain and/or keep. Rand's definition is neutral between competing theories. Rand formulates this definition to orient our thinking to the subject of values. She then proceeds to identify the facts of reality that give rise to the concept of "value." Rand believes that once we know the facts that ground the concept, we can identify what one ought to act to gain and/or keep.[4]

For Rand, value is the *object* of action; it is *that* which one acts to gain and/or keep. Values can be physical goods, such as a shirt, a phone, a car, or a family heirloom. Values can also be states of affairs, such as a vacation, good health, a romantic relationship, or a particular politico-economic system.[5]

A value denotes an object whose benefit depends on or is enhanced by our actions; it is that which *one acts to gain and/or keep.*[6] An object that benefits us is not a *value* unless the benefit results from our actions. A romantic relationship is a value because romantic relationships depend on the actions of the people in the relationship. Other people can give us relationship advice; however, in the end, the people in the relationship are the ones who have to do the work. For evidence, observe elderly couples who are in loveless marriages because they stopped putting in the effort needed to sustain the relationship.

A value conceptualizes a *factual relationship* between the actor and the object of his or her actions. The object is a value because it possesses specific properties that redound to the benefit of the actor when he or she takes the appropriate actions. Water is a value to someone who needs to rehydrate. Water's value is grounded in facts about water and the biology of the person who is to drink it.

An object's value depends on this relationship. Water is of value to a person who needs to rehydrate. Water is not of value to someone with severe hyponatremia. To such a person, water can be deadly. Value is relative because values conceptualize relationships and, as a matter of fact, that which benefits a person under specific conditions may not benefit him under different conditions. Water is of benefit to a person when he is dehydrated, not when he suffers from hyponatremia.

A value presupposes an *evaluation* by the person who has to act to gain and/or keep the object. A person must be intellectually convinced that the object is worth going after before he or she will take the necessary actions.[7] The factual relationships that ground values exist independent of our grasp of them. We will not act to gain and/or keep an object unless we grasp these relationships, however. A person with hyponatremia needs a sports drink to restore sodium levels in his blood. He will not reach for a sports drink unless he grasps that he needs the drink to restore his sodium levels.

The pursuit of values is a do-it-yourself affair. Values are that which *one* acts to gain and/or keep. Values are not that which *others* act to gain and/or keep on our behalf. Other people can identify the factual relationships that ground values and can point out these relationships to us. In the end, however, the object is only a value when we grasp these relationships ourselves.

Rand observes that whenever someone asserts that an object is a value, there are two questions that one must immediately ask: "of value to *whom* and for *what*?" (emphasis in original).[8] These questions ground value-claims in the relevant facts of reality. The first question (*Of value to whom?*) recognizes that an object is of value to particular individuals. The second question (*Of value for what?*) recognizes that these individuals must grasp the end that the object is to serve.

Consider the value of insulin injections. Human beings need insulin to regulate glucose levels in the blood. Most people produce insulin naturally. Diabetics do not produce sufficient insulin. Before insulin injections became available, diabetics attempted to regulate their glucose levels using diet. Most died within a year of diagnosis. In the late 1970s, medical doctors discovered how to synthesize human insulin, revolutionizing diabetics' lives.

Insulin injections are a value—*to* diabetics, *for* the purpose of regulating glucose levels in the blood. The value of insulin injections is grounded in facts about human biology and synthesized insulin. Insulin injections are only of value in this context. Insulin injections are not of value to a hypoglycemic. Injecting a hypoglycemic with insulin lowers the glucose levels of someone already with low blood sugar, placing them into a potentially fatal coma.

So far, we have identified the factual basis of the claim that insulin injections are a value. Insulin injections are not yet of value. A value is that which *one acts* to gain and/or keep. For insulin injections to be of value to a diabetic, the diabetic must grasp the benefit of insulin injections and take the necessary actions to gain and/or keep them.

A doctor can save the life of an unconscious diabetic by injecting him with insulin. An insulin injection, after all, will regulate the glucose levels in a diabetic's blood, whether or not the diabetic grasps the benefit of the injection. This injection is not a *value*, however.

Consider a diabetic who does not grasp the benefit of insulin injections. Perhaps this diabetic is a conspiracy theorist who thinks that diabetes is a fantasy concocted by drug companies looking to profit from selling insulin. This diabetic will not act to gain and/or keep insulin injections and so will not benefit from the insulin.

A doctor can inject insulin in emergencies, such as when a diabetic is found on the street unconscious. A doctor cannot continually stand next to a diabetic, knocking him out or forcibly restraining him every time the doctor needs to administer a glucose level test or an insulin injection. The benefit of insulin depends on the diabetic acting to gain and/or keep this benefit, and the diabetic will only do so if he first grasps that insulin is of benefit.

The anti-vaccination movement is a real-life example of people who refuse to act to gain and/or keep a benefit. The vaccine provides a real benefit to the people who are vaccinated, saving millions of lives. The vaccine is not a *value* in the lives of the anti-vaxxers, however. An anti-vaxxer does not gain the benefit of the vaccine because he refuses to take the actions needed to gain this benefit. If the government tried to compel him to receive this benefit, he would actively fight against it.

Rand did not oppose helping others, contrary to her critics' assertions. Rand believes that the help we can provide others is necessarily limited to emergencies because we cannot provide others with values. We can, rightly, save a stranger from drowning or provide financial assistance to a friend, if there is no sacrifice. We cannot *evaluate* for someone else.[9] As much as it may pain us to watch a friend or loved one refuse the vaccine, in the end, the pursuit of values is something that each one of us must do for ourselves.

AN OBJECTIVE THEORY OF VALUE

Rand's theory is an *objective* theory of value. For Rand, a value is the form in which we conceptualize specific facts about the world. A value is not a thing that exists out there in the world independent of us. Rand recognizes that values are subject-dependent. At the same time, Rand recognizes that we must form our values by disciplining our thinking to grasp facts about the world which exist independent of us.[10] The facts that ground our values are not subject-dependent. As Leonard Peikoff explains in his summary of Rand's position: "the good designates *facts* . . . as *identified conceptually*, and *then evaluated by human consciousness* in accordance with a rational standard of value" (emphasis mine).[11]

Rand's use of the word "objective" to designate subject-dependent values may strike some readers as odd. Today, "objective" is usually used to refer to objects that exist independent of thought. Historically, "objective" denoted the act of bringing an object before the mind.[12] For Rand, "objective" refers to the act of disciplining one's thinking to grasp independently existing facts, which is what we must do to form values.

The pursuit of values is intellectually demanding. Rand differentiates between two types of abstractions—*cognitive abstractions*, through which a thinker grasps the facts of reality; and *normative abstractions*, through which a thinker integrates cognitive abstractions to form goals and identify the means to these goals.[13] Both types of abstractions are implicit in Peikoff's summary: "the good designates facts . . . as identified conceptually [*cognitive abstractions*], and then evaluated by human consciousness in accordance with a rational standard of value [*normative abstractions*]."

HUMAN LIFE AS THE STANDARD OF VALUE

Rand argues that we must hold human life as our ultimate value and standard of value.[14] We shall consider why Rand thinks that an ultimate value is needed. We shall then consider why she thinks that human life is the ultimate value.

Most of our values are *instrumental*, meaning that they are values because they are a means to an end. If someone were to assert, "You ought to study for tomorrow's exam," a legitimate question to ask in response is, "Why?" To which the person might answer, "You ought to study for tomorrow's exam so that you can pass the course." This person claims that the end of passing the course justifies studying for tomorrow's exam. To this ought statement, you can also ask, "Why?" To which the person might respond, "You ought to pass the course to meet your graduation requirements." The end justifies the means, and the end itself is justified as a means to a further end. You can keep asking why until you reach an ultimate end that justifies the subservient ends.

All of our value chains must end at the same place. An ultimate end is a cognitive integrator.[15] We need a sole ultimate end to integrate our value chains and thereby avoid contradictions in the pursuit of our ends. We must not place ourselves in a position whereby we are pursuing contradictory ends because then achieving one of our values will sabotage the achievement of our other values.

Rand argues that life is the only candidate for being an ultimate end because life, metaphysically, is an end in itself.[16] Life is a process. The processes that constitute life are the means to life. Life is both end and means.[17] Anatomically, our heart pumps blood through our veins as a means to the end of continuing that state whereby our heart pumps blood through our veins. The pumping of blood is a means to its own end.

Furthermore, Rand argues that life is a conditional form of existence and that life's conditionality necessitates our pursuit of ends. Rand's claim is not that life is the ultimate end because we need to be alive to pursue ends.[18] Rand's point is that we must achieve ends in the face of the alternative between life and death. The end of life is conditional on our actions. If the life-death alternative did not confront us, there would be no grounds on which to choose one end over another. Life's conditionality gives rise to the concept of "value" and establishes that which we ought to act to gain and/or keep.

Life is fundamentally different from physical matter. Living organisms face the possibility of non-existence. Matter does not. If you were to throw a porcelain vase against a brick wall, it would smash into shards. The matter that constitutes the vase no longer has the form of a vase. Still, the matter continues to exist in a different form.[19] The loss of a life is not like a smashed vase. Death is non-existence. When a grandfather dies, the person who liked milk with his coffee, who played peek-a-boo with his grandchildren, who enjoyed evening walks in the park, and who liked to read detective fiction on a wet Sunday afternoon is gone.

Rand does not reduce survival to the body's physical needs. For the reasons explained in the next chapter, Rand is not a materialist. Rand recognizes that the mind is our tool of survival, so our psychological needs are as real as our physical needs. For evidence, observe that a person's mental state affects his or her survival. Depression can be lethal because the depressed person is not motivated to take the actions he or she needs to live.

The value of an object is not self-evident. Values are not objects out there in the world. We must form our values by grasping facts about the world and evaluating these facts by the standard of human life. Is a dishwasher a value? The survival value of a dishwasher is not obvious. After all, some people seem to live perfectly well without one. Conceptual work is needed to grasp how a dishwasher can further a person's life by freeing his time to chat with friends, take a jog, or read a book.

Rand rejects the is-ought dichotomy.[20] David Hume argues that we cannot deduce an *ought* from an *is* because a deductive argument cannot get out of a premise that which is not already there.[21] Hume's observation is interpreted to mean that normative claims cannot be grounded in the facts of reality. Rand does not attempt to *deduce* normative conclusions from factual premises. Rand *induces* normative conclusions by using cognitive abstractions as a basis for goal-directed thinking. Rand recognizes that normative abstractions involve a different chain of concepts from cognitive abstractions. We must evaluate facts. We do so by reference to a standard that is itself based on the facts, namely the fact that life is a conditional form of existence.

Rand contrasts her *objective* theory of value with what she calls the *intrinsic* and *subjective* theories. The intrinsic theory holds that value is a property of a thing and that this property exists out there in the world independent of us. The subjective theory holds that values are the product of consciousness independent of facts. The intrinsic and subjective theories assume that if values are real, then they must exist as properties of things, like color, texture, solidity, odor, and sound. The intrinsicist claims to have found this property. The subjectivist claims not to be able to find it. Rand challenges the assumption that values must be properties of things to be real. According to Rand, values are products of consciousness that enable us to grasp specific facts about the world. For Rand, values are not *out there* (as they are for the intrinsicist) or *in here* (as they are for the subjectivist) but are the *"out there" as grasped by the "in here."*[22]

BUSINESSMEN CREATE OBJECTIVE VALUES

In the first chapter, we saw that businessmen are creative because they bring into existence new goods and new states of affairs. A computer manufacturer brings together components to create a laptop. A hairdresser cuts and styles his client's hair. We can now observe that there is an intellectual act that stands behind a businessman's creativity—the forming of *normative abstractions*.

Businessmen must engage in goal-directed thinking to produce goods or services. Businessmen must conceptualize the ends that his or her goods or services will serve. The computer manufacturer needs to think about the ends that the laptop will serve to determine how the laptop ought to be configured. The hairdresser needs to think about his client's goals to determine how he must manipulate the scissors.

Entrepreneurs form new normative abstractions. Scientists identify the facts of reality by forming cognitive abstractions. The entrepreneur is creative because he or she takes the discoveries of scientists and integrates them to conceptualize new ends and new goods and services that are to serve these ends. As Rand explains, "The businessman carries scientific discoveries from the laboratory of the inventor to industrial plants, and transforms them into material products that fill men's physical needs and expand the comfort of men's existence."[23]

Businessmen commercialize scientific discoveries. Commercialization consists of businessmen conceiving of the ends that scientific discoveries make possible, ends of which no one had previously thought.

Businessmen create values in the sense that they form the conceptual chains involved in normative thought. Consider how businessmen created the *value* of the internet. Businessmen did not create the internet. The internet was a government project. Among other factors, Vinton Cerf and Robert E. Kahn invented the TCP/IP protocol while working on a government grant. This protocol is the backbone of the internet. The internet does not possess value because of this protocol, however. Businessmen created the internet's value by conceptualizing the ends that this protocol makes possible, such as online stores (Amazon), video and music streaming services (Netflix and Spotify), social media platforms (Facebook and LinkedIn), and search engines (Google).

When talking about businessmen creating value one must be careful not to illicitly convert *objective value* into *intrinsic value*. A businessman creates value in the sense that he conceptualizes the factual grounds of objective values and, on this basis, produces goods or services that he believes his customers will judge to be of value. The goods or services that a businessman produces are *not* objective values until his customers *evaluate them as being of value in the context of their lives*. Recall, an object is only an objective value to the person who evaluates it as being of value and acts to gain and/or keep it. A businessman cannot evaluate for his customers. A businessman creates goods or services that are capable of being objective values should his customers concur with his evaluation.

Apple created the iPhone because Apple's designers judged that a smartphone would be of value to Apple's customers. These designers had to form *normative abstractions*. For the iPhone to be of objective value, Apple's customers had to grasp what the designers grasped within the context of their own lives. Apple does not create the iPhone's value status. Apple creates an object that serves certain ends and is capable of being valued by its customers. Without the iPhone, there would be nothing for Apple's customers to evaluate. From the customer's standpoint, Apple created one of his or her values.

PROFIT SIGNALS THE CREATION OF OBJECTIVE VALUE

In the first chapter, we saw that the demand for a good or service reflects the aggregate value judgments of individual customers. We can now observe that these aggregate value judgments are *objective*. Rand coined the term "socially objective value" to denote the value status of goods and services sold in the marketplace. Rand defines "socially objective value" as "the sum of the individual judgments of all the men involved in trade at a given time, the sum of what *they* valued, each in the context of his own life" (emphasis in original).[24] The iPhone is of socially objective value because millions of individuals judged the iPhone to be of value in the context of their own life. The iPhone's financial success is the social expression of these individual judgments.

In a free market, *profit* is the sign that a businessman has correctly judged the value of the goods or services that he or she offers for sale. *Loss* is the sign that a businessman has misjudged the value of these goods or services. The market mechanisms of profit and loss are the only means by which businessmen can discover the objective value of their goods or services. How did Apple learn that iPhones are of socially objective value? It made a profit. How did Blackberry learn that its phones were no longer of objective value? It made a loss.

Value is objective, not intrinsic. A businessman can identify how his goods or services further human ends. The status of a businessman's goods or services as objective values, however, depends on the judgments of the individuals who choose to purchase the good or service. To learn whether his goods or services are of objective value, a businessman needs to know the value judgments of the individuals in the marketplace. The market provides businessmen with this knowledge through his profit and loss statement.

CAUSALITY PROMOTES OBJECTIVE JUDGMENTS

Why do profit and loss signal the *objective* value of a good or service? Why not the *subjective* value judgments of customers? Systemic forces within a market system encourage individuals to make objective value judgments. In particular, the law of cause and effect functions as a feedback mechanism, helping individuals to learn from their mistakes.

Misjudgments of value adversely affect individuals' lives. A value is that which one acts to gain/and or keep. An individual who misjudges value is acting to gain and/or keep that which harms his or her life. The alcoholic who acts to gain a bottle of bourbon has misjudged the value of that bottle. Reality provides feedback in the form of hangovers, the loss of his job, the mortgagee-sale of his house, and the loss of his family. An obese man who acts to subsist on a diet of beer, doughnuts, and pizza has misjudged the value of this food.[25] Reality provides feedback in the form of an expanding waistline and type two diabetes.

Profit is a sign that a good or service is of socially objective value, and socially objective value is an aggregate of the value judgments of hundreds, thousands, or even millions of individuals. For a businessman to make a profit from a good or service that people mistakenly judge to be of value, these individuals must continue to value the good or service in defiance of the negative consequences for their own life.

A good's or service's status as a socially objective value implies that in the aggregate individuals find the good or service to be of genuine value, not that *everyone* finds it to be of value. Alcohol companies are profitable because most people are not alcoholics and know how to drink responsibly. Pizza companies are profitable because most people are not obese and know how to eat a balanced diet, treating themselves to pizza on special occasions.

The evidence that profit signals socially objective value can be found in the history of unprofitable products. Products are unprofitable when individuals in the marketplace do not judge these products to be of value. Apple's products have been cited several times as examples of products that are of socially objective value. Still, not all of Apple's products have been profitable. In 1994, Apple introduced the QuickTake camera, one of the world's first digital cameras. The QuickTake did not have an in-camera display. To see how a photo looked, you first had to transfer the image to your computer. The camera had memory capacity for eight photos. Imagine being on a family holiday. You snap eight photos. You cannot take any more photos until you return home. In comparison, a film camera allows you to swap the film and keep snapping. For the QuickTake to be profitable, millions of people would have had to purchase the camera in defiance of its apparent limitations.

The market is a process. Market mechanisms transmit individuals' judgments, and it can take time for people to think through the evidence and work out the value of a good or service. Value is not self-evident. A businessman can temporarily make a profit from a good or service that is *not* of objective value—while individuals work to figure out its value. Similarly, a businessman can temporarily make a loss from a good or service that *is* of objective value. A snapshot of the market does not tell us whether businessmen can make a profit from goods or services that are not of objective value. We need to look at how the profitability of a good or service develops over time.

The market transmits the judgments of investors as well as customers. A business's market value reflects investors' judgments about a company's future profitability. Amazon and Netflix ran at a loss for many years. These companies' market value did not reflect their *current* profitability but investors' judgments about *future* profitability. Investors judged that customers would come to find value in these companies' services, with future profits offsetting early losses.

Rand's account of socially *objective* value has striking similarities to Carl Menger's account of *subjective* value. Menger wrote before Rand had identified the objective-intrinsic-subjective trichotomy. Menger called his theory "subjective" because he wanted to emphasize that value is subject-dependent, in contrast to previous theories, which treated value as the intrinsic property of objects.[26] Like Rand, Menger recognizes that economic value judgments must be grounded in the relevant facts of reality. Menger's use of the word "subjective" is misleading. Menger has really provided an objective account of value. He did not classify his account as "objective" because he believed the intrinsic and subjective accounts to be the only classifications. He did not recognize an objective account as an option.

Profit and loss signal the socially objective value of a good or service—*in a free market*. Today, states regulate all economies. No economy is a free market. Government regulations distort the transmission of information about the value of goods and services provided by the economic mechanisms of profit and loss. We shall consider the implications for the moral status of profit maximization later in this chapter.

RAND'S ACCOUNT OF VIRTUE

Rand defines "value" as "that which one acts to gain and/or keep" and "virtue" as "the act by which one gains and/or keeps it."[27] Values identify the ends that we ought to pursue. Virtues identify the actions that we ought to take to achieve these ends.

According to Rand, a virtue is an action informed by a principle. Principles being the cognitive tool by which we grasp the actions that we must take to achieve our values. Rand defines "principle" as "a fundamental, primary, or general truth, on which other truths depend."[28] The principle of honesty, for example, identifies the general truth that "the unreal is unreal and can have no value."[29] Among other things, this means that there is no value in plagiarizing an essay, misrepresenting one's skills on a CV, or engaging in shenanigans with an intern in the Oval Office. The principle of honesty is grounded in the metaphysical fact that existence has primacy over consciousness, so pretending that the facts are otherwise does not change them. The evidence for the principle of honesty is to be found in studying past acts of honesty and dishonesty, observing the consequences, and grasping why these consequences must follow from these acts.

Principles do not perform the same cognitive function as rules. A principle is an abstract guide that moral agents must apply to specific situations. A rule is an injunction to take (or to refrain from taking) a specific action in a specific place. Courtesy is a principle. A "No Smoking" sign indicates a rule that is only applicable in the room in which the sign hangs. The principle of courtesy subsumes a range of situations, from not smoking in public places, to holding doors open for people, waiting your turn in line, and not parking in front of someone else's garage. Judgment is not needed to understand and follow a rule. The principle of courtesy, in contrast, requires the actor to exercise judgment. Should guards hold doors open for their prisoners, as a courtesy? Should an ambulance driver refrain from parking in front of someone else's garage in an emergency? The individual in the situation must make these judgments.

Rand's account of virtue may appear idiosyncratic. After all, contemporary virtue ethicists treat virtue as a *character trait*, not as an *action*. They also distinguish a virtue-approach to ethics from a principled-approach. Still, Rand's account is not as far removed from contemporary virtue ethics as may first appear. Rand recognizes that a virtue is a character trait. Rand stresses the action-aspect of virtue because she recognizes that action cultivates virtuous character traits and that the justification for cultivating a virtuous character is that so doing disposes a person to act virtuously.[30]

Rand embraces virtues and principles because she recognizes that the actions that cultivate a virtuous character are those actions informed by moral principles. A person needs principles to know what actions to take. Moreover, understanding why these actions are virtuous disposes him to act virtuously. A virtuous person would be repulsed at the thought of lying because he grasps the principle of honesty and so understands that there can be no value in dishonesty. To the virtuous person, who thinks in principles, there is no more incentive to lie than there is to cross a busy road blindfolded.

THE VIRTUE OF RATIONALITY

Rand argues that the basic virtue is *rationality*. She writes: "The virtue of *Rationality* means the recognition and acceptance of reason as one's only source of knowledge, one's only judge of values and one's only guide to action" (emphasis in original).[31] Implicit in Rand's definition are the two types of abstractions discussed above. Reason as one's only source of knowledge identifies our need to form cognitive abstractions. Reason as one's only judge of values and one's only guide to action identifies our need to form normative abstractions.

Rand recognizes that human consciousness possesses identity, just like physical objects. Francis Bacon observes that "Nature to be commanded must be obeyed."[32] Rand recognizes that we must obey the nature—or identity—of our consciousness to grasp the facts of reality. Rand discovered her theory of concepts by observing how consciousness functions through introspection.[33] The field that teaches us how to use our minds properly is called *epistemology*.

Rand holds that reason is our only means of grasping the facts of reality. There is no alternative. Either we act on reason, or we act blind. Emotions are sometimes treated as though they are an alternative. Rand, however, points out that "emotions are not tools of cognition."[34] Our emotions are grounded in our evaluation of the facts. Emotions provide us with important information. Paying attention to someone's emotions provides us with insight into his or her values. Emotions do not tell us whether or not an evaluation is justified. Both sides of the Brexit referendum had equally strong emotional responses to the outcome. Knowing a person's emotional response tells us their evaluation of Brexit; it does not tell us whether their evaluation is right or wrong.

Rand honors the crucial role of emotions in life. Rand recognizes that a person with reality-based values will have a rich emotional life. When our values are grounded in reality, there are no contradictions between our values. We feel passionate about our values and react angrily when our values are threatened. A person with conflicting values will have conflicting emotions, undercutting his or her emotional life. Reason and emotion are complimentary, for Rand, because she believes that rational thought leads to strong emotions.

THE BASIC VIRTUES

Rand identifies seven basic virtues. In addition to rationality, there are the virtues of independence, honesty, integrity, justice, productiveness, and pride.[35] These virtues subsume all of the actions that we need to obtain our values. Whatever we are acting to gain and/or keep, our actions need to instantiate these virtues.

The virtue of *independence* recognizes that we must think for ourselves. We must use *our* brains to discover knowledge, judge our values, and guide our actions. Other people can present us with their conclusions and the evidence that led them to these conclusions. These conclusions are not knowledge, for us, until we have grasped the factual basis of these conclusions for ourselves. A physicist can study Newton's work. Newton's discoveries are not knowledge for this physicist, however, until he grasps the truths of Newton's discoveries for himself.

We have already seen the role of independence in the earlier discussion of objective value. The pursuit of value is something that we must do ourselves because objective value depends on us grasping the value of the object that we are acting to gain and/or keep. Other people cannot grasp the value of an object on our behalf. As we saw earlier, a doctor's grasp of the vaccination's value does not put this knowledge into the head of an anti-vaxxer. The anti-vaxxer has to be intellectually convinced that the vaccine is worth going after before the vaccine will be of objective value to him.

The virtue of *honesty* recognizes that we must face the truth, the whole truth, and nothing but the truth.[36] Honesty is not a social virtue for Rand. She recognizes that a person can lie to himself by turning his mind away from uncomfortable facts. The unreal is unreal. Values must, therefore, be achieved in reality and cannot be achieved in a fantasy world of our own making. A student who has a midterm tomorrow can tell himself that he is prepared and does not need to study. However, if he has not mastered the material, then he has not mastered the material, and telling himself otherwise will not change this fact.

The virtue of *integrity* recognizes that we must put principles into practice. A value is that which one *acts* to gain and/or keep. A person who conceptualizes values but does not act on them does not really hold these ends as values. Stephen R. Covey's daughter tells the story of how Covey and she spent months planning a "date" together when she was twelve. When leaving the convention center, where Covey was giving a presentation on the day of their big night out, Covey met an old college friend he had not seen in many years. The friend invited Covey and his daughter to dinner. Covey thanked him for the invitation but declined, explaining that he has a "special date" planned with his daughter. Covey's daughter later said that this moment bonded them together forever because her father demonstrated that in his hierarchy of values, she mattered most.[37] Covey exhibited integrity because he acted on his values.

The virtue of *justice* recognizes that a person's character is a fact of reality. A person is not born with a particular character. He had to create his character through his choices and actions, and, within certain limits, he can change his character if he so chooses, for better or for worse. So long as a person has a particular character, we must treat him accordingly.[38] The scholarship should be given to the student who has demonstrated his aptitude for university through his academic performance. We should not go into business with a partner who has a record of cheating his clients. We should not marry a man with a history of philandering.

The virtue of *productiveness* recognizes that we should not adjust to the world but should adjust the world to us by remaking the world in the image of our values. We create a world fit for human life through the production of goods and services. We recognize the value of reading, so we create printing presses, publishing houses, bookstores, and e-book readers. We value seeing clearly, so we create eyeglasses and optometrists. We value health, so we create medical schools, hospitals, pharmacies, and life-saving drugs. We value entrepreneurship, so we create mechanisms for raising funds, such as limited liability corporations and stock markets on which to sell and buy shares in these corporations.

The virtue of *pride* recognizes that we must create a character that is worthy of achieving values. A value is that which *one* acts to *gain and/or keep*. A person will not act to gain and/or keep an object when he does not regard himself as a worthy beneficiary. A student will not put in the work needed to master a subject for a midterm exam when he believes that he is academically hopeless. A woman will not work to create a romantic relationship when she believes that she is unlovable. According to Rand, we must earn our own esteem by cultivating a virtuous character.

PROFIT MAXIMIZATION REQUIRES VIRTUE

Profit maximization requires businessmen to cultivate a virtuous character.[39] Profit is a sign that a businessman has created a good or service that is of socially objective value, and the virtues are the actions that a businessman must take to create such goods or services. Among other things, businessmen practice the virtue of rationality when they discipline their thinking to conceptualize life-furthering ends and the goods and services that can serve these ends.

We can find evidence for the role of rationality in profit maximization in studies of business success and failure. Jaana Woiceshyn's study of nineteen oil company CEOs found that those CEOs rated as "effective" by their peers made decisions based on facts, not emotion. These CEOs had a reputation for checking the quality of information before acting. As Woiceshyn explains, "The CEOs kept asking questions to get facts and to integrate them with their existing 'knowledge,' instead of relying on routine 'scripts.'"[40]

Edwin A. Locke's study of "prime movers" in business also found that successful businessmen were committed to the facts—and only to the facts. Locke notes that ineffective CEOs, in contrast, attempted to achieve business success in defiance of the facts. He gives the example of Macy's CEO, Edward Finkelstein, who intimidated subordinates and spent freely on perks while telling himself that an imaginary economic upturn would save the company.[41]

The virtue of rationality requires an active mind. The virtues are actions, and the virtue of rationality requires mental action. A businessman committed to using his mind to obtain knowledge and guide his actions must be an active thinker. John Allison was CEO and chairman of BB&T for twenty-three years. BB&T operated thirty-three community banks. Allison would visit each bank periodically and have lunch with board members, who were also local business leaders. Allison writes: "I never had a boring lunch. These individuals were always asking questions, expressing opinions, engaged, challenging, discussing, in gear. It was easy to see why they were successful. They were paying attention to life."[42]

The importance of virtue in business is perhaps best illustrated by a moral hazard that businessmen face daily—the temptation to lie. A businessman invests his life savings into starting his own business, a company that is to produce a new type of good. He genuinely believes that his future customers will judge this good to be of objective value. He invests all of his money. He also invests his time and makes an emotional commitment to the success of the business. The stakes are high. If the business fails, this man may lose his car, his house, and his reputation. As this man proceeds to develop the product, he encounters facts that should cause him to rethink the success of his venture. The temptation is for this man to mentally pull back from identifying the implications of these facts, so as not to confront the possibility that his venture will fail.

Of course, a virtuous businessman will not be tempted to evade facts. The virtuous businessman confronts the implications because he recognizes that the facts are what they are, and refusing to confront them now is self-defeating. He will recognize that if the venture is going to fail, it is best that he cuts his losses now and moves to a new venture instead of engaging in a futile attempt to hold off the inevitable.

Contrary to the assumptions of critics, few businessmen have the character of a Kenneth Lay or Elizabeth Holmes. Businessmen are more likely to lie to themselves than to their customers or investors. Consider Iridium's failure. Iridium was a consortium of aerospace and communication companies that set out to blanket the world with a network of satellites so that a person could make a phone call from anywhere on the planet. Motorola conceived of Iridium in 1987, when cell phones were rare. In a world dominated by corded phones, the evidence indicated that satellite phones would be of socially objective value. By the time Iridium opened for business, the world of portable communication had changed dramatically, with cell phones now commonplace. A year after opening for business, Iridium filed for bankruptcy.[43] Iridium's executives must have been aware of the changes in the communication market but persisted in trying to make Iridium a success in defiance of the facts.

THE MORALITY OF SELF-INTEREST

Rand's ethics is an ethics of self-interest. Rand defines "value" as "that which *one* acts to *gain and/or keep*." This definition implies that the actor must be the beneficiary of his or her actions. As we have seen, the pursuit of value requires the actor to grasp the value of the object that he or she acts to gain and/or keep. An object is only of value to the person who grasps its value and acts to gain and/or keep it. An object is not of value outside of this context. We can act to gain and/or keep objects that are of value to us. We cannot act to gain and/or keep objects that are to be of value to other people. The conclusion that values must be of benefit to the person who acts to gain and/or keep them is implicit in the pursuit of values.

We saw earlier that a doctor cannot provide a skeptical diabetic with the *value* of insulin. For insulin to be of value, the diabetic must grasp that insulin is an object worth pursuing. A doctor can benefit an unconscious diabetic by injecting him with insulin. A doctor cannot constantly be on standby with a syringe in his or her hand, however. The diabetic must hold insulin as a value to benefit from insulin injections. The insulin, therefore, can only be of value to the person who acts to gain and/or keep it.

Rand does not claim that people should not act to gain values for others. Instead, Rand claims that values are not the type of thing one person can give to another. The only conceivable way for one person to provide another with values is to get inside his head and coerce him into making the necessary intellectual identifications, which is impossible. We cannot coerce someone into intellectually grasping an object's value. All we can do is present a person with the evidence and then let him make up his own mind.

Self-interest is not the foundation of Rand's ethics but a corollary of her objective theory of value. Jan Österberg states that egoism is usually taken to be an answer to the question, "What, fundamentally, ought one to do?"[44] Rand's egoism is an answer to the question, "Who ought to benefit from what one, fundamentally, ought to do?" For Rand, self-interest is about benefiting from the achievement of *values*, values that the actor has conceptualized based on facts about the relationship between the objects of his or her actions, and the requirements of human life.

Philosophy textbooks and newspaper columns often caricature Rand's ethics as a type of ethical egoism. Still, some academic philosophers have acknowledged that Rand's ethics does not resemble ethical egoism as it is usually understood. John Hospers observes that if Rand's ethics "is to be called egoistic at all, it is a very different brand of egoism from the traditional variety."[45] Michael Heumer observes that nowhere in Rand's works "will one find a statement that looks like" ethical egoism.[46]

Rand's egoism does not resemble the ethical egoism of the philosophy literature because moral philosophers interpret egoism as an answer to the question of whose interests should have priority when interests conflict.[47] Egoism, on this interpretation, holds that a person should choose his or her own interests at the expense of others' interests.

Rand's egoism does not require that we pursue values at others' expense. On the contrary, we should expect others to benefit from our pursuit of values. Working to sustain a romantic relationship with our spouse benefits us, our spouse, and our children.

The standard objections to ethical egoism do not apply to Rand's egoism. James Rachels asserts that the problem with egoism is that it is unacceptably arbitrary. He claims that egoists advocate dividing the world into two categories—us and all the rest. The egoist then maintains that we should regard the interests of the first group (us) as more important than the interests of the second group (all the rest). For Rachels, egoism belongs in the same category as anti-Semitism, nationalism, sexism, ageism, and all the other forms of group-ism.[48]

Rand does not divide people into groups. The point of Rand's egoism is that a value is an object that can only be of benefit to the person who acts to gain and/or keep it. There is nothing in the pursuit of values that requires other people to lose for us to benefit. Valuing is not a zero-sum game. The pursuit of values benefits ourselves and others. When we maintain our house, so doing is a value to us and a benefit to our neighbors.

Rand does not believe that we can provide other people with *values*. A value is not the only type of benefit possible, however. "Value" and "benefit" are not synonymous. "Value" denotes a class of benefits that depend on us acting to gain and/or keep them. We can benefit other people in our pursuit of values even though this benefit is not a value to the beneficiary of our actions.

TRADE

Profit is the market mechanism through which businessmen learn that they have created a good or service that is of socially objective value. Rand's argument implies that businessmen cannot provide their customers with values. Nevertheless, businessmen appear to be doing so when they sell goods or services.

Businessmen do not provide their customers with *values*. Businessmen *trade* with their customers, and trade requires customers to *evaluate* the good or service as an object worth acting to gain. The goods and services that businessmen offer for sale are not objective values until their customers make an evaluation.

Apple produces the Apple Watch because its designers judge that the Apple Watch possesses properties that will further the lives of its customers, such as monitoring its wearer's heartbeat and alerting emergency services in the event of a fall. Apple's designers may have correctly identified the factual grounds for thinking that the Apple Watch will be of value. The Apple Watch is *not* an objective value at this point, however. The Apple Watch only becomes an objective value when its customers grasp these facts for themselves and evaluate the Apple Watch as a good worth purchasing. A trade requires customers to make such an evaluation.

The moral beauty of the trading relationship is that through a trade, we can obtain values created by other people. A trade demands that both parties make an evaluation. The seller and buyer have to evaluate what the other is offering. The trade goes ahead only when both sides judge that the other is offering an object worth acting to gain.[49]

Profit is a businessman's reward for correctly judging the value of a good or service. Profit is itself an objective value to the businessman who acts to gain and/or keep it. The word "profit" means "advantage" or "benefit." The excess of revenues over expenses came to be called "profit" because people recognized that this excess is of benefit to the business's owners. Profit is often thought to be self-interested because a businessman is maximizing cash in his bank account. This understanding is superficial. We find the self-interest of profit in the division of labor, which is what enables a businessman to pursue his values by creating goods and services that are of value to his customers.

PROFIT MAXIMIZATION MEETS THE *WHAT* AND *HOW* CONDITIONS

Profit is a businessman's reward for creating goods or services that are of socially objective value. Profit maximization meets the *what* condition because businessmen need to conceptualize how their goods and services can serve human ends in order to maximize profit. Profit maximization meets the *how* condition because creating goods and services that are of socially objective value requires businessmen to cultivate the virtues. The pursuit of profit is morally demanding, requiring businessmen to discipline their thinking as they work to create goods and services that will be of objective value to their customers.

A businessman who fails at the task of profit maximization can still be moral. Rand recognizes that the chain of concepts involved in forming normative abstractions is more complex than the chain involved in forming cognitive abstractions.[50] Intellectually, the businessman who sets out to create goods and services that are of objective value has a more challenging task than the research scientist. A virtuous businessman can work diligently to create a good or service that he or she believes will further human life—and be mistaken.

When evaluating a businessman, the moral standard is whether a businessman *seeks* to create goods or services that are of socially objective value by cultivating the virtues and conceptualizing the ends that his goods or services are to serve. If a businessman correctly identifies the value relationships, his reward is profit. If a businessman fails, he will not make a profit, but he is no less moral.

The *what* and *how* conditions are not separate. These conditions are different perspectives on the single act of creating value. The *what* condition pertains to the end. The *how* condition pertains to the means. Cultivating a vicious character is not a means of creating goods and services that are of socially objective value. A businessman fails to meet the *what* condition when he or she fails to meet the *how* condition. A person with a vicious character is irrational, unthinking, dishonest, hypocritical, unjust, lazy, and lacks self-worth. A businessman with these characteristics cannot create objective value.

IMMORAL PROFIT

Profit is a sign that a businessman has produced goods or services that are of objective value because the law of cause and effect constitutes a feedback mechanism that encourages people to make better decisions. Nevertheless, a businessman can make a profit from goods and services that are not of objective value to the extent that irrational beliefs persist in a society. The efficacy of reality's feedback mechanism depends on a person grasping the relationship between his or her actions and the effects of those actions. An irrational person is not capable of grasping the causal relationship. To the extent that people within a society embrace the irrational, a businessman can make a profit from running a psychic hotline, running a New Age bookstore that sells healing crystals and books on astral projection and reincarnation, or by providing alternative medicine, such as aromatherapy, reflexology, and Reiki.

Let us set aside the issue of whether these goods or services would exist in a free market. One could make a case that these goods and services are profitable today because the state-mandated education system has been systematically undermining children's ability to think conceptually.[51] George Walsh observes that primitive people embrace mysticism in those areas of life where they lack a sense of control.[52] The products of an anti-conceptual education system turn to mysticism for a similar reason; their minds are not competent to grasp the facts of reality, and so they seek solace in belief systems that purport to provide them with knowledge of the world without the mental discipline required for conceptual thought. Considering why these beliefs persist is outside of this book's scope. For our purposes, the question is the moral status of the profit a businessman makes by catering to these beliefs.

The businessman who seeks to maximize profit by creating objective value is not engaged in the same task as the businessman who seeks to maximize profit by catering to the irrational. A moral businessman seeks to grasp the facts of reality. He disciplines his thinking to grasp factual relationships between the properties of specific goods and services and the end of human life. A "New Age" businessman turns away from the facts of reality. He pretends that he is creating value for his customers by evading all of the facts to the contrary. A moral businessman accepts reason as his only source of knowledge, his only source of values, and his only guide to action. A New Age businessman rejects reason in favor of some form of extrasensory knowledge. A moral businessman is committed to the truth, the whole truth, and only the truth. A New Age businessman brushes aside evidence that would call into question the value of his goods or services.

Reiki healers, for example, claim to create value for their clients by transferring universal energy through their palms to their patient's body. There is no scientific evidence for this energy's existence or Reiki's effectiveness. Reiki healers harm their clients. At best, clients are spending their wealth on a useless service instead of on goods or services that are of objective value. At worst, clients are sabotaging their health and possibly even threatening their lives by shunning conventional medicine.

The profits of New Age businessmen are immoral because these businessmen are not seeking to create objective value, and they are not instantiating the virtues.

Some New Age businessmen are not businessmen but con artists. These people do not believe that they are creating value for their clients. Instead, they are preying on their clients' credulity to convince them to part with their money. These "businessmen" are fraudsters. The "profit" of these "businessmen" is not immoral because it is not *profit*. The cash that these "businessmen" alleviate from their clients is properly designated *loot*.

ENTREPRENEURIAL JERKS

The entrepreneur who is a "brilliant jerk" might seem to be counterevidence to my claim that a businessman needs to meet the *how* condition to meet the *what* condition. Steve Jobs seems to be an example of a businessman who violated the *how* condition while creating goods and services of socially objective value.

A virtuous businessman is not necessarily someone who is going to be liked. Russell T. Davies is a successful television producer and scriptwriter. Davies describes how, during his career, he had to sack actors, rewrite writers, and banish directors. He writes: "I know of one script editor, who I had booted off a show years ago, who still calls me the Devil incarnate. But he was rubbish. So he was removed. Good."[53] This script editor labeled Davies the "Devil incarnate" because of his virtues. Virtuousness is not the same as niceness. While Davies is not a businessman, we should expect businessmen to be similarly criticized for maintaining the moral standards demanded by the pursuit of value.

One must be cautious about public reports of a person's character. Portrayals of well-known people often generalize one or two incidences as though they represent the total of a person's life. Examining the facts about Jobs's character is outside the scope of this book. All we can do here is note that those who worked closely with Jobs have challenged the popular portrayals. Tim Cook, for example, had the following to say about the Walter Isaacson biography, which presented Jobs as a flawed genius: "The person I read about there is somebody I would never have wanted to work with over all this time. Life is too short. . . . It's emphatically untrue that he wasn't a great human being, and that is totally not understood."[54]

WHY BUSINESSMEN SHOULD MAXIMIZE PROFIT

In the first chapter, we saw that there is a distinction between the morality of *profit* and the morality of profit *maximization*. Why should businessmen seek to *maximize* profit? What is wrong with a *satisfactory* profit?

Profit maximization is foremost an intellectual enterprise. To maximize profit, a businessman must have an active mind. A self-imposed limit on profit is a self-imposed limit on thought. A businessman reads a magazine article on a new type of material produced by NASA called memory foam. His mind goes to work. He projects how memory foam could improve human life by being cast in the form of pillows, mattresses, and protective headgear. Now, imagine that this businessman is already making a satisfactory profit from his current enterprises. To avoid maximizing profit, he would have to push these thoughts aside and go back to reading his magazine.

Calls for profit satisfaction seem plausible if one assumes that the pursuit of profit is a zero-sum game. In this view, a businessman who seeks to maximize profit is like a child who seeks to maximize his share of a cake. Instead of taking a satisfactory amount and leaving the rest for his siblings, he takes the largest possible slice for himself. Businessmen do not *take* profit. Businessmen *create* profit by creating goods and services that are of socially objective value. We should want businessmen to maximize profit because when they do, we are all better off.

Business ethicists treat profit maximization with suspicion because they confuse profit *maximization* with profit *prioritization*. To maximize something means to get as much of that thing as possible. Business ethicists fear that the profit-maximizing businessman will seek to prioritize profit above more important values, such as human life. Chapter 5 explores the distinction between profit *maximization* and profit *prioritization*. For now, we shall just note that the fear of a conflict between profit and human well-being is misguided. A businessman who seeks to maximize profit seeks to maximize his or her reward for creating goods and services that are of objective value, which means goods and services that *further human life*. We should no more fear the businessman who seeks to maximize profit than we should fear the scientist who seeks to maximize knowledge.

PROFIT IN A REGULATED ECONOMY

Profit signals the creation of socially objective value—*in a free market*. Profit does not necessarily signal the creation of socially objective value in a regulated economy.

In a free market, reality's feedback mechanism encourages people to make better judgments because they must confront the consequences of their actions. In a regulated economy, the state cushions people from the consequences, depriving them of a learning opportunity.

A couple reapplied for welfare. The man is thirty and unemployed. The woman is twenty-five and works in a daycare center. When a welfare worker reviewed their spending, she found that the couple spent $36 each month at a fitness center. The welfare worker was not surprised. She finds that people who cannot afford necessities keep their cable subscription and call waiting.[55] People do not have to adjust their spending to fit within their financial constraints when the state provides them with food and shelter.

This problem is not restricted to welfare beneficiaries. The state also cushions corporate executives from the consequences of their bad choices. In the aftermath of the 2008 financial crisis, Congress voted to provide $700 billion of financial assistance to corporations to protect them from the natural consequences of their bad judgments. Under the Troubled Asset Relief Program (TARP), J. P. Morgan Chase received $25 billion, Wells Fargo $25 billion, AIG $40 billion, Bank of America $45 billion, and CitiGroup $50 billion.[56]

In a regulated economy, a businessman cannot know whether his profits signify the objective judgment of his customers or a subjective judgment that appears to be efficacious because customers are cushioned from the consequences. Goods and services that are profitable today may not exist in a free market. Psychic hotlines are profitable, today. In a free market, a person who attempted to run his or her life by the advice of psychics would soon come up against reality's feedback mechanism. In a regulated economy, this person can return to psychics for advice safe in the knowledge that the welfare state will meet his or her basic needs.

In a free market, market mechanisms transmit the judgments of individuals. In a regulated market, market mechanisms transmit the judgments of bureaucrats.

Consider the Natural Gas Crisis of 1977. Natural gas was selling at the market rate of $2 per thousand cubic feet in the states in which it was produced. In other states, the price of natural gas was set by the Federal Power Commission, which imposed a maximum price of $1.42 per thousand cubic feet. In a free market, price signals value judgments. Normally, the price of $2 per thousand cubic feet would have signaled to businessmen that the customers in these states value natural gas more than the customers where the price is $1.42 per thousand cubic feet. In this case, the price in other states did not reflect the value judgments of customers, but the judgments of the bureaucrats in the Federal Power Commission. The winter of 1977 was exceptionally cold in some states. The customers in these states would have happily paid more than $2 per thousand cubic feet, signaling the value of the natural gas to them. The government prevented them from paying a market rate, however. Consequently, customers in these states were deprived of an objective value—and froze.[57]

In a free market, businessmen have to create objective value to maximize profit. In a regulated economy, a businessman can maximize profit by taking advantage of government regulations.

The Union Pacific Railroad was founded to take advantage of government favors granted under the Pacific Railroad Act of 1862. Under this act, the United States government provided the Union Pacific with twenty alternate sections of land free and government loans for each mile of track laid. The Union Pacific's profits depended on the miles of track laid not on whether the track was of socially objective value, so the Union Pacific laid winding roads to increase the mileage.[58]

The Union Pacific's profits depended on executives pleasing politicians not on furthering the ends of their customers. As a result, executives invested in politicians, wining and dining senators, ambassadors, and government bureaucrats, serving them Chinese duck and Roman goose while an orchestra played. Free railroad passes were distributed to members of Congress and state legislatures.[59]

Profits that result from government favors do not meet the *what* and *how* conditions and are, therefore, *immoral*. These profits do not meet the *what* condition because they do not signify the creation of objective value. These profits do not meet the *how* condition because the character traits needed to schmooze politicians are not the same traits needed to create objective value. Among other things, such a businessman is more concerned with getting into favor with the government of the day instead of accurately conceptualizing the relevant facts of reality.

In a free market, competition is a good thing because businessmen are competing against each other and against themselves to create goods or services that are of objective value. Apple competes against Samsung to see who can offer the greatest value to customers. Apple also competes against itself because customers will only purchase a new iteration of a product when they judge the product to be of greater value than previous iterations. As a result, the market operates to continually introduce new goods and services of greater socially objective value.

In a regulated economy, businessmen can hobble their competitors through regulation. In some states, funeral directors use the law to prevent retailers from competing in the sale of caskets and urns. A funeral director might sell a stainless steel casket for $3,494. The same casket would sell in a retail store for $1,499. To prevent retailers from competing, funeral directors teamed up with local legislatures to mandate that only licensed funeral directors can sell caskets.[60] The profits of these funeral directors do not signify the creation of objective value, but their success at closing this market to competitors.

Profits that result from businessmen using the law to prevent competition are *immoral*. Customers purchase these businessmen's goods or services not because they judge their goods or services to be of superior value, but because other options have been legally closed to them.

Businessmen have a moral obligation to advocate for free markets. A free market does not necessarily favor businessmen. Some businessmen may find that businesses that are profitable in a regulated economy will not be profitable in a free market. Nevertheless, businessmen should advocate for free markets because they need market mechanisms to know whether they have created goods or services that are of socially objective value.

VALUE IN CONTEMPORARY BUSINESS ETHICS

The moral case for profit maximization depends on Rand's objective theory of value. Rand was a passionate advocate for the profits of businessmen because she recognizes that values are objective, not intrinsic or subjective. Contemporary business ethicists do not recognize the morality of profit maximization because they do not recognize that values are objective. Business ethicists treat values as *collective* and *subjective*.

In the first chapter, we saw that the *raison d'être* of contemporary business ethics is to solve the problem of how to subject an artificial entity to moral obligations. We can now add that business ethicists think that corporations have a moral obligation to promote the *values of society*.

These values are not the aggregation of the value judgments of individuals, but the values of society considered as a whole. Business ethicists do not attempt to validate these values by appealing to the facts of reality. The values of society are the values that the self-appointed spokesmen for society believe should be of social importance, such as feeding the homeless or raising awareness of climate change.

The assumption that value is collective and subjective is evident from the examples that business ethicists cite of businessmen who create value. As we saw in the introduction, the proponents of CSR cite Ben & Jerry's support of a campaign to raise awareness of the threat of global warming as an example of how businessmen can use their companies to do good.[61] They do not mention the objective value of Ben & Jerry's ice cream.

Throughout the business ethics literature, CSR's proponents assume that the businessman who cares about *creating value* is the businessman who gives his or her employees time off to feed the homeless, not the businessman who creates smartphones; the businessman who founds an organization to fund research into breast cancer, not the businessman who creates driverless cars; the businessman who raises awareness of income inequality, not the businessman who creates a sports drink to refresh athletes.

There is a respect in which the moral case for profit maximization shares the same concern as contemporary business ethicists, namely the belief that businessmen should be concerned with creating value. Business ethicists do not recognize that businessmen are already creating value through the production of goods and services because their understanding of value is flawed. In chapter 7, we explore the philosophical assumptions that ground their understanding of value.

THE EVIDENCE

Profit maximization is moral because profit is a businessman's reward for creating goods or services that are of objective value. The pursuit of profit is moral when businessmen seek to conceptualize value relationships that are grounded in the facts of reality. The pursuit of profit is not moral when businessmen cater to people's irrationality or take advantage of government regulations.

This chapter has outlined the moral case for profit maximization. Chapter 3 provides evidence that profit maximization meets the *what* condition by looking at how businessmen maximize profit by creating goods and services that serve human ends. Among other things, this chapter shall consider the role of the intellect in the creation of the wheel, the refrigerator, and the shipping container.

Chapter 4 provides evidence that profit maximization meets the *how* condition by examining the biographies of three historical businessmen. We shall see that J. P. Morgan, John D. Rockefeller, and Thomas Edison possessed the character traits needed to create goods and services that are of objective value. As evidence that these virtues are needed to create value in all areas of life, we shall consider the character traits of Louis Pasteur, which are strikingly similar to the character traits of the foregoing businessmen.

NOTES

1. Louis P. Pojman and James Fieser, *Ethics: Discovering Right and Wrong*, 7th ed. (Boston, MA: Wadsworth, 2012), 81. Pojman and Fieser open their chapter on egoism with a quote from Rand's *The Virtue of Selfishness*. They then proceed to discuss the case of Nestlé allegedly using manipulative advertising techniques to sell baby formula to third-world mothers. According to Nestlé's critics, the mothers mixed the formula with contaminated water resulting in the deaths of millions of infants. Pojman and Fieser describe the Nestlé case as one of the "most notorious examples of selfishness in the business world." Juxtaposing Rand's endorsement of selfishness with the description of the Nestlé case as an example of selfishness in business implies that Rand would have approved of Nestlé's alleged actions. Cf. Robert White, "Profit Maximization Does Not Necessitate Profit Prioritization," *The Journal of Ayn Rand Studies* 17, no. 2 (December 2017): 223n6. For a critique of the popular accounts of the Nestlé case, see Fred D. Miller Jr., *Out of the Mouths of Babes: The Infant Formula Controversy*

(Bowling Green, OH: The Social Philosophy and Policy Center, 1983). Chapter 5 discusses the Nestlé case.

2. Michael Szenberg, "Philosophical Pattern Comparisons among Eminent Economists," *The American Economist* 37, no. 1 (Spring 1993): 19n23; Archie B. Carroll et al., *Corporate Responsibility: The American Experience* (Cambridge: Cambridge University Press, 2012), 225.

3. Ayn Rand, "The Objectivist Ethics," in *The Virtue of Selfishness: A New Concept of Egoism* (New York: Signet, 1964), 16.

4. For a discussion of Rand's method, see Leonard Peikoff, *Objectivism through Induction* (Irvine, CA: Ayn Rand Institute, 1997), lecture ten.

5. Tara Smith, *Viable Values: A Study of Life as the Root and Reward of Morality* (Lanham, MD: Rowman & Littlefield Publishers, 2000), 84.

6. Tara Smith, "The Importance of the Subject in Objective Morality: Distinguishing Objective from Intrinsic Value," in *Objectivism, Subjectivism, and Relativism in Ethics*, ed. Ellen Frankel Paul, Fred D. Miller Jr., and Jeffery Paul (Cambridge: Cambridge University Press, 2008), 138.

7. Ibid., 137.

8. Rand, "The Objectivist Ethics," 16.

9. Ayn Randa, "The Ethics of Emergencies," in *The Virtue of Selfishness: A New Concept of Egoism* (New York: Signet, 1964), 52–53. Ethicists are often too quick to assume sacrifice because they conflate *forgoing* a value with *sacrificing* a value. Rand recognizes that forgoing a value is not a sacrifice when the result is the achievement of a higher value. Thus, Rand argues that helping a friend in financial trouble is not a sacrifice but an act of integrity because a friend's well-being should be more important than buying a gadget for oneself.

10. Smith, "The Importance of the Subject in Objective Morality," 141.

11. Leonard Peikoff, *Objectivism: The Philosophy of Ayn Rand* (New York: Meridian, 1993), 243.

12. Henry B. Veatch and Francis H. Parker, *Logic as a Human Instrument* (New York: Harper & Row, 1959), 25n12.

13. Ayn Rand, "The Psycho-Epistemology of Art," in *The Romantic Manifesto: A Philosophy of Literature*, revised ed. (New York: Signet, 1975), 18.

14. "The Objectivist Ethics," 17.

15. Robert Tarr, "Economic Theory and Conceptions of Value: Rand and Austrians versus the Mainstream," in *Foundations of a Free Society: Reflections on Ayn Rand's Political Philosophy*, ed. Gregory Salmieri and Robert Mayhew (Pittsburgh: University of Pittsburgh Press, 2019), 330–31.

16. Rand, "The Objectivist Ethics," 18.

17. Tara Smith, *Ayn Rand's Normative Ethics: The Virtuous Egoist* (New York: Cambridge University Press, 2006), 32.

18. Peikoff, *Objectivism*, 212–13.

19. Cf. Robert White, "Egoless Egoists: The Second-Hand Lives of Mad Men," in *Mad Men and Philosophy: Nothing Is as It Seems*, ed. Rod Carveth and James B. South (Hoboken, NJ: John Wiley & Sons, 2010), 81–82.

20. Rand, "The Objectivist Ethics," 18 and 24.

21. David Hume, *A Treatise of Human Nature*, ed. L. A. Selby-Bigge (Oxford: Clarendon Press, 1958), 423. For a discussion of Hume's argument, see Charles R. Pigden, "Naturalism," in *A Companion to Ethics*, ed. Peter Singer (Oxford: Blackwell Publishers, 1993), 423. For a discussion of how Rand overcomes Hume, see Smith, *Viable Values*, 101–103; Tibor R. Machan, *Ayn Rand* (New York: Peter Lang, 1999), 59–63.

22. Peikoff, *Objectivism*, 112.

23. Ayn Rand, *For the New Intellectual: The Philosophy of Ayn Rand* (New York: Signet, 1961), 27.

24. Ayn Rand, "What Is Capitalism?" in *Capitalism: The Unknown Ideal* (New York: Signet, 1967), 24–25.

25. This example is suggested by Yaron Brook and Don Watkins, *Free Market Revolution: How Ayn Rand's Ideas Can End Big Government* (New York: Palgrave Macmillan, 2012), 70.

26. Tarr, "Economic Theory and Conceptions of Value," 347–48 and 359–60.
27. Rand, "The Objectivist Ethics," 27.
28. Rand, "The Anatomy of Compromise," 144.
29. Rand, *For the New Intellectual*, 129.
30. Smith, *Ayn Rand's Normative Ethics*, 48–52.
31. Rand, "The Objectivist Ethics," 28.
32. B. H. G. Wormald, *Francis Bacon: History, Politics and Science, 1561–1626* (Cambridge: Cambridge University Press, 1993), 168.
33. Ayn Rand, *Introduction to Objectivist Epistemology*, ed. Harry Binswanger and Leonard Peikoff, expanded second ed. (New York: Meridian, 1990), 307.
34. Rand, *For the New Intellectual*, 55.
35. Ibid., 128.
36. Peikoff, *Objectivism*, 267–68.
37. Greg McKeown, *Essentialism: The Disciplined Pursuit of Less* (London: Virgin Books, 2014), 133–34.
38. Ayn Rand, "The Metaphysical Versus the Man-Made," in *Philosophy: Who Needs It* (New York: Signet, 1984), 31.
39. For examples of how the virtues promote profit maximization, see Jaana Woiceshyn, *How to Be Profitable and Moral: A Rational Egoist Approach to Business* (Lanham, MD: Hamilton Books, 2012).
40. Jaana Woiceshyn, "Lessons from 'Good Minds': How CEOs Use Intuition, Analysis and Guiding Principles to Make Strategic Decisions," *Long Range Planning* 42, no. 3 (2009): 305–306.
41. Edwin A. Locke, *The Prime Movers: Traits of the Great Wealth Creators*, second ed. (Irvine, CA: The Ayn Rand Bookstore, 2008), 40.
42. John A. Allison, *The Leadership Crisis and the Free Market Cure: Why the Future of Business Depends on the Return to Life, Liberty, and the Pursuit of Happiness* (New York: McGraw Hill, 2015), 38–39.
43. Donna Greiner and Theodore B. Kinni, *Ayn Rand and Business* (New York: Texere, 2001), 62–63.
44. Jan Österberg, *Self and Others: A Study of Ethical Egoism* (Dordrecht: Kluwer Academic Publishers, 1988), 14.
45. John Hospers, "Ayn Rand's Philosophical Significance," *Reason Papers*, no. 23 (Fall 1998): 92.
46. Michael Huemer, "Is Benevolent Egoism Coherent?" *The Journal of Ayn Rand Studies* 3, no. 2 (Spring 2002): 277.
47. Kurt Baier, "Egoism," in *A Companion to Ethics*, ed. Peter Singer (Oxford: Blackwell Reference, 1991), 201–202; Kai Nielsen, *Why Be Moral?* (Buffalo, NY: Prometheus Books, 1989), 169–70.
48. James Rachels and Stuart Rachels, *The Elements of Moral Philosophy*, 5th ed. (New York: McGraw-Hill, 2007), 87. Stuart Rachels took over the book with the fifth edition, following his father's death. James Rachels originated the arbitrariness argument against egoism. Rachels' argument is curious because it is altruism that divides the world into "us" and "all the rest" and holds the second group to be more important than the first. Altruism would, therefore, seem to suffer from the very group-ism for which Rachels criticizes egoism.
49. For a discussion of the nature of the trading relationship, see Robert White, "Ayn Rand Versus Adam Smith," *The Journal of Ayn Rand Studies* 7, no. 1 (Fall 2005): 148.
50. Rand, "The Psycho-Epistemology of Art," 18.
51. Ayn Rand, "The Comprachicos," in *Return of the Primitive: The Anti-Industrial Revolution*, ed. Peter Schwartz, new expanded edition of *The New Left: The Anti-Industrial Revolution* (New York: Meridian, 1999). For a comparison of the state of education in early America with the state of education today, see Andrew Bernstein, "Heroes and Villains in American Education," *The Objective Standard* 13, no. 3 (Fall 2018).
52. George Walsh, *The Role of Religion in History* (New Brunswick, NJ: Transaction Publishers, 1998), 17.

53. Russell T. Davies and Benjamin Cook, *The Writer's Tale: The Final Chapter* (London: BBC Books, 2010), 97.

54. Brent Schlender and Rick Tetzeli, *Becoming Steve Jobs: The Evolution of a Reckless Upstart into a Visionary Leader* (New York: Crown Business, 2015), 392. Schlender and Tetzeli present Jobs as an *immature* genius who matured during his years away from Apple. The Jobs presented by Schlender and Tetzeli confirms the argument made in this chapter about the relationship between character and value.

55. David Kelley, *A Life of One's Own: Individual Rights and the Welfare State* (Washington, DC: Cato Institute, 1998), 105.

56. Thomas Sowell, *The Housing Boom and Bust*, revised ed. (New York: Basic Books, 2010), 84.

57. George Reisman, *Capitalism: A Treatise on Economics* (Ottawa, IL: Jameson Books, 1998), 222–23.

58. Burton W. Folsom, *The Myth of the Robber Barons: A New Look at the Rise of Big Business in America*, 5th ed. (Herndon, VA: Young America's Foundation, 2007), 18.

59. Ibid., 20–21.

60. See, for example, the case brought by the Institute of Justice against the Alabama Board of Funeral Service, https://ij.org/case/alabama-caskets/.

61. Philip Kotler and Nancy Lee, *Corporate Social Responsibility: Doing the Most Good for Your Company and Your Cause* (Hoboken, NJ: John Wiley & Sons, 2005), 55.

Chapter Three

The Objective Value of Goods and Services

This chapter provides evidence that businessmen produce goods and services that are of objective value. The first chapter established that the morality of profit maximization depends on businessmen producing goods or services that are of genuine value. The second chapter established the theoretical basis for concluding that profit signifies the production of goods and services that are of objective value. Drawing upon the histories of the wheel, the refrigerator, and the shipping container, this chapter demonstrates that businessmen engage in the type of goal-directed thinking that characterizes the conceptualization of objective value.

This chapter then considers an implication of the value status of goods and services, namely that pursuing profit is not materialistic. We reject the mind-body dichotomy, which impedes people's recognition of the role of values in profit maximization. We then consider how a person's purchasing decisions express his or her values.

This chapter concludes by considering why opposition to the production of goods and services is opposition to the pursuit of values.

WHEELS

Chapter 2 argued that businessmen produce goods and services that are of objective value, which requires businessmen to form normative abstractions. In the histories of the wheel, the refrigerator, and the shipping container, we see individuals conceptualizing facts and integrating these facts to conceptualize new ends.

We could have looked at any three objects. We look at these goods because of their physicality. People do not usually think of these goods as instantiations of human values, like Victor Hugo's *Les Misérables* or Ludwig von Beethoven's ninth symphony; yet, that is what they are.

The invention and adoption of the wheel required the conceptualization of ends and the means to these ends. Today, the benefits of the wheel are so evident that we do not pause to reflect on whether we need wheels to achieve our ends. We drive to work on wheels. We sit on wheeled chairs. We push our shopping around a supermarket in a cart that moves on wheels. At the weekends, we may relax by going for a bike ride in the park, on wheels, while our son or daughter rides a scooter next to us, on wheels. We pull our luggage to planes on wheels. Wheels are such a ubiquitous part of modern life that it may seem no thought is required to grasp the wheel's value. History shows otherwise.

People carried objects before the invention and adoption of the wheel. When there were too many objects for a single person to carry the task was divided among different people. In some countries, animals were used to carry objects, or dogs dragged the objects along the ground on a travois.[1]

These transportation methods were not only used by societies that had yet to discover the wheel. They were also used by societies that knew about the wheel but did not grasp its value. The Olmec people in Tres Zapotes knew about the wheel; their children played with toy dogs that rolled along on wheels. Still, they did not grasp the transportation value of the wheel.[2]

The wheel does not impress knowledge of its value onto us. In chapter 2, we saw that normative reasoning is distinct from cognitive reasoning. We have to know facts about the wheel before we can conceptualize how the wheel can serve human ends. The value status of the wheel is not evident from these facts alone, however. The wheel was not of value to the Olmec people because they did not conceptualize the ends that the wheel could serve, aside from entertainment as part of a children's toy.

Richard W. Bulliet argues that the wheel was invented when people were confronted by an end that could not be achieved by traditional methods of transportation. According to Bulliet, people confronted this possibility in the copper mines of the Carpathian Mountains in Eastern Europe.[3] The end was moving copper ore out of the mines. Traditional transportation could not achieve this end efficiently, prompting an unknown inventor to look for an alternative. He or she proposed transporting the copper ore out of the mines in a basket that rolls on wheels.[4]

For evidence of the role of values in the adoption of the wheel, observe that mistaken value judgments prevented the adoption of the wheel in some societies, even when they widely used wheeled transportation. The peoples of some German nations, for example, rejected the carriage as a means of transportation because, in their judgment, traveling on wheels undermines the manly virtues of dignity, courage, honor, and loyalty.[5] Carriages were only adopted in these countries after cannons were mounted on wheels, demonstrating that wheels could serve a manly purpose.[6] These people accurately identified facts about the wheel. Still, mistakes in normative reasoning prevented them from grasping the wheel's value. Similarly, rickshaws were adopted in some countries and not in others, because people in the latter countries believed that rickshaws reduced the puller to the level of a farm animal.[7]

The inventors of the wheel needed to conceptualize the ends that the wheel was to serve and a wheel that could achieve these ends. A wheel is not just a round object that rolls along the ground. There are different types of wheels. The original wheel used in the copper mines of the Carpathian Mountains was a *wheelset*.[8] A wheelset consists of two wheels fixed to the ends of an axle that turn in unison. Turning one of the wheels turns the other wheel as well. One can observe wheelsets on locomotives.[9] Wheelsets usually move along on tracks. Wheelsets were not designed to be easily steered because the tracks determine the carriage's direction.

Wheelsets were designed to achieve the end for which they were invented—transporting copper ore out of mines. Steering was not part of their design because steering was not needed to achieve this end. A new type of wheel had to be invented to achieve an end that could not be achieved by the wheelset. This new type of wheel is a *stationary axle*. The end was a mobile home.

A stationary axle consists of two wheels fixed to the ends of an axle in which the wheels rotate independently, like the wheels of a car.[10] The wheels on a stationary axle can turn at different angles, so that the outer wheel can follow a longer path around a corner than the inner wheel, preventing the vehicle from rolling.[11]

According to Bulliet, the stationary axle was invented when hydrographic and climate changes forced the Black Sea residents to adopt a nomadic lifestyle.[12] Wheels designed to be steered by tracks were not suitable for mobile homes that needed to be steered by their drivers. The conceptualization of a new end prompted the redesign of the wheel because a new type of wheel was needed to serve as a means to this end.

The most recent wheel is the *caster*. The advantage of the caster is that it can role and pivot enabling the wheel to be pulled or pushed in any direction.[13] The caster made possible a range of ends, such as shopping carts, wheelchairs, and baby strollers.

The conceptualization of values was required to invent the wheelset, the stationary axle, and the caster. The formation of normative abstractions was required to conceptualize ends and to conceptualize wheels that could serve as instrumental means to these ends. Goal-directed thinking was also required to create the context in which these wheels can serve our ends.

Wheeled vehicles might appear to be an advantage to walking on foot or riding on a horse. We make this judgment in the context of the twenty-first century, a world designed for wheeled transportation. Wheeled vehicles did not always have an advantage over walking or horse riding. Wheeled vehicles were not an advantage in cities designed for foot traffic. Cities had to be redesigned to take advantage of wheeled vehicles. Visit an ancient city that was constructed before the adoption of wheeled transportation, such as Fes el-Bali in Morocco. You will find narrow streets, sharp curves, and steps. Local businesses still use animals to transport goods. Contrast Fes el-Bali with almost any city in New Zealand, which was built well after the adoption of wheeled transportation.[14] You will find wide roads, with sufficient space for cars to travel simultaneously in both directions, even when cars are parked on both sides.

REFRIGERATORS

Integrating cognitive abstractions forms normative abstractions. Scientists had to conceptualize the facts of reality that make refrigerators possible before businessmen could integrate these facts to conceptualize the refrigerator. Isaac Newton first identified the laws of cooling in his 1701 treatise, *Principles of Natural Philosophy*.[15] In 1755, William Cullen, a professor of medicine at Edinburgh Medical School, created a vacuum in a container of diethyl ether, which, when boiled, absorbs heat from the surrounding air and creates a small amount of ice.[16]

In 1758, Benjamin Franklin, a founding father of the United States, and John Hadley, a professor of chemistry at Cambridge University, conducted an experiment in which they wet the bulb of a thermometer with ether and used bellows to evaporate it. With each subsequent application, the thermometer registered a lower temperature until ice one-quarter inch thick formed on the surface of the bulb.[17]

These experiments demonstrate that it is possible to create artificial ice. Before the modern refrigerator, people used ice to preserve perishable food. A "refrigerator" meant a wooden box filled with ice. The ice was cut from lakes, the only source then available. The natural ice trade was a big business just over one hundred years ago. Icemen would deliver natural ice blocks to the door in the same way as couriers deliver parcels today.[18] The problem with natural ice is that it can become contaminated by pollutants from the lake, and the availability of ice depended on the weather.[19] A warm winter could result in what was called at the time an "ice famine."[20]

While scientists discovered the principles by which to create artificial ice, it took an American steam engineer by the name of Oliver Evans to reflect on their experiments and conceive of a machine that could produce artificial ice.

Evans conceived of his machine in 1805 but never built it.[21] Evans's machine would eventually be built twenty-nine years later by the American inventor and mechanical engineer Jacob Perkins.[22] While Perkins's machine only produced a small amount of ice, he demonstrated that ice could come from a machine. Over one hundred years after Newton identified the laws of cooling, Perkins's machine was the first attempt to transform a scientific principle into a material product that can improve human life.

A mechanical refrigerator for the home was not the goal. The goal was to create artificial ice that icemen could transport to people's homes for use in their wooden refrigerators. Businessmen did not conceive of a mechanical refrigerator for the home at this time. In a pre-Edison world, artificial ice had to be produced by giant machines powered by a steam engine, which was not practical for home use.

The first commercial refrigerator was not designed for the home, but to support existing businesses. John Gorrie was a doctor who set out to create a machine that could cool his sick patients' homes. Gorrie established artificial ice as his business's goal because making ice was the only commercial application of a mechanical refrigerator at this time. Gorrie boasted that his machine could make ice on any part of the Earth at any time of the year.[23] Gorrie's primary market was brewers who wanted to make lager beer all year-round. Brewers recognized the importance of mechanical refrigeration to their business and provided the financial basis for the nascent mechanical refrigeration industry. Brewers would remain the primary market for mechanical refrigeration until 1890.[24]

Entrepreneurs observed Gorrie's success in the brewing industry and grasped that mechanical refrigeration opened up possibilities of which they had not previously conceived. In 1800 New Zealand, sheep were raised solely for their wool. When wool prices dropped by one third, a crisis for New Zealand farmers ensued. Canadian entrepreneur William Soltau Davidson had emigrated to New Zealand a few years earlier. He recognized that Britain's rising population increased demand for meat and that mechanical refrigeration provided the means for New Zealand sheep farmers to meet this demand. In 1882, a ship with a steam-powered refrigeration unit was used to ship meat from Port Chalmers in Dunedin to London. This trip was the world's first commercially successful refrigerated shipment, giving New Zealand an early lead in the refrigerated shipment industry.[25]

By the early 1900s, engineers began to conceive of small mechanical refrigerators that could be installed in shops and restaurants. These mechanical refrigerators enabled businesses to produce their own ice instead of buying from icemen.[26] Today, we do not think of refrigerators as machines for the production of artificial ice. Engineers of the early 1900s thought of mechanical refrigerators in these terms because what people wanted was ice, and engineers sought to conceptualize a new means to this end.

Frigidaire (a company then owned by General Motors through one of its subsidiaries) produced the first mechanical refrigerator for the home in 1921. The machine and the motor were concealed at the bottom below the food compartment. The refrigerator was plain and white and cost $10,100 in today's dollars.[27] Despite the price, the Frigidaire was so popular that the profits covered the entire dividend for GM preferred stock that year, signaling to General Motors and other manufacturers the socially objective value of home refrigerators.[28] The word "fridge" would become synonymous with refrigerators. The Frigidaire was commercially successful because people grasped the value of being able to keep perishable food cold without having to purchase ice.

Cognitive reasoning was required to identify the physical laws of cooling. Cognitive reasoning was required to discover how to apply these laws to the creation of artificial cooling. Normative reasoning was required to take these discoveries and apply them in the form of a machine that could churn out artificial ice; to grasp that an artificial ice machine could serve the needs of businessmen and consumers better than natural ice; and to conceive of a box that kept its content cool without using ice.

The goal of the refrigerator's inventors was to create artificial *ice*. They created artificial *cold*. Future innovators looked at this achievement and conceptualized ends that had not occurred to the refrigerator's inventors, such as ice-skating rinks,[29] artificial snow,[30] the embalming of bodies,[31] the frozen food industry,[32] MRI machines (which require liquid helium),[33] the freezing of male sperm and female eggs,[34] and the transportation of donated human organs.[35]

SHIPPING CONTAINERS

Shipping containers seem to have little to do with human values. Value judgments do not appear necessary to conceive of transporting a good from one location to another physically. We pick up a box and move the box from one side of the room to the other—an exercise in brute physical strength. A shipping container seems to do the same thing on a larger scale. The opposite is the case, however. Shipping containers are a significant achievement in the conceptualization of values.

Shipping containers are a recent innovation. Before the 1950s, ships were loaded and unloaded using the bulk break method. Longshoremen loaded and unloaded each cargo item separately. A person standing on the wharf, at the time, would have seen longshoremen walking up and down the plank carrying loads of bananas on their backs or bags of coffee in their hands. Freight had to be tightly stowed because if an item broke loose, it could damage the other cargo or even capsize the ship.[36]

At this time, trucking, railroads, and shipping were regarded as separate industries. A manufacturer in midland United States who wanted to ship its goods to a city in midland Europe would need to hire a trucking or railroad company to transport its goods from its warehouse to the docks. The manufacturer would then need to pay a shipping company to transport its goods from the United States to Europe, where the manufacturer needed to pay another trucking or railroad company to transport its goods from the European docks to its final destination. Manufacturers would sometimes hire a freight forwarder who specialized in putting together the different pieces of the transport puzzle.[37]

Since the goods were transported using the bulk break method, each item would be individually loaded into the truck, then unloaded at the docks, where the items might have to wait in a transit shed for the ship to arrive and unload, before being loaded onto the ship, and then unloaded at the European docks before being loaded onto the European truck ready for its final destination. Items could number in the thousands. Aside from the sheer workforce and time needed to ship goods, damage and theft were significant transportation risks.[38]

For these reasons, most manufacturers found that it was not cost-effective to sell internationally. Manufacturers thought locally, producing goods locally for the local market. Manufacturers that shipped their goods internationally located near docks to simplify the receipt of raw materials and the shipment of the finished goods.[39] People who grew up before the invention of the shipping container had to purchase goods produced by local manufacturers.

The shipping container revolutionized domestic and international transportation. Today, transportation costs are so negligible that they do not even factor into a company's decision where to manufacture. A United States–based company can manufacture its goods anywhere in the world and sell directly to any customer in the world. Even private individuals, shopping online, barely consider the shipping costs when purchasing goods from other countries. As a result, businessmen, who once competed with businessmen in the same city or country, now compete with businessmen across the globe.

Malcolm Mclean invented the shipping container.[40] The shipping container enables a manufacturer to transport goods without filling and refilling them at each stage of the journey. The container is filled at the warehouse and may not be opened again until it reaches its final destination. The container is then loaded onto the back of a truck and driven to the docks. A crane transfers the container from the truck to the ship. The longshoreman does not touch the contents and may not even be physically located at the wharf. Instead, a modern longshoreman may operate a crane from an office some distance away. When the ship arrives at the next dock, a crane transfers the container from the ship to a truck, which transports the container to its final destination.

The shipping container is revolutionary. Mclean's real revolution, however, was in reconceptualizing the context in which the shipping container operates. Mclean believed that the business of a transport company was not in operating a truck, a railroad, or a ship, but in *moving freight*.[41] Mclean's insight was that transport companies should be selling *transportation*, instead of renting space in their trucks, locomotives, or ships.[42]

Before the shipping container, trucking, railroads, and shipping were regarded as separate industries. In enabling the seamless transition from trucks to railcars and to ships, the shipping container opened up the possibility of treating these heretofore *separate* industries as aspects of a *single* industry.

Reconceiving these industries created the need to develop logistical systems to determine how to transport goods. Where previously, manufacturers had to decide which trucking company to hire and which ship to transport their goods on, today computers coordinate the complex network of transport routes. When a manufacturer or private individual pays a company such as DHL or UPS to ship their goods, these companies' logistical systems determine the most efficient route for the goods to reach their destination. These systems determine that the goods need to be transported by this truck, that the truck needs to be at the dock at this time, that the crane needs to load the containers in this order, and so on, with such a degree of efficiency that these companies can accurately predict the day and time at which the goods will arrive at their final destination.[43]

The objective value of the shipping container was made possible by the mind of the man who conceived of using the box to ship goods, who conceived of creating a transport industry to move the box from one location to another, and who conceived of the logistical systems needed to coordinate the movement of different boxes around the planet.

Critics of profit maximization like to celebrate the local production of goods sold to local markets. Localism is not desirable, however. The shipping container means that a young child today can purchase goods that without the shipping container would either only be accessible to the ultra-rich, who can afford the transport costs or would not have been produced at all due to the absence of a local market. In conceptualizing the transport industry, Mclean has helped people across the world obtain values that distance would otherwise close to them.

PROFIT MAXIMIZATION

The histories of the wheel, the refrigerator, and the shipping container evidence the role of value judgments in the production of goods and services. These histories also evidence the value of *maximizing* profit. A businessman can achieve a *satisfactory* profit by following the lead of other businessmen.

To *maximize* profit, however, a businessman has to be an industry leader, which means that he or she has to conceptualize new value relationships. The individuals who pioneered the above goods did not seek to profit by repeating the activities of previous generations. These active-minded individuals sought to conceptualize new ends.

The unknown person who first thought of using wheels to transport ore out of the copper mines of the Carpathian Mountains did not settle for traditional methods of transportation. He or she grasped that wheels could be used to achieve an end to which they had not heretofore been put. William Soltau Davidson did not accept the financial loss that came with a drop in New Zealand wool prices. He responded by creating a new industry—refrigerated shipments. Malcolm Mclean did not accept that trucking, railroads, and shipping must be separate industries. He conceived of uniting these industries into a single transportation system.

BUSINESSMEN ARE NOT MATERIALISTS

The role of values in the production of goods and services challenges a widely accepted myth—that profit-maximizing businessmen are materialists.[44] Businessmen produce physical stuff. The goods that businessmen produce are physical entities that we can see or touch. You can slide the tip of your finger across a mobile phone or around the base of a kettle. The services that businessmen produce are physical activities that use physical goods to effect changes in the physical world. A hairdresser manipulates the comb and scissors in his hands to alter the physical length of his client's hair. Still, businessmen are not materialists because a businessman's value judgments shape the production of material goods and services.

The above histories demonstrate why the materialist assumption is false. Nevertheless, we must explicitly challenge this assumption because not doing so can impede our ability to accept the role of values in profit maximization fully.

THE MIND-BODY DICHOTOMY

Businessmen are labeled "materialists" because of cultural assumptions inherited from Classical Greece. Plato imagined that living in the material world is like living in a dark cave. His *Republic* tells the story of a group of men imprisoned in a cave from birth. The men are chained so that they can only see the wall in front. Puppeteers walk behind, casting shadows. The prisoners assume that these shadows are the real world. One of the prisoners is freed and exits into the light. As the prisoner's eyes adjust, he sees the real world for the first time. He recognizes this new world as superior to the world of shadows. When the prisoner returns to the cave, he tells his fellow captives about the outside world. To their ears, his words sound like the ramblings of a madman, and they conclude that leaving the world of shadows is dangerous.[45]

Immanuel Kant proffered the same idea. Kant divided existence into two realms—the *noumenal* and the *phenomenal*.[46] The noumenal realm is the world outside of Plato's cave—the real world—the world as it exists independent of us. The phenomenal realm is the world of shadows—the world that our brains create for us. According to Kant, knowing does not consist in the mind *apprehending* objects in reality, but in the mind *molding* the raw material of sensation to create the material world, like a sculptor molds a statue out of marble.[47]

Kant's predecessors recognized that we see with human eyes and hear with human ears. We do not see as a bee sees or hear as a bat hears. Kant recognized that the same observation applies to how we think. We think with a human brain. We do not think like a bee or a bat. We can, therefore, only know the world as it appears to us, not the world as it exists independent of our senses.

The *mind-body dichotomy* is the name given to this metaphysical split.[48] The mind and body, in this view, belong to different worlds. "Idealists" embrace the mind side of the dichotomy. "Materialists," the body side.

The mind-body split can be observed everywhere in our culture. John Gray's bestselling book in popular psychology *Men Are from Mars, Women Are from Venus* reflects the cultural assumption that men and women are from different worlds.[49] Traditionally, men are placed on the body side and women on the mind side. The assumption being that the proper role of a man is to tend to this-worldly matters and that the proper role of a woman is to tend to allegedly higher concerns, such as looking after the home and raising children.

Within many universities, there has been a long-standing conflict between business and art students. This conflict is usually heightened in liberal arts universities where business students are seen as interlopers by professors teaching traditional liberal arts subjects, such as literature and politics.[50]

The mind-body split can be observed in the movie *Dead Man Walking*.[51] Based on a true story, the movie dramatizes the relationship between Sister Helen Prejean and convicted murderer Matthew Poncelet. Prejean's commitment to the Christian principle of unconditional love leads her to sympathize with a man who murdered a teenage couple and is now sitting on death row. Prejean expresses agape love for a man who is unlovable because she does not love the physical Poncelet who viciously murdered two people. She loves the noumenal Poncelet stripped of all his actions in the physical world.

THE INTELLECTUAL AND THE MATERIAL ARE INTEGRATED

The problem with the mind-body dichotomy is that everywhere we see the integration of the intellectual and the material. The integration of mind and body does not call for an explanation because they are not separate in the first place. Consider the role of the body in the creation of products that have traditionally been placed on the mind side of the dichotomy.

Books are regarded as intellectual achievements. Still, a book is a physical entity that we can see or touch. We can flick through a book's pages. We can run the tip of our finger across a book's page and feel the ink's indentation. Book lovers are familiar with a secondhand bookshop's distinctive odor. Light reflects off the ink and strikes our retinas, causing an electric signal to transmit the sensation to our brain. The content of a book is intellectual. A book gives this content physical existence. When we read *Les Misérables*, we are reading Victor Hugo's thoughts. We can do so, 134 years after Hugo's death, because *Les Misérables* gives his thoughts physical existence.[52]

Painting is similarly placed on the mind side of the dichotomy. Still, a painting is a physical entity that we can see or touch, like a book. We can hold a painting between our hands. We can hang a painting on a wall. Though perhaps not recommended, we can run our fingertip across the canvas and feel the paint's indentation. An artist creates a painting by mixing paint on a palette, dipping his brush into the paint, and brushing the paint on a canvas as it leans against an easel. Like books, a painting's content is intellectual; and like books, painting gives this content physical existence. When we contemplate the *Mona Lisa*, we are contemplating Leonardo da Vinci's view of existence. We can do so because the *Mona Lisa* gives da Vinci's view physical reality.

Music might appear to be the least material of the arts, belonging uncontroversially on the mind side of the dichotomy. After all, we cannot run our fingertip along Beethoven's fifth symphony. Still, we see the integration of mind and body in music. We experience music through sound waves vibrating our ears. Physical instruments produce these sound waves, and the waves can be measured using a sound level meter. An orchestra reads notes from music sheets. The notations on these sheets give physical existence to music. We cannot run our fingertip along the sound waves that transmit Beethoven's fifth symphony. We can, however, run our fingertip across the ink on a sheet of music just as we can with the page of a book. Recordings give physical existence to music in the form of grooves on vinyl records or compact discs. Like books and paintings, the content of music is intellectual. Still, we can experience content created by long-dead composers because their music has been given physical existence.

We can observe the integration of mind and body across our lives. You walk home late at night. You take a shortcut through a park. You hear what sounds like a twig snapping. You make an intellectual judgment—someone might have stepped on the twig—someone walking behind you—a stranger—a mugging was reported in this park last week—danger! Adrenalin floods your body. Your heart rate escalates. Your breathing becomes labored. You perspire.

Consider the construction of a bridge. A bridge is a physical entity that we can walk or drive across. Still, a bridge is not exclusively physical. The thinking of the engineer who designs a bridge determines its form. The bridge stands because the engineer correctly grasped the engineering principles that determined how the bridge needed to be built to withstand the weight of the traffic crossing it. If an engineer's judgment is mistaken, then the bridge will not stand. Tragic evidence of the integration of mind and body in bridge construction can be found in the collapse of the pedestrian bridge at Florida International University in 2018, killing six people. The engineer who designed the bridge made an intellectual error, and people died.

The goods and services that businessmen produce are just more examples of the integration of mind and body. We see this integration in the fact that businessmen produce goods and services through a creative process no different from the writing of a novel or the composition of a symphony. We also see this integration in the fact that customers express their values through the goods and services that they choose to buy.

GOODS AND SERVICES OBJECTIFY OUR VALUES

The goods and services that a person purchases objectify his or her values. A person purchases a good or service as an instrumental means to one or more of his or her ends. These ends are a person's values. The goods and services that we purchase express our values and signal our values to others.

You enter a department store. You cast your eyes across the goods on the shelves. You will be interested in some goods and indifferent to others. You will be interested in those goods that you judge might be able to serve your ends, but not those goods that are irrelevant to your ends. If you are childless, you may be indifferent to the toy section of department stores because these goods are irrelevant to your ends. After you have a child, you will find that the toy section piques your interest because now these toys have the potential to serve a vital end—your child's happiness.

The goods and services that we purchase express our hierarchy of values. When we purchase *this* good or service, the money we spent is not available to purchase *that* good or service. One of the costs of a purchase is the opportunities forgone. Economists call this choice "opportunity cost." When we purchase a good or service, we serve some of our ends at the cost of not being able to serve other ends. We make an implicit judgment that the ends we serve are more important to us than the ends we forgo.

When we purchase a *good*, we make a judgment that this good possesses the characteristics needed for the good to serve our end. When we purchase a *service,* we make a judgment that the person providing the service possesses the characteristics needed for his or her actions to serve our end.

Few people engage in *explicit* means-end reasoning when they go shopping. Nevertheless, means-end reasoning is *implicit* in a person's purchasing choices. A person may not say to himself, "I am buying this *in order* to achieve that." Still, at the back of a person's purchasing choices, there is an end that he or she wants to achieve. You buy a basketball—in order to get fit. You buy a textbook—in order to prepare for your law exams. You buy a hamburger—in order to satiate your hunger. The exception is when people purchase on a whim. For the reasons discussed in chapter 2, such choices cannot dominate an economic system, at least in a free market.

GOODS AND SERVICES EXPRESS OUR VALUES

The goods and services that we purchase express our values and, in so doing, make our values visible to others. Our values are part of what makes us the particular person we are. In objectifying our values, our purchasing decisions solidify our personal identity. Nathaniel Branden distinguishes between our "*species* identity" and our "*personal* or *individual* identity" (emphasis in original).[53] Our species identity consists of those characteristics that make us a human being, such as the fact that we walk on two legs, have opposable thumbs, and have hair on top.[54] Our personal identity consists of those characteristics that make us the particular person we are, such as the fact that we enjoy science-fiction movies, reading classic fiction, and strolling in the park.

Consider the clothes that we choose to buy. We all buy clothes. We do not all buy the same *style* of clothes, however. We buy clothes that serve our values. A lawyer who wants to project a professional image might buy a three-piece suit. A man who enjoys surfing might buy sleeveless shirts and board shorts. A woman who enjoys bicycling might buy a Lycra outfit. Of course, a person can buy different styles of clothes. A lawyer may enjoy surfing or bicycling at the weekends. The purchaser's range of values determines the range of styles from which he chooses.

Television and movie directors understand this point. The character's clothes transmit his or her personal identity to the audience. James Bond's suits express Bond's character. A Bond dressed like Del Boy from the television series *Only Fools and Horses* signals a different character from the Bond of the Ian Fleming novels.

Defense attorneys also understand this point. The accused who appears in court is dressed differently from the accused arrested a few days (or even a few hours) earlier. A suit and tie replace black shirts and ripped jeans. The defense attorney dresses his client to transmit to the judge the character signaled by a suit and tie, which may be the opposite of the character signaled by his client's regular clothes.

Members of a subculture also understand this point. Their choice of clothes expresses their common identity and signals to other people their membership in this subculture. We can tell that a person embraces the values of a hippie, a punk, a goth, or a hipster through the way he or she dresses. A self-described goth who dresses like a hipster is not a goth.

Conmen also understand this point. When Frank Abagnale dressed as a pilot to cash fake checks, he used the pilot's uniform to signal to the teller his trustworthiness.[55]

Recipients of unwanted birthday or Christmas gifts also understand this point. If you have received clothes that you would not purchase yourself, you might have thought, "This shirt is not me."

The saying that one cannot judge a book by its cover is not true. There is a sense in which one can judge a book by its cover. The cover we choose for ourselves is one of the mechanisms through which we express our values and thereby signal our values to others. Though some people attempt to send a false signal, they can do so only because a signal is being sent.

Consider the goods we choose to populate our homes. Television and movie directors recognize that a character's home is one of the mechanisms by which the character's identity is transmitted to the audience, like a character's clothes. If you walk into a new acquaintance's living room and observe that the chairs and couches are arranged to facilitate conversation, this tells you that conversation is an important value to your acquaintance. If, on the other hand, your acquaintance's living room is decorated with framed posters from the *Star Wars* movies, this tells you that these movies are of value to your acquaintance.

The purchase of goods and services is one of the means by which we achieve psychological visibility. We can observe our physical self in a mirror. We cannot similarly observe our psychological self. We experience our psychological self through our interactions with other people. When other people see us in a way that accords with how we see ourselves, we feel visible. If not, we feel invisible.[56] Through the choices we make in the purchase of goods and services, we objectify our personal identity and thereby signal our values to others.

EXPANDING OUR ENDS

Businessmen are not slaves to their customers' preexisting ends.[57] The productive role of businessmen is to expand our ends by conceptualizing new ends and new goods and services to serve these ends. We purchase goods and services because they are an instrumental means to our ends. We do not hold an end unless there is a means. Ends without means are fantasies, not values. Innovations in goods and services open up the possibility of ends that had not previously been achievable.

One hundred years ago, spending a fortnight's vacation on the other side of the world was not of value because there were no means of achieving this end. Traveling by ship from one side of the planet to the other took over forty days. Jet travel made it possible for a person to value such a vacation.

Today, holidaying on Mars is not a realistic end. Anyone who holds this end as a serious value is fantasizing. Entrepreneurs are working toward making this end a reality, however. If successful, they will have expanded the range of ends from which we can select our values. These entrepreneurs will have opened up a new value to us.

EXPRESSING VALUES THROUGH PRODUCTION

The goods and services that consumers purchase reflect their personal identity. The goods and services that businessmen produce also reflect their personal identity. Jeff Bezos's work with Amazon is part of what makes Bezos, Bezos. A Jeff Bezos who chose to become a lifeguard on Bondi Beach in Australia would have been a different Jeff Bezos from the one who founded Amazon.

A businessman does not produce goods or services for his consumption. His goods or services are intended to serve his customers' ends. Steve Jobs produced computers for his customers, not for his personal use. Nevertheless, the ends of a businessman's customers are ends that he judges to be worth pursuing. These ends are part of a businessman's values just as they are part of his customers'.

A businessman does not have to enter a particular field. Jeff Bezos could have become a lifeguard; Steve Jobs, a sheep farmer; Mark Zuckerberg, a newspaper editor. These businessmen chose their particular fields because, in their hierarchy of values, promoting these specific ends was more important to them than the other ends that they could have chosen.

Consider Apple's *Think Different* campaign.[58] Apple was primarily a computer company at the time. Nevertheless, the *Think Different* campaign does not mention computers. The *Think Different* campaign celebrates the ends to which Apple's computers are the means. Jobs regarded computers as bicycles for the mind.[59] *Think Different* celebrates this end; it celebrates the intellectual achievements that computers can help us achieve. The *Think Different* campaign tells Apple's prospective customers: this is the *end* for which we make our computers.

The claim is not that businessmen should be passionate about their customers' ends *instead of* profit maximization. Profit measures the value created by the production of goods and services. The concrete form of a businessman's passion for profit maximization is a passion for the ends to which his or her goods or services will be put. Profit maximization is an abstraction. A businessman's passion for profit maximization is to be found in Jeff Bezos's passion for retailing, Steve Jobs's passion for consumer electronics, and Mark Zuckerberg's passion for social networking.

A passion for customers' ends is usually posited as an alternative to a passion for profit. The implication being that a businessman must choose.[60] The mistake is to confuse a passion for *profit* with a passion for *cash.* A businessman can have a passion for accumulating cash without caring about the ends to which his or her goods or services will be put. A businessman cannot have a passion for profit separate from a passion for the ends, because the former signifies the achievement of the latter.

A businessman cannot be passionate about profit maximization as such. Profit maximization is an abstraction. A passion for profit maximization would be like a passion for an abstract love independent of the love for a particular person. Concretely, a businessman needs to be passionate about the ends to which his or her goods or services will be put. A businessman need not identify this passion as a concrete instance of passion for profit. The job of philosophers is to take a conceptual step back and observe that a passion for profit maximization unites a passion for retailing, a passion for computers, and a passion for social networking.

THE CASE AGAINST "STUFF"

Let us conclude by considering several of the standard arguments against the production of goods and services. Critics of profit maximization often seek to diminish the importance of goods and services by dismissing them as mere "stuff." As Annie Leonard explains in her book *The Story of Stuff: How Our Obsession with Stuff Is Trashing the Planet, Our Communities, and Our Health*, "When I say 'Stuff' in this book, I mean manufactured or mass-produced goods. . . . Stuff as I define it here is also known as 'crap.' You could substitute the word 'goods' every time you see the word 'Stuff,' but since goods are so often anything but good . . . I don't like to use that term."[61]

Production is about the pursuit of values. When critics, like Leonard, diminish the importance of goods and services, they diminish the importance of our values. Anti-stuff arguments can be found in a range of sources. We shall focus on the arguments as presented by Leonard because she surveys the standard arguments against "stuff."

NATURAL RESOURCES

Leonard's fundamental argument is that natural resources are limited and that we are coming up against this limit.[62] Leonard's other arguments assume that we urgently need to limit our consumption of natural resources.

Leonard argues that before the Industrial Revolution, all work was carried out by the physical labor of human beings with some assistance from animals. She argues that our physical limitations imposed a natural limit on our ability to exploit the Earth's resources. The introduction of machines abolished this limit. Machines, Leonard argues, enable human beings to exploit natural resources without limit. Now, we have reached the point where we have almost exhausted all of the Earth's natural resources, threatening our very existence.[63]

This argument is not original to Leonard. In 1798, Thomas Malthus warned that we must curb population growth, or we would come up against the limit of natural resources to sustain the population, leading to mass famine and starvation.[64] The same argument appears more recently, in Paul R. Ehrlich's *The Population Bomb* and The Club of Rome's *The Limits of Growth.*[65] *The Limits of Growth* used computer modeling to give its predictions legitimacy. *Business Week*'s review conceded that "practically everyone agrees that on a finite planet, growth must end sooner or later."[66]

Profit maximization consists of the maximization of valued goods and services, which ultimately come from natural resources. If Leonard is correct, then the maximization of profit uses up our finite resources, threatening human life.

Fortunately, Leonard is not correct. Leonard does not understand what a natural resource is. Though Leonard does not think it necessary to define a "natural resource," her argument implies that a natural resource is one that exists in nature independent of human effort. There is no such thing. Resources do not exist in nature *as resources*. The raw materials that we label "resources" exist in nature. Their status as a resource does not. Human intelligence transforms these objects into resources by discovering how to exploit them in the service of human life.

Leonard conjures up the image of human beings extracting resources from the Earth and pumping them into factories where they are transformed into the "stuff" she so loathes. We cut down trees and transport them to factories where they become paper, chairs, and tables. This description is not accurate, however. Trees exist in nature independent of us. We give trees their status as a resource by cutting them down and turning them into paper, chairs, and tables. Trees do not exist *as a resource* independent of our ability to make use of them.

Oil is the classic example of a "natural resource" that was not a resource until fairly recently. For millennia, oil existed in the ground untouched by human hands. This oil was not a resource. On the contrary, farmers regarded oil as a nuisance. Oil only became a "natural resource" when human beings discovered how to extract oil from the ground to light their homes and fuel their cars.[67]

Leonard's self-contradiction is that she wants us to preserve our natural resources by ceasing to use them. When we cease to use a natural resource, however, it loses its status as a resource. Leonard claims that she wants us to *preserve* our natural resources. Actually, Leonard proposes to *abolish* them.

There is no limit to natural resources. Since human ingenuity is the source of our resources, we can create new ones. The universe is packed with stuff that has the potential to become a resource.[68] One recent example is human perspiration. Entrepreneurs have invented a machine that can turn perspiration from worn clothes into clean drinking water.[69] Just a few years ago, perspiration was not a resource for a person searching a desert for drinking water. This machine turns perspiration into a resource.

Ehrlich's *The Population Bomb* was published in 1968 and predicted that during the 1970s, India would face mass starvation as a result of population growth. Ehrlich was wrong. India was exporting food to other countries by the time Ehrlich had predicted that India would be unable to feed its population. What happened? Scientist Norman Borlaug revolutionized food production in India by creating a new type of wheat. Borlaug increased India's natural resources, enabling it to feed a growing population.[70]

CHERISHING GOODS

Leonard's other arguments are based on the assumption that we need to preserve natural resources. Leonard argues, for example, that we should care more about the stuff we have. Though Leonard praises people who purchase organic and fair-trade clothes, she does not think they go far enough. Leonard argues that people should cherish the clothes that they already own and not purchase new ones. Leonard thinks that people should care for the stuff they already have with the same love they would have for a family heirloom.[71]

Leonard clothes her argument in the language of values. She uses words such as "cherish" and "love." Leonard, however, is not arguing that we should *value* the goods we own. She concludes that we should not be purchasing new goods. Purchasers of organic and fair-trade clothes do not go far enough in Leonard's view because they bought *something* when the ideal is not to buy anything. Hence Leonard's endorsement of the World War II saying, "Use it up, wear it out, make it do, or do without."[72]

The organizers of Buy Nothing Day share Leonard's antipathy to buying new goods. Buy Nothing Day is an international day of protest against consumption. It is held on Black Friday, one of the busiest shopping days in the United States. The protest is supported by Adbusters, an international organization that promotes a lifestyle committed to buying less. Among other things, activists wander around shopping malls with a blank stare during what they call a "Zombie Walk," and encourage people in shopping malls to cut up their credit cards.[73]

The goods we purchase are instrumental values. We should value these goods because they are the means to our ends. Instrumental values are conditional. They are of value *if* they serve our ends. Goods cease to be values when the conditional clause no longer applies.

Physical goods wear out over time, or new goods that better serve our ends supersede them. We should, therefore, expect that our belongings will cease to be of value over time. In accounting, the concept of *depreciation* recognizes this phenomenon. The new MacBook Pro that we love today will be junk in five years. While Leonard thinks this a problem, this phenomenon merely reflects the fact that every good is a means to an end, and therefore necessarily ceases to be of value to the purchaser when it ceases to serve the end for which it was purchased.[74] Goods do not possess intrinsic value.

Indifference is the proper attitude toward goods that cease to serve our ends. We should not care what happens to them. We could turn our old clothes into rags, as Leonard suggests, or we could donate them to charity or sell them through eBay. We should not deny ourselves goods that serve our ends in order to hold onto worthless goods to which we should be indifferent. Though Leonard invokes the language of values, she is arguing for *self-denial*. We deny ourselves values when we deny ourselves the means to our values.

HAPPINESS

Leonard does not recognize the contribution that goods make to our happiness. Leonard acknowledges that we need to consume to live and that a hungry or cold person needs more stuff to be happy. Leonard also acknowledges that some stuff beyond our basic needs can make life sweeter, such as a bottle of wine to share with friends. Leonard, however, thinks that we need family and friends to make us happy, not more stuff.[75]

Leonard endorses the movements known as "downshifting," "enough-ism," and "voluntary simplicity," in which people choose to have less stuff in their lives.[76] Leonard thinks that Americans should be more like Europeans, who, she imagines, live in small houses and prefer to socialize with friends and neighbors in public places instead of watching hours of television in big houses filled with possessions.[77] Leonard is not the first person to lionize the European lifestyle. Amitai Etzioni similarly claims that European societies produce and consume less because he thinks that Europeans have adopted a lifestyle that privileges leisure time and visits to coffee shops over income.[78]

We find happiness in the fulfillment of our values. Purchasing goods makes us happy when those goods fulfill our values. Merely purchasing more stuff will not make us happy. More stuff makes us happy when it is a means to our ends. Our ends, therefore, are the standard by which to judge how much stuff we need to be happy. A basketball enthusiast may find happiness in purchasing a basketball and a hoop to attach to his or her garage. A racing car enthusiast may find happiness in purchasing a sports car.[79]

The moral approach is *selectivity according to one's values*. We should be selective in our purchases because, as we have seen, when we purchase *this*, the funds are no longer available to purchase *that*. The inability to purchase *that* is one of the costs of the purchase of *this*. Selectivity ensures that we are fulfilling our *highest* values.

We cannot stipulate that a person needs more or less stuff in order to be happy. A spendthrift who is irresponsible in his purchasing habits may need to purchase less of *this* in order to have the funds available to purchase the goods that serve his values. A miser who denies himself purchases that would serve his values may need to purchase more stuff to be happy.

Scott Pape is a syndicated columnist and radio commentator in Australia, where he provides financial advice to young people. Pape argues that a person on an average income can live like a multimillionaire if they spend consciously. When Pape's home burned to the ground, his family had to replace everything. Pape realized that much of what he owned was cluttering up space, so Pape and his wife decided not to replace these things. Pape also realized that some things made a big difference in his family's life, so they spent more money on them. Pape argues that we should cut out the things that we buy unthinkingly and "spend extravagantly" on those things that add value to our lives.[80] Pape is advocating that his readers spend selectively according to their values.

Stuff is not a substitute for having values. Stuff is a *means* to an end. Purchasing stuff will not give the purchaser an end that he or she does not possess. A person must first establish his or her values and then make purchasing decisions that accord with these values. Purchasing stuff does not make a person happy. Purchasing stuff that *fulfills one's values* does.

Leonard thinks that people can find happiness in spending less because she is evaluating other people's purchases by the standard of her values. Leonard acknowledges that purchasing a bottle of wine to share with friends is an acceptable purchase because this purchase is a means to *her* ends. Leonard refuses to recognize that other people do not share her ends and may find happiness in owning goods that serve ends other than her own.

Leonard endorses the "downshifting," "enough-ism," and "voluntary simplicity" movements because she presumes that we are reaching the limits of our natural resources and, therefore, must reduce our consumption. These movements are not advocating *selectivity* but *self-denial*. There may be people who need to downshift or live more simply in the sense that they need to be more selective in their purchasing decisions. These movements, however, are not advocating that we should only purchase goods that serve our values. These movements advocate forgoing our values.

PLANNED OBSOLESCENCE

Leonard argues that businessmen deliberately design their products to become obsolete sooner than necessary in order to prompt their customers to purchase a new iteration of the same product before they really need to.[81] "Planned obsolescence" is the name given to this supposed policy. This argument has an intuitive appeal because businessmen maximize profit through repeat purchases. Apple, for instance, maximizes profit through the owners of its iPhone XR upgrading to the iPhone 11 Pro Max. By designing the iPhone XR to become obsolete before the end of its useful life, Apple, it would seem, can sell more phones. Klaus Bosselmann, a professor of law at the University of Auckland, claims that from "a business point of view, it makes sense to deliberately shorten the life cycle of a product . . . to stimulate consumption," when from a "sustainability perspective, such a business strategy is obscene and should be banned."[82]

Today, critics invoke the phrase "planned obsolescence" to condemn any instance of a company producing a new iteration of a product that is still functional. The phrase did not originally refer to such practices, however. "Planned obsolescence" was coined to refer to the practice whereby a company produces a new iteration of a product that is *functionally identical* to the previous product but looks different. A new refrigerator, for example, might have the same functions as the previous model. Still, the manufacturer introduces a silver façade to encourage customers to replace the previous model, which has a white façade. The introduction of the new façade is planned obsolescence. "Planned obsolescence" did not refer to the introduction of a new model that was *functionally different* from the previous one.[83]

The phrase "planned obsolescence" was coined when the importance of industrial design was just being recognized. Designers could not project a time when technological progress would advance rapidly, as it does today, so they assumed that the only way to encourage customers to purchase a new iteration of a product was to change its appearance.

Leonard's target is not such changes. Her target is goods that are *functional advances* over previous iterations. Manufacturers compete with themselves by producing new iterations of products that they expect their customers to judge to be of higher value than previous iterations. The iPhone 11 Pro Max is competing against the iPhone XR (and all of Apple's previous models). Self-competition encourages manufacturers to innovate in their products' functionalities.

Contrary to Leonard's assumption, customers do not mindlessly purchase the latest iteration of a product. They make a value judgment. A customer who purchases the Pro Max will not have this money available to purchase other goods. One cannot spend money twice. The customer, therefore, must decide whether the Pro Max is sufficiently better than the XR to justify the purchase. Even if a customer's current phone is still functional, the purchase may be justified if the Pro Max's new functions better serve this person's values. A professional photographer, for instance, might decide that advances in the Pro Max's camera make the purchase worthwhile in relation to his or her values.[84]

Had Leonard's target been advances in industrial design, she still would not have a basis for complaint. A product's appearance is a legitimate value. Consider the first iMac. The iMac's revolution was not in its functionalities, which were not substantially different from any other computer at the time, but in its design. The multi-colored translucent casing made the iMac the first computer that could fit the décor of one's living room.[85] The iMac was a computer designed for the home. The importance that we place on industrial design reflects the fact that goods serve our values.

ADVERTISING

Chapter 2 emphasized the role of judgment in purchasing decisions. The status of a good or service as an objective value depends on customers being free to make value judgments. Leonard challenges this assumption, arguing that businessmen use advertising to manipulate customers into purchasing products that they would not otherwise buy. Leonard asserts that it would take "a will of steel" to resist Amazon's lure and purchase books from a local bookstore.[86]

Leonard argues that companies such as Apple, the Gap, and Nike sell brands, not goods. According to Leonard, these companies do not make goods but purchase goods that other companies have made and merely slap on their brand.[87]

Leonard owes an intellectual debt to John Kenneth Galbraith, the foremost critic of advertising in the anti-capitalist literature. In *The Affluent Society*, Galbraith argues that businessmen use advertising to manufacture wants for their goods and services.[88] Galbraith argues that businessmen cannot justify the production of goods and services by appealing to consumer demand when they manufacture that demand.

Businessmen do not use advertising to manufacture wants. Businessmen produce goods and services and use advertising to inform potential customers of their value. As we have seen, innovative products open up the possibility of values that customers had not previously conceived. The creation of mechanical refrigeration, for example, opened up the possibilities of ice rinks and artificial snow. Businessmen are not manufacturing *wants*; they are conceptualizing values. Advertising is the mechanism by which businessmen explain the value of their goods and services to potential customers. Businessmen need to do so because customers have not conceptualized these values themselves. The anti-advertising literature fails to recognize that the productive role of businessmen is to conceptualize *new values*.[89]

Businessmen do not sell brands *instead* of goods or services. Though the companies Leonard list do not manufacture goods themselves, they design the goods that they hire other companies to produce. Apple does not *physically* combine the components that constitute its laptops or phones. Apple, nevertheless, *directs* the combination of these components.

The importance of brands reflects the role of values in the marketplace. A company's brand is its statement of values. The brand is how a company transmits to its customers its passion for the ends that it expects its goods or services to serve. Nike's brand, for instance, celebrates physical fitness because its clothes are designed as a means to this end.

At the root of all of these objections is an ignorance of the objective conception of value. Businessmen are not *exploiters* of Earth's natural resources, as critics assume. Businessmen are *creators* of resources—expanding the range of raw materials that can be of benefit to human life. Natural resources do not possess intrinsic value. Preserving these resources does not preserve something of value. Natural resources become of value through businessmen conceptualizing facts and integrating these facts to conceptualize ends and the goods and services that can serve these ends. Far from being a threat to sustaining life on Earth, profit maximization is a businessman's reward and motivation for expanding the resources upon which all of our lives depend.

CONCEPTUALIZING VALUES

The first chapter established that the morality of profit maximization depends on two conditions. To be moral, businessmen must maximize profit through producing goods and services that are of legitimate value ("the *what* condition"), and they must do so virtuously ("the *how* condition"). The second chapter established the theoretical basis for concluding that profit maximization meets both conditions. Through the histories of the wheel, the refrigerator, and the shipping container, this chapter has established that businessmen engage in the goal-directed thinking needed to produce goods and services of objective value. The next chapter shall provide historical evidence that businessmen possess the character traits needed to conceptualize objective value.

NOTES

1. Richard W. Bulliet, *The Wheel: Inventions & Reinventions* (New York: Columbia University Press, 2016), 37.
2. Ibid., 38.
3. Ibid., 51 and 57.
4. Ibid., 57.
5. Ibid., 151–52.
6. Ibid., 160.
7. Ibid., 186.
8. Ibid., 67.
9. Ibid., 1 and 15.
10. Ibid., 1 and 3.
11. Ibid., 13.
12. Ibid., 71.
13. Ibid., 210–13.
14. I visited Morocco three months after visiting New Zealand. Having just finished Bulliet's book, I paid attention to the roads in both countries. The Fes el-Bali alleyways were obviously designed for foot traffic and the New Zealand roads for wheeled transportation.
15. Carroll Gantz, *Refrigeration: A History* (Jefferson, NC: McFarland & Company, 2015), 17.
16. Ibid., 32.
17. Ibid., 33.
18. Ibid., 3.
19. Ibid., 53 and 72.
20. Ibid., 26.
21. Ibid., 33–34.
22. Ibid., 34.
23. Ibid., 39–41.
24. Ibid., 68.
25. Ibid., 60. New Zealand would continue to ship meat to the United Kingdom until the United Kingdom entered the European Union.
26. Ibid., 91.
27. Ibid., 99–101.
28. Ibid., 100.
29. Ibid., 61–62.
30. Ibid., 238.
31. Ibid., 72.

32. Ibid., 177.
33. Ibid., 226.
34. Ibid., 227.
35. Ibid., 239.
36. Marc Levinson, *The Box: How the Shipping Container Made the World Smaller and the World Economy Bigger*, second ed. (Princeton, NJ: Princeton University Press, 2016), 21–22 and 26.
37. Ibid., 11–12.
38. Ibid., 36–37, 110, and 225.
39. Ibid., 21.
40. Ibid., 48.
41. Ibid., xii.
42. Ibid., 227.
43. Ibid., 14.
44. James Twitchell, "Two Cheers for Materialism," in *The Consumer Society Reader*, ed. Juliet B. Schor and Douglas B. Holt (New York: The New Press, 2000); Debi Ghate, "The Businessmen's Crucial Role: Material Men of the Mind," in *Why Businessmen Need Philosophy: The Capitalist's Guide to the Ideas Behind Ayn Rand's* Atlas Shrugged, ed. Debi Ghate and Richard E. Ralston (New York: New American, 2011), 46–47. Karl Marx is this view's source. Edwin A. Locke, "The Traits of Business Heroes in *Atlas Shrugged*," in *Perspectives on Ayn Rand's Contributions to Economic and Business Thought*, ed. Edward W. Younkins (Lanham, MD: Lexington Books, 2018), 213. The assumption that businessmen are materialists is evident in complaints against our so-called "consumer society." See, for example, the essays in Juliet B. Schor and Douglas B. Holt, eds., *The Consumer Society Reader* (New York: The New Press, 2000).
45. Plato, "Republic," in *Plato: Complete Works*, ed. John M. Cooper (Indianapolis: Hackett Publishing Company, 1997), 1132–35.
46. Immanuel Kant, *Critique of Pure Reason*, trans. Norman Kemp Smith (London: MacMillan, 1929), 257–75. For a two-world interpretation of Kant's argument, see Peter Simpson, *Goodness and Nature: A Defence of Ethical Naturalism* (Dordrecht: Martinus Nijhoff Publishers, 1987), 122.
47. John Wild and J. L. Coblitz, "On the Distinction Between the Analytic and the Synthetic," *Philosophy and Phenomenological Research* 8, no. 4 (June 1948): 656–57.
48. For a discussion of the mind-body dichotomy, see Leonard Peikoff, *Objectivism: The Philosophy of Ayn Rand* (New York: Meridian, 1993), 28–30 and 148–50; Peikoff, *Understanding Objectivism: A Guide to Learning Ayn Rand's Philosophy* (New York: New American Library, 2012), 25–28.
49. John Gray, *Men Are from Mars, Women Are from Venus: The Classic Guide to Understanding the Opposite Sex*, 20th anniversary ed. (New York: Harper, 2012).
50. During a visit to Oberlin College, I spoke with a group of administrators about Oberlin's plan to introduce a business program. They told me that faculty strongly oppose the plan because they believe that adding a business program will compromise Oberlin's values as a liberal arts college.
51. Tim Robbins, *Dead Man Walking* (Gramercy Pictures, 1995). While watching this movie, the following quote from Rand came to mind: "pity for the guilty is treason to the innocent." Ayn Rand, "Bootleg Romanticism," in *The Romantic Manifesto: A Philosophy of Literature*, revised ed. (New York: Signet, 1975), 131.
52. The integration of mind and body explains why free minds and free markets go together. When the government controls the economy, it necessarily has to decide which books will be published, because the government controls the printing presses and allocates ink and paper. Cf. George Reisman, *Capitalism: A Treatise on Economics* (Ottawa, IL: Jameson Books, 1998), 23.
53. Nathaniel Branden, "Alienation," in *Capitalism: The Unknown Ideal*, ed. Ayn Rand (New York: Signet, 1967), 289–90.
54. Of course, there are human beings who do not have two legs, opposable thumbs, or hair on top. These variations are recognized in the way we use language to classify our observa-

tions. When we see a person walking down the street, we do not say, "There goes a two-legged man," because the concept of "man" subsumes the fact of being two-legged. When we see a person who has lost a leg, however, we might say, "There goes a one-legged man," because in so doing, we recognize that this individual has all of the characteristics of a man except for the fact that he has one leg.

55. Jeff Nathanson, *Catch Me If You Can* (DreamWorks, 2002).

56. For an explanation of psychological visibility, see Nathaniel Branden, *The Psychology of Self-Esteem: A Revolutionary Approach to Self-Understanding That Launched a New Era in Modern Psychology*, 32nd anniversary ed. (San Francisco: Jossey-Bass, 2001), 194–204. See also Edwin A. Locke and Ellen Kenner, *The Selfish Path to Romance: How to Love with Passion and Reason* (Doylestown, PA: Platform Press, 2011), 6–8 and 11n5.

57. The consumer sovereignty movement appears to be based on this assumption. The idea is that a free market requires businessmen to follow consumer desires. Ludwig von Mises expresses this view when he states that the consumer is the captain of a free market. Ludwig von Mises, *Bureaucracy*, ed. Bettina Bien Greaves (Indianapolis: Liberty Fund, 2007), 17. Not all proponents of the free market accept that the consumer is sovereign. M. Northrup Buechner, for example, claims that capitalism is a system of *producer* sovereignty, not of consumer sovereignty. M. Northrup Buechner, *Objective Economics: How Ayn Rand's Philosophy Changes Everything About Economics* (Lanham, MD: University Press of America, 2011), 204–205. Discussions of free markets should avoid talk of group sovereignty. There is one sovereign in a free market—the individual.

58. Walter Isaacson, *Steve Jobs* (London: Little, Brown, 2011), 327–32. For a discussion of the philosophical significance of the *Think Different* campaign, see Robert White, "Two Sides of Think Different," in *Steve Jobs and Philosophy: For Those Who Think Different*, ed. Shawn E. Klein (Chicago: Open Court, 2015).

59. Isaacson, *Steve Jobs*, 115.

60. Businessmen who are passionate about the value that they create for their customers are sometimes said to be running "purpose-led" or "values-led" companies. See, for example, John Izzo and Jeff Vanderwielen, *The Purpose Revolution: How Leaders Create Engagement and Competitive Advantage in an Age of Social Good* (Oakland, CA: Berrett-Koehler Publishers, 2018), 53.

61. Annie Leonard, *The Story of Stuff: How Our Obsession with Stuff Is Trashing the Planet, Our Communities, and Our Health—and a Vision for Change* (New York: Free Press, 2010), xxxiii.

62. Ibid., xix.

63. Ibid., xix and 101.

64. T. R. Malthus, *An Essay on the Principle of Population* (Mineola, NY: Dover Publications, 2007).

65. Thomas Robertson, *The Malthusian Moment: Global Population Growth and the Birth of American Environmentalism* (New Brunswick, NJ: Rutgers University Press, 2012), 61 and 180.

66. Quoted in ibid., 181.

67. Reisman, *Capitalism*, 64.

68. Ibid., 65. For a discussion of why there is no limit to natural resources, see Julian L. Simon, *The Ultimate Resource 2*, revised ed. (Princeton, NJ: Princeton University Press, 1996); Matt Ridley, *The Rational Optimist: How Prosperity Evolves* (London: Fourth Estate, 2011); Peter H. Diamandis and Steven Kotler, *Abundance: The Future Is Better Than You Think* (New York: Free Press, 2012).

69. The Sweat Machine was built by Swedish engineer Andreas Hammar and uses membrane distillation to let steam through but keep other substances out.

70. Audra Hilse, "Norman Borlaug: The Man Who Taught People to Feed Themselves," *The Objective Standard* 5, no. 1 (Spring 2010).

71. Leonard, *The Story of Stuff*, 51.

72. Ibid., x.

73. Jessica Ketcham Weber, "Buy Nothing Day," in *Encyclopedia of Activism and Social Justice*, ed. Gary L. Anderson and Kathryn G. Herr (Thousand Oaks, CA: SAGE Publications, 2007).

74. Goods that have sentimental value may be an exception. The good no longer serves the end for which it was purchased. However, the good now serves another end, maintaining a physical connection with memories of the past. Businessmen do not produce sentimental values, and such values cannot be bought and sold. For this reason, sentimental goods are often said to be *priceless*, meaning that the sentimental value of the good cannot be priced.

75. Leonard, *The Story of Stuff*, 148.

76. Ibid., 158.

77. Ibid., 157. I have lived in Europe for the last twelve years and do not recognize the Europe that Leonard describes. The Europeans I know who live in small houses do so because they cannot afford a larger house. Grandmothers spend hours watching Turkish soap operas. Televisions are constantly on in the background at restaurants and even in people's homes when they entertain visitors.

78. Amitai Etzioni, "Introduction: Voluntary Simplicity—Psychological Implications, Societal Consequences," in *Voluntary Simplicity: Responding to Consumer Culture*, ed. Daniel Doherty and Amitai Etzioni (Lanham, MD: Rowman & Littlefield, 2003), 12.

79. Ayn Rand, *Atlas Shrugged* (New York: Signet, 1992), 384.

80. Scott Pape, *The Barefoot Investor: The Only Money Guide You'll Ever Need* (Milton, Queensland: John Wiley & Sons, 2017), 49–55.

81. Leonard, *The Story of Stuff*, 161–62.

82. Quoted in Kamila Pope, *Understanding Planned Obsolescence: Unsustainability through Production, Consumption and Waste Generation* (London: Kogan Page, 2017), i.

83. Gantz, *Refrigeration*, 157.

84. I evidence this claim. I currently own an iPhone 6. Since this iteration of the iPhone serves my ends, I have judged that there is no need to upgrade.

85. Isaacson, *Steve Jobs*, 355.

86. Leonard, *The Story of Stuff*, 118.

87. Ibid., 108–109.

88. John Kenneth Galbraith, *The Affluent Society* (Cambridge, MA: Riverside Press, 1958), 127. Galbraith is challenging the doctrine of consumer sovereignty. For a discussion of Galbraith's "dependence effect" and a response, see Jerry Kirkpatrick, *In Defense of Advertising: Arguments from Reason, Ethical Egoism, and Laissez-Faire Capitalism* (Claremont, CA: TLJ Books, 2007), 25 and 70–71; Tibor R. Machan, *The Morality of Business: A Profession for Human Wealthcare* (New York: Springer, 2007), 75–76; Tibor R. Machan, *The Promise of Liberty: A Non-Utopian Vision* (Lanham, MD: Lexington Books, 2009), 112–13.

89. Robert Tarr, "Economic Theory and Conceptions of Value: Rand and Austrians versus the Mainstream," in *Foundations of a Free Society: Reflections on Ayn Rand's Political Philosophy*, ed. Gregory Salmieri and Robert Mayhew (Pittsburgh: University of Pittsburgh Press, 2019), 372–73.

Chapter Four

The Virtues of Businessmen

This chapter provides evidence that businessmen possess the character traits needed to produce goods and services that are of objective value. The first chapter established that the morality of profit maximization depends on businessmen producing goods and services virtuously. The second and third chapters established that businessmen produce goods and services that are of objective value by conceptualizing facts and integrating these facts to form values. The second chapter also provided the theoretical basis for concluding that businessmen need to cultivate specific virtues in order to be successful at this task. This chapter provides evidence that businessmen possess these virtues by examining the biographies of three historical businessmen who maximized profit successfully—J. P. Morgan (1837–1913), John D. Rockefeller (1839–1937), and Thomas Edison (1847–1931).

Chapter 2 identified the virtues that businessmen need to produce goods and services that are of objective value—the virtues of rationality, independence, honesty, integrity, justice, productiveness, and pride. Since the conceptualization of objective values is an intellectual task, our primary concern is to demonstrate that these businessmen exhibited a commitment to reason in their business lives.

After considering the virtues of these businessmen, we shall consider the character traits of the research scientist Louis Pasteur (1822–1895). The striking parallels between Pasteur's character and the characters of these businessmen evidence the role of virtue in the creation of objective value across all fields.

This chapter then considers criticisms that have been leveled against these businessmen that call into question their characters. We defend these businessmen against unjust criticisms and consider the respects in which their characters are mixed.

This chapter concludes by observing that these businessmen are role models for a well-lived life. The virtues that we observe in their lives are virtues that we should want our children to emulate.

MORGAN, ROCKEFELLER, AND EDISON

Morgan was a banker who financed entrepreneurs, and who saved the United States continental railroad system by transforming railroad management. Rockefeller founded the first modern corporation, which enabled him to conduct business on an unprecedented scale. Rockefeller's operation achieved economies of scale that enabled him to sell clean, safe kerosene at a price affordable for families on average incomes, allowing them to light their homes at night. Edison made a business out of invention. His "scientific factory" churned out inventions that transformed the world, including the phonograph, the motion picture camera, and the electrical distribution system.

We could have looked at the lives of contemporary businessmen, such as Warren Buffett, Jeff Bezos, or Steve Jobs. For our purposes, a businessman's race, gender, nationality, or the era in which he or she lived is unimportant. We are looking at the lives of these three men because we can observe their lives with an impartiality that we cannot bring to the lives of contemporary businessmen.[1] At the same time, we can still appreciate the significance of these men's achievements because they did not live during a time far removed from our own.

MORGAN AS A TALENT SPOTTER AND FINANCIAL DOCTOR

Morgan maximized profit through channeling wealth from Europe to entrepreneurs in America who had promising ideas for new businesses, but who lacked the wealth to finance the businesses themselves. Today, we would call the men Morgan invested in "entrepreneurs," though the term was not in widespread use in Morgan's time.[2] When deciding whether to invest in an entrepreneur, Morgan had to judge whether a sufficient number of prospective customers would judge the good or service to be of value for the business to be profitable. Morgan also had to judge whether the individual had the character needed for the business to succeed. When Morgan provided Edison with the financing Edison needed to found the company that would become General Electric, he was investing in Edison, the man, not just in an electrical distribution system.

Morgan was a talent spotter. His banking business consisted of accurately identifying individuals with the character needed to start their own business, and getting them money.[3] In this sense, Morgan is no different from the sports recruiter whose job it is to spot the next Michael Jordan, the conductor whose job it is to spot the next Enrico Caruso, or the casting agent whose job it is to spot the next Elisabeth Moss.

Morgan was once described by one of his critics as the "boss croupier of Wall Street."[4] The implication being that Morgan investing in entrepreneurs like Edison is the same as a gambler throwing dice in a casino. Morgan was not a gambler who happened to have successive decades of extraordinary good luck. Morgan invested based on reasoned judgment. He took a risk. His risk, however, was not the same as a gambler's. A gambler's risk is grounded in chance. The gambler cannot, at that moment, know all of the factors acting on the dice, and therefore cannot make a judgment about which side will come up. Morgan staked his investment on the soundness of his judgment.

Morgan was also a financial doctor. Sometimes businesses fail because they offer goods or services that prospective customers do not judge to be of value. Sometimes businesses offer goods or services that are of objective value to their customers but still fail because of mismanagement.

Mismanagement was a problem for America's fledging continental railroad companies. Railroads transformed lives. The railroad meant that if a farmer's crops failed, instead of his family facing starvation that winter, he could source food from other parts of the country. Despite the railroad's value, companies were failing under incompetent management. The Reading Company operated a railroad in southeast Pennsylvania and neighboring states. It could not raise funds to carry on business, so it turned to Morgan. His bank bought the controlling stock, and he took charge of their finances. Morgan raised $20 million in new bonds, saving the company. He did so during a depression.[5] Morgan was able to raise funds for a failing business during a depression because investors trusted his judgment, a trust earned through decades of sound judgment.

ROCKEFELLER AS CORPORATE RADICAL AND PIONEER

Rockefeller created value by using economies of scale to reduce the cost of producing kerosene. In Rockefeller's time, lighting one's home at night was the prerogative of the rich. The oil burned to light homes was sourced from whales, which was expensive to obtain. Cheaper alternatives, such as lard oil, or wicks dripping in fat, were not clean or safe.[6] After Edwin Drake demonstrated that oil could be found by drilling into the ground, fly-by-night businessmen entered the oil business, looking to make a quick profit. These owner-operated refineries were expensive to operate and produced oil of variable quality. Rockefeller's Standard Oil raised the quality of oil (hence the name, *Standard* Oil), and through the size of its operation reduced the price of kerosene from 23.5 cents per gallon to 5 cents. In raising the quality of oil and reducing its price, Rockefeller brought light within reach of hundreds of thousands of households.

Rockefeller founded a company that would become a model for future business organizations. Today, we take for granted corporations the size of Amazon, Apple, Columbia Pictures, Disney, Samsung, and Xerox. Corporations of this size did not exist in Rockefeller's day. Standard Oil emerged in a world in which corporations only had a legal existence in the state in which they were incorporated. Among other things, this meant that corporations could not own property in other states. To translate the legal situation of Rockefeller's day into our context, it would be as if Apple only had a legal existence in California and could not conduct business in other states. Rockefeller challenged America's antiquated corporate laws, paving the way for modern corporations. As an executive at Standard Oil observes, "He not only envisaged a new system of business upon a grand scale but he also had the patience, the courage and the audacity to put it into effect in the face of almost insuperable difficulties, sticking to his purpose with a tenacity and confidence [that were] simply amazing."[7]

Rockefeller conducted his business in a fundamentally different way from the businessmen who ran owner-operated refineries. Rockefeller invested in railroad facilities such as warehouses, terminals, and loading platforms.[8] Owner-operators were not concerned with long-term investments. Rockefeller negotiated preferential rates with the railroads. Owner-operators were not in a position to negotiate preferential rates because their businesses were not profitable for the railroads, whose trains had to stop to pick up single carloads of oil repeatedly.[9] Rockefeller employed scientists to find new ways to refine oil.[10] Owner-operators were out to make a quick profit with minimal effort, and so were not the type of people to take an interest in science. Rockefeller could achieve considerable savings by making minuscule changes in the production process. Reducing the amount of solder on cans by one drop saved Standard Oil hundreds of thousands of dollars over several years.[11] Though owner-operators could have made such changes, there was no point in even considering them, because the impact on the bottom line would have been negligible.

Rockefeller founded a business of astonishing size, even by today's standards. Twenty thousand wells poured oil into four thousand miles of pipelines, which carried the oil to the seaboard or five thousand tank cars. Standard Oil employed over one hundred thousand workers and exported fifty thousand barrels to Europe every day. When Standard Oil was broken up by the United States government, its constituent companies became Exxon, Mobil, Amoco, and Chevron, as well as some lesser-known names.[12]

Rockefeller had to pioneer new management practices to manage a corporation of this size effectively. In Rockefeller's day, businesses were managed by men who could directly perceive every aspect of the business. So doing was physically impossible in the case of Standard Oil. Rockefeller, therefore, had to manage the company through the numbers in the ledger books.

Rockefeller was the first person to think of conducting business on this scale. In this respect, Rockefeller was like Beethoven, who was the first person to think of adding the human voice to a symphony; Sir Arthur Conan Doyle, who was the first person to think of using the same characters in multiple stories; and Bill Gates, who was the first person to think of separating a computer's operating system from its hardware.[13]

EDISON AS INVENTOR-BUSINESSMAN

Edison maximized profit through inventing goods and services that he expected other people to judge of value in the context of their own lives. In Edison's day, inventors were presumed to possess something like a sixth sense, which gave them unique insight through which they could grasp that which had not been grasped before. Edison demonstrated that invention is a this-worldly process that can be brought under conscious control.

Edison's invention of the phonograph, for example, came about through a series of observations. Today, in the world of radio, podcasts, Alexa, and Siri, we think nothing of hearing the human voice emanating from inanimate objects. In Edison's day, no one had thought of recording sound. When Edison first recorded the human voice, one of his workmen made pious exclamations in German, and skeptics believed the voice to be a ventriloquist's trick.[14] The idea of a phonograph did not exist before Edison invented it. He was thinking about a machine that had not been thought of before. Edison did not start there, however. He started with what he already knew.

First observation. Edison was working on an automatic telegraph. He designed a device that could record and repeat telegraph messages at speeds of two hundred words a minute. The telegraph receiver embossed the dots and dashes of Morse code on a disk. When the disk was placed in a similar machine, the message was repeated on another telegraph wire.[15]

Second observation. Edison was working on Alexander Graham Bell's telephone receiver when he noticed that its diaphragm vibrated with his voice. The vibrations were of sufficient size that it could be made to do mechanical work. Edison attached a needle to the diaphragm and rested his finger on it. When Edison spoke into the diaphragm, the needle pricked his finger.[16]

Third observation. When Edison's automatic telegraph raced along at high speed, the movement of the arm over the dots and dashes made sounds similar to those emitted by Bell's first telephone.[17]

Edison then put these observations together. He reasoned that if he could record the movements of a diaphragm on a disk, as he was doing with the dots and dashes from the telegraph receiver, he could use the indentations to set another diaphragm in motion, thereby reproducing the sounds that had vibrated the first.[18] In so doing, Edison was not acting like a fantasy novelist, dreaming of a contraption with no basis in reality. On the contrary, Edison came up with the phonograph by taking note of the facts of reality and then grasping the logical implications, something he had spent years training his mind to do.

Edison is usually classified as an inventor instead of as a businessman. He was something much more profound—an inventor-businessman. As one German economist observed, Edison is "the outstanding example of a man who *made a business of invention itself*" (emphasis in original).[19]

Edison founded Menlo Park as a "scientific factory." His ambition was to turn out a minor invention every ten days and a major invention every six months.[20] Though Edison's ambition was optimistic, the number of inventions to emanate from Menlo Park is nonetheless remarkable. In addition to the phonograph, there was the microphone, the incandescent light bulb, the electrical distribution system, the motion picture camera, concrete houses (the precursor of today's prefabricated houses), and industrial batteries, among others. In conducting invention as a business, Edison laid the foundation for the research and development laboratories of modern corporations.[21]

MEN OF THE MIND

Morgan, Rockefeller, and Edison were thinkers. Except for Edison, they were not professional intellectuals and therefore did not keep a record of their thinking. Morgan's motto was *think a lot, say little, write nothing.*[22] We do not need a record of their thinking, however, to grasp the intellect's role in their lives. While their intelligence may not be evidenced through monographs or journal articles, as it would be with a professional intellectual, we can find evidence through how they conducted their lives.

Morgan's success depended on his ability to accurately identify specific facts of reality, in particular, the facts of an individual's character. When deciding whether to invest in someone, Morgan had to ask himself, in effect, whether this person had the character needed to make this business a success. For Morgan, a person's character was more important than collateral or social standing. Morgan was known to invest a million dollars in a man without a cent in the world if he had the right character.[23]

Morgan invested in failing businesses because he recognized that their failure was caused by the characters of the men managing the company and that the business could be turned around if he replaced them with different men.

Morgan was a successful banker because he was able to do something few people can do well; he could identify the characters of men accurately. Human beings have free will. We choose our character. We did not have to have our character, and, within certain limits, we can change. So long as a person has a particular character, however, his character is a fact of reality. Through our identification of this fact, we can predict his future behavior. We can predict whether he would make a good husband, whether we should purchase a used car from him, whether we should entrust him with our children, or whether we should invest money in his business.[24]

Morgan's intelligence was apparent from an early age. He was regarded as a mathematical prodigy. As a high school student, he could calculate cube roots in his head.[25] As a university student, he was invited by one of his professors to pursue a career as a professor of mathematics.[26] Though the ability to judge other people's characters may seem far removed from the field of mathematics, both demand that Morgan develop and use his intellect.

Rockefeller used the ledger books to identify the financial health of Standard Oil's operations and to diagnose the cause of an operation's profit or loss. If an operation was making money, the numbers told him why. If an operation was losing money, the numbers pointed him to the problem. The numbers on the ledger books' pages were signs pointing Rockefeller to the relevant facts of reality. Through the numbers, Rockefeller could manage every aspect of Standard Oil's operations without stepping foot on an oil field. Rockefeller's management strategy differentiated Standard Oil from other companies of the time. As Rockefeller recognized, "Many of the brightest kept their books in such a way that they did not actually know when they were making money on a certain operation and when they were losing."[27]

Rockefeller was not always rational outside of business, as we shall soon see. Rockefeller respected his mind when he was seeking to maximize the production of oil, however. When writing business letters, for instance, Rockefeller would go through several drafts until every superfluous word was eliminated.[28] Given that grammar is one of the tools of conceptual thought, this is evidence of a well-ordered mind at work.

Edison was an inventor, so he kept extensive scientific journals which recorded his thinking. Nevertheless, the breadth of Edison's knowledge is striking. After Edison quit school, his mother home-schooled him. She had Edison read Edward Gibbon's *Decline and Fall of the Roman Empire*, David Hume's *History of England*, and Barnas Sears's *History of the World*, as well as literary classics such as William Shakespeare and Charles Dickens.[29] At the age of fifteen, Edison joined the Detroit Free Library, and read the entire collection, starting with the first book on the first shelf, and ending with the last book on the last shelf. Edison's favorite was Victor Hugo's *Les Misérables*.[30]

Edison dismissed the importance of formal education, in his later years, and opposed the teaching of the liberal arts, claiming that America needs practical engineers and industrial men, not graduates trained in the "ninny" subjects of Latin and philosophy.[31] Edison had internalized the widely accepted dichotomy between theoretical and practical subjects, and in choosing the life of a practical inventor, he saw himself as standing on the practical side of the dichotomy. He was mistaken. Edison did not recognize that he had given himself a liberal arts education and that he brought extensive theoretical knowledge to bear on solving what he saw as purely practical problems.

Edison trained his mind from an early age to identify solutions. Edison worked as a telegrapher at the Western Union Office in Cincinnati, before becoming a full-time inventor. Rats menaced the office. Other people observed this problem, shrugged, and continued with their work. Edison observed this problem and identified a solution. He invented a device consisting of two metal plates connected to a battery. He named his device a "rat-paralyzer."[32]

Similarly, Edison was reporting on roll calls in Congress for the press wire, when he observed the time wasted waiting for voice votes. Edison was not the first person to observe the loss of time. He was the first to think of a solution. He invented the first electronic vote recorder.[33]

RESPECTING FACTS

A rational thinker recognizes, at least implicitly, that facts are what they are independent of what anyone thinks or wishes. We must conform to the facts. We cannot expect the facts to conform to us.[34] Morgan, Rockefeller, and Edison respected facts throughout their business lives.

Morgan recognized that the facts of a man's character exist independent of social convention. As a result, Morgan made hiring decisions that were considered unconventional for the time. Morgan's father wanted to found a banking dynasty based on family ties, like the Rothschild's. Morgan built a banking dynasty based on merit.[35] He recognized that familial relationships do not determine a man's character. Morgan, therefore, rejected family members and people from socially respectable families as partners, hiring, instead, men of integrity who had the appropriate professional qualifications.[36] For instance, Morgan offered the presidency of a major enterprise to a German Jew. He did so in 1904, a time when most American business leaders were casually anti-Semitic.[37]

Rockefeller's respect for the numbers in his ledger books was a respect for the facts signified by those numbers. These numbers were signs pointing to specific facts about Standard Oil's operations. Though mistakes are possible, they are easy to ferret out. Just as there cannot be contradictions in reality, there cannot be contradictions in the numbers. When Rockefeller found a contradiction, he knew that a mistake had been made. Rockefeller did not personally observe Standard Oil's day-to-day activities. Instead, he relied on reports from his subordinates. He could check their claims against the numbers, which means, he could check their claims against the facts of reality as grasped through means of the numbers.

Rockefeller, sadly, was not consistent in his respect for the facts of reality. He had a blind spot for homeopathy. Though Rockefeller would go on to fund the establishment of Johns Hopkins Hospital, which led the fight against homeopathy, he initially insisted that the medical institutions he funded treat homeopaths with respect.[38] Rockefeller maintained his support of homeopathy even when mainstream doctors cured his hydrocele, a condition that his homeopath had maintained was incurable.[39]

Edison respected the absolutism of reality when identifying the facts that made the phonograph, the motion picture camera, and the electrical distribution system possible. Consider, for instance, Edison's experiments to find a suitable filament for the incandescent light bulb. Edison tested thousands of materials before he found what he wanted. Either the material possessed the characteristics he needed, or it did not. If it did not, he moved on to the next material.

Edison sometimes got the facts wrong. When Edison developed his electrical distribution system, he opted for direct over alternating current because he wanted to bring electricity into people's homes. He was, therefore, obsessed with demonstrating the safety of electricity. At the time, direct current was safer. Technological advances, however, addressed the safety issues with alternating current. Edison's mistake was to maintain his support for direct current even though the basis of his opposition to alternating current no longer applied. Though Edison was irrationally obstinate on this particular issue, he eventually conceded that he had made a mistake.[40]

INDEPENDENT THINKERS

A rational thinker recognizes, at least implicitly, that he must think for himself. A rational thinker is necessarily an independent thinker because thinking is a do-it-yourself activity, like digestion.[41] An independent thinker is not necessarily original. If he is studying physics, he has to grasp for himself the truths of physics, so that he sees these truths through his own eyes. Independence does not require that he make discoveries of his own. An independent thinker sees the truth of Newton's discoveries in reality, not on the pages of the *Principia*.

An independent thinker is not a contrarian. He does not disagree for the sake of disagreement. Nevertheless, maintaining one's position in the face of others' opposition often calls attention to a person's independence, because a person who grasps the truth for himself maintains his position independent of others' opinions.[42]

Morgan appears to have been acutely aware of the importance of intellectual independence from an early age, perhaps because his father exercised extraordinary control over his life. In a school assignment, Morgan noted that he intended "to act and think in all cases for myself."[43] These were not empty words. Morgan financed Edison's electrical distribution system in defiance of his father's opposition.[44] He would go on to become the first person in history to illuminate his residence entirely by Edison's light.[45]

Rockefeller explicitly endorsed the importance of independent thought. When asked by an assistant superintendent, "If you were me, what would you do?" Rockefeller replied, "I would do what I thought best."[46] Here, Rockefeller is declaring that he acts on his judgment while, at the same time, declaring that he expects others to do the same.

Rockefeller's independence is evident in his support for Lima crude. Lima crude gave off a noxious smell, which one newspaper observed smelled "like a stack of polecats," rendering it unsuitable for home use.[47] Rockefeller was convinced that his scientists would find a way to remove the smell, making Lima crude commercially viable. His Board of Directors disagreed. Rockefeller, therefore, decided to stake his own money on his judgment. He told the Board: "I will build this improvement out of my own funds and underwrite it for two years. . . . At the end of that time if it is a success the company can reimburse me. If it is a failure, I will take the loss."[48] The Board decided to stand with Rockefeller and invest in Lima crude. Rockefeller's scientists found a way to remove the noxious smell, and Standard Oil made a fortune from what had been previously worthless oil.

Edison always sought to understand things for himself. Consequently, he demonstrated remarkable independence from an early age. When Edison's schoolmaster declared his mind "addled," Edison did not internalize this judgment as many children of his age might; he ran home and refused to return. Edison would later say that he found his education repulsive because he needed to see things for himself.[49] He wanted to learn about bumblebees by studying bumblebees, not by memorizing a list of facts about bumblebees chalked on the blackboard by his schoolmaster. For this reason, Edison endorsed the Montessori method of education.[50]

Edison's early independence provided him with the intellectual skills needed for a career as an inventor-businessman. It also inoculated him against the opposition he would face from the newspapers and the scientific community. Morgan and Rockefeller faced public criticism because of their immense wealth. Edison faced public criticism because he did not think like other men. When Edison founded Menlo Park, the newspapers declared that his "scientific factory" would be a failure, because, they claimed, a man without formal education could not conduct scientific research.[51] The phonograph, the incandescent light bulb, and the motion picture camera would prove them wrong.

Nothing would compare with the criticism Edison faced when pursuing the invention for which his name would be forever associated, the incandescent light bulb. Edison did not invent the light bulb. The ability to turn electric current into illumination was discovered in 1808, thirty-nine years before Edison was born.[52] By the 1860s, when Edison was about thirteen, electricity lit England's lighthouses, and electric candles lit Paris's streets.[53] These systems used arc lights, which gave out a blinding glare and emitted noxious gasses, making them suitable for remote lighthouses, but impractical for home use. Furthermore, arc lights were wired to a dynamo in a series, so all the lights had to be turned on and off simultaneously. Edison's contribution was to conceive of the *subdivision of light*. He projected a system of many small lights in which each one could be turned on and off separately. His aim was nothing less than a duplication of the gas-distribution industry with electricity.[54] Edison would be condemned for conceiving of the subdivision of light.

A leading scientific journal declared that Edison's talk of the subdivision of light showed that he was ignorant of the fundamental principles of electricity and dynamics.[55] The value of gas stocks declined after Edison announced his work on the electric light. In response, the British Parliament convened a committee to investigate Edison's work, in case his lighting system posed a threat to British gas. (Britain's Gas Light and Coke Company was the world's first public gas works.) British scientists advised that Edison's electric light project is "unworthy of the attention of practical or scientific men."[56]

Some newspapers asserted, without any basis in fact, that Edison's work on light had brought him to the point of death and that he lay in a state of despair. Other newspapers declared that Edison was a "charlatan" and that his work on light "smirched" his reputation as a scientist.[57]

Edison responded to these criticisms by letting his inventions speak for themselves. He gave the criticisms no thought, quietly soldiering on with his work.

Edison had been working from principles that the scientific community had yet to grasp. He had conceived of a fundamental change in the form of the electrical circuit, which made the subdivision of light possible.[58] For this reason, the continuing glow of Edison's light bulb sent shockwaves through the scientific community.[59]

SELF-MADE MEN

Morgan, Rockefeller, and Edison were self-made men. The phrase "self-made man" usually denotes a man who started with nothing and with minimal help from others made a fortune. Rockefeller and Edison were self-made in this sense. Morgan was not because he was born into a wealthy family and entered the family business. "Self-made man" has a deeper meaning, however, and in this deep sense, all three were self-made.

In chapter 3, we saw that a person has a *species* identity and a *personal* identity.[60] A person's *species* identity pertains to his nature as a human being. A person's *personal* identity pertains to his particular character. A person's "self" is his personal identity. A person is "self-made" in the sense that he makes his self by choosing the values that form his character.

Not everyone forms a self. There is such a thing as psychological stillbirth. Such a person does not develop a personal identity. Instead, his personal identity is an extension of someone else's, such as his mother or father. We see psychological stillbirth in cases of narcissistic parents, who do not permit their children to make their own decisions, so the child fails to develop a separate identity.[61]

Profit maximization is egoistic because the conceptualization of value demands that a person acts on his own judgment, thereby shaping a personal identity of his own making. Morgan, Rockefeller, and Edison were self-made men in the sense that they were rational, independent thinkers, who made their *selves*.

Morgan made himself into J. P. Morgan through choosing which entrepreneurs to invest in, which Board of Directors to replace, and with whom to replace them. As a wealthy heir, Morgan could have coasted on his father's money, like many wealthy heirs of his generation. Morgan's father expected him to go into the family business. Still, Morgan could have parroted his father's decisions while living off a guaranteed income. Had Morgan done so, we would not know his name today. There would have been no J. P. Morgan. There would have been a psychologically empty vessel waiting to be filled by his father's ideas. Morgan valued his intellectual independence and made his own decisions, even when they conflicted with his father's. For this reason, there are biographies of Morgan and not of the other sons of wealthy bankers, whose names have been lost to history.

Rockefeller made himself into John D. Rockefeller through choosing to invest in the oil industry, through choosing to consolidate the oil industry at a time when it was dominated by small owner-operated businesses, through choosing to use well-maintained ledger books to manage Standard Oil, through choosing to hire scientists to discover a way to commercialize Lima crude, and through countless other decisions.

Edison made himself into Thomas Edison through choosing to reject his schoolmaster's assessment of his intelligence, through choosing to read an entire library of books, through choosing to pursue a career as an inventor-businessman (not an obvious choice for a deaf boy from a poor family), through choosing to be alert to the world around him, and through choosing to follow the logical implications of his observations.

Morgan, Rockefeller, and Edison were able to make superlative profits because of the traits that they incorporated into their characters. Through these men's lives, we see that profit maximization is morally demanding. In chapter 2, we saw that profit signifies a businessman's success at conceptualizing goods or services that are of socially objective value. Conceptualizing value requires a commitment to reason. Without the virtue of rationality, these men would not have been able to maximize profit. A person of lesser virtue may have been able to make a satisfactory profit. To create value on an unprecedented scale, these businessmen had to conceptualize new value relationships, which required them to cultivate a character that was up to the task.

PASTEUR AS RESEARCH SCIENTIST

Let us now consider the character traits that Pasteur needed to create objective values in medical science. Though Pasteur was not a businessman, he possesses the same character traits that we have seen in the lives of Morgan, Rockefeller, and Edison. We should not be surprised by this striking parallel. These character traits are not peculiar to profit-maximizing businessmen. Anyone who sets out to create objective value must cultivate these virtues.

Pasteur wanted to improve the quality of French beer. In Pasteur's day, animal and human waste contaminated water, rendering it unsafe for consumption. Alcoholic beverages provided a safe alternative. Speaking of alcohol, Pasteur observed that wine is "the most healthful, the most hygienic of beverages."[62] For Pasteur, alcohol quality was a health issue.

Brewers, at the time, knew that beer had to be clear to be healthy and tasty. They did not understand why, however, and they showed no interest in finding out. Brewing was regarded as an art, so it would not have occurred to them to understand the biological process by which beer is made.[63]

Pasteur sought to understand why beer sometimes goes off in order to prevent the alternation from occurring. He discovered that parasitic germs from the air infected the yeast, causing the alternation.[64] Pasteur's solution was to kill the germs by heating the beer during fermentation. The heat did not alternate the beer, and the heated beer kept indefinitely. Pasteur patented this process, which he named *pasteurization*.

When Karl Jacobsen built a new brewery in 1870, he incorporated Pasteur's theories into the manufacturing process. Consequently, Jacobsen's brewery went from exporting four million deciliters of beer per year to two hundred million. In honor of Pasteur's contribution to brewing, Jacobsen erected a marble bust of Pasteur at the entrance of the street leading to his brewery. The brewery's name is Carlsberg.[65]

While pasteurization began as a process for improving the quality of beer, its significant impact would be in improving the safety of a different beverage. The milk we pour over our cereal each morning is safe to drink because it has been *pasteurized*.[66]

Pasteur's biggest impact, however, would be in his discovery of the vaccine. The vaccinations we receive as children have eliminated once common childhood diseases, thereby significantly raising average life expectancy. Many of us are alive today, thanks to Pasteur.

Pasteur did not discover vaccination. The process of immunizing a person against smallpox had been around for centuries. Edward Jenner demonstrated, about a hundred years before Pasteur's experiments, that inoculating a person with the cowpox vaccine made them immune to smallpox.[67] (The word "vaccination" comes from the French word for cow, *vache*.) Vaccination, at this time, was equated with the *smallpox* vaccine, and the ability to inoculate against smallpox was not thought to have implications for other diseases.[68] Pasteur's contribution was to grasp the process of vaccination, thereby enabling him to manufacture vaccines against a range of diseases.

Pasteur's assistants were culturing microbes in the laboratory when the start of the academic year interrupted their work. When they inoculated chickens with the bacteria, the chickens did not become sick as expected. Pasteur decided to inject these chickens with a new dose of active microbes. The chickens resisted the disease. Chickens who had not been inoculated with the aged bacteria died.[69] Pasteur grasped that he was seeing the same process Jenner had observed with smallpox. Pasteur understood the implications: by manipulating the virulence of a germ, he could manufacture a vaccine.

Pasteur was not satisfied. He could prevent someone who never had the disease from developing it. Pasteur, however, wanted to go a step further. He wanted to cure a disease *after* the person had contracted it. He decided to experiment with rabies.[70] Rabies was not a common disease, but it was frightening, and its symptoms stirred the public imagination. Pasteur's challenge was to develop a vaccine that would act more quickly than the disease, so that the vaccine could act after the germ had entered the organism, but before the disease became symptomatic.[71]

Joseph Meister was nine years old when a rabid dog bit him on both thighs, both legs, and on the hands, making rabies inevitable. Joseph's mother brought him to Pasteur, who inoculated him with the rabies vaccine. Joseph became the first person in history to survive a rabies infection. Pasteur watched over Joseph as he grew up, giving him a job at the Institut Pasteur as a security guard. Many years later, as an old man, Joseph stood guard over Pasteur's crypt, beneath the Institut, as the Nazis invaded Paris.[72]

PASTEUR AS A THINKER

Pasteur, like Morgan, Rockefeller, and Edison, was a *thinker*. Brewers, throughout history, observed the alternation of beer. Pasteur was the first person to identify the cause, which enabled him to bring the brewing process under conscious control.

Pasteur observed that chickens inoculated with weak bacteria did not develop the disease. He did not stop there. He asked, "What would happen if we inoculate the same chickens with a virulent version of the same bacteria?" When Pasteur saw that the inoculated chickens survived, while the uninoculated chickens died, he recognized that he was observing the same process as occurs in the smallpox vaccine. In so doing, Pasteur was able to identify the biological process behind vaccination.

PASTEUR RESPECTED THE FACTS OF REALITY

Pasteur, like Morgan, Rockefeller, and Edison, treated *the facts of reality as absolutes*. Fermentation was considered a chemical synthesis in Pasteur's time. When Pasteur observed fermentation, he saw that the amyl alcohol that rotated the plane of light came from the ferment rather than from the sugar, as had been supposed. Pasteur knew from his earlier discoveries in chemistry that only life rotates the plane of light. He concluded that ferment is alive.[73] Pasteur realized that ferment had been misconceptualized, and he proceeded to reconceptualize everything that he knew about fermentation in light of this discovery. Pasteur concluded that fermentation is the act of reproduction of the living germs that constitute yeast. The sugar is merely the food that allows the yeast to reproduce.[74] Pasteur adjusted his thinking to conform to the facts. He did not attempt to adjust the facts to fit his presuppositions.

PASTEUR AS AN INDEPENDENT THINKER

Pasteur, like Morgan, Rockefeller, and Edison, was *an independent thinker*. After Pasteur demonstrated the efficacy of vaccination, he was condemned by the medical profession, because he was not a physician. Michel Peter, from the Académie de médecine, proclaimed, "M. Pasteur's excuse is that he is a chemist who, inspired by the desire to be useful, wanted to do something for medicine, to which he is a total stranger."[75] The implication being that Pasteur's vaccine could not work because Pasteur was a chemist, not a physician. The opposite was the case. Pasteur's success lay, in part, in his ability to take discoveries from one field and apply them to what had heretofore been treated as a separate field.

Pasteur would leave the hall of the Académie trembling in anger at those who chose not to grasp the proof of his vaccine.[76] Though Pasteur was affected by this injustice in a way that Edison never was, he did not allow his hurt feelings to affect his assessment of the facts. Pasteur solved the problem by refusing to attend further meetings.

Animal rights activists also condemned Pasteur. Curiously, Pasteur was not condemned for using animals to produce vaccines, but for being a lousy scientist. The president of the Antivivisectionist League declares: "It will have taken almost a century to demonstrate the errors of [the] vaccine, but it will take only a fourth of this time to annihilate the fantastic doctrines of M. Pasteur, which contradict the laws of general biology. . . . Science does not recognize in the great discoveries of M. Pasteur anything but a tissue of dogmatic conceptions and unsuccessful attempts more apt to ruin than to enrich the country that would adopt them."[77] Opposition to vaccination today is from a scientifically ignorant minority. This statement reflects the views of mainstream scientists.

PASTEUR POSSESSES A SELF

Pasteur, like Morgan, Rockefeller, and Edison, was a *self-made man*. Pasteur made himself into Louis Pasteur by choosing to study physics, by choosing to apply his knowledge of physics to chemistry, by choosing to apply his knowledge of physics and chemistry to biology, by choosing to investigate the alternation of beer, and by choosing to make the connection between the smallpox vaccine and his own experiments in the inoculation of chickens.

UNJUST ACCUSATIONS

Morgan, Rockefeller, and Edison, like most people, have a mixed character. These men were virtuous in certain areas, such as business, but not in other areas, such as their home life. We have focused so far on the areas in which they were virtuous. Out of justice to them, we must acknowledge the areas that are not so admirable. Before we do, we must first sweep aside some unjust accusations. Though all three men are open to legitimate criticisms, prominent critics attack them for their *virtues*, not for their vices.

Morgan's wealth is taken as all the evidence needed to call into question his moral character, as though what is important, morally speaking, is how much money a man possesses, not how he obtained it. Morgan believed that opposition came from the "occult mechanisms" of high finance, and innocently believed that if people understood his work, they would see it as a national service.[78] The opposition was not grounded in ignorance of high finance, however. It was based on the assumption that Morgan has no moral right to the wealth that he created.

One commentator asserts that America would be better off without men like Morgan: "I can't quite understand a man like Mr. Morgan making money out of his country's need. . . . The fewer of such men we have in this country the better I say. Dullness which is contented with smaller profits is better in the long run."[79] This person implicitly recognizes that Morgan's intellect is the source of his wealth, and in response, elevates *dullness* above *intelligence* as an ideal. Without the intelligence of a Morgan, there would be *smaller* profits, which means *less* wealth, which means *fewer* goods and services available for people to purchase. This person is implying, whether he realizes it or not, that America would be better off as an *impoverished* country.

Pope Francis articulates the moral premise here (quoting Saint John Chrysostom): "Not to share one's wealth with the poor is to steal from them and to take away their livelihood. It is not our own goods which we hold, but theirs."[80] On this premise, businessmen are charging their customers for goods or services that are rightfully theirs. Imposing a price on customers, on this view, is like charging someone rent for living in their own home. Morgan has the intelligence to create wealth. Given this, Morgan should have created wealth as a favor to the country, to whom his wealth rightly belongs.

Rockefeller, like Morgan, was condemned for his wealth. Rockefeller was also convicted in a court of law of violating specific laws, and this conviction is cited to give legitimacy to moral condemnations of his wealth. These laws, however, should not have existed. If they still existed today, the companies that have raised our living standards, such as Apple and Microsoft, would not have been possible. Rockefeller should be praised for acting in defiance of these laws, not condemned. In a mixed economy, where businessmen are forced to act in the face of a plethora of unjustified and immoral laws, we cannot take a conviction as evidence of a bad character. We must first ask whether the breached law was valid.

Standard Oil acted like a modern corporation. It was not a corporation in the eyes of the law, however. Standard Oil was a *combination* of corporations. Corporations, at this time, only had a legal existence in the state in which they were incorporated. Rockefeller created Standard Oil by purchasing the stock of different corporations and transferring ownership to Standard Oil's Board of Directors, who held the stock in *trust*. When New Jersey amended its corporate laws, allowing corporations in New Jersey to own the stock of other corporations, this stock was transferred to Standard Oil of New Jersey. This combination was the mechanism through which Rockefeller was able to create a business on the scale of modern corporations within the confines of an antiquated legal system.[81] For this reason, Standard Oil was sometimes referred to as a *trust* or as a *combination*. The Sherman Anti*trust* Act, under which Standard Oil was convicted, takes its name from the trust established to hold stock in Standard Oil's constituent corporations.[82]

Imagine what Apple would look like had it been organized along the same lines as Standard Oil. Apple would not be a single corporation but a combination of corporations. There would be Apple of Texas, Apple of New York, Apple of Alaska, and so forth, with the stock of all of these separate corporations held by Apple of California. The Board of Directors of Apple of California would coordinate the activities of Apple's constituent corporations.

Now, imagine that Apple is prosecuted under the Sherman Antitrust Act for engaging in anti-competitive practices. Of what would these anti-competitive practices consist? Of outperforming Microsoft or Nokia? No. The anti-competitive practices would consist of Apple of California suppressing competition between the Apple corporations in the different states. The combination is preventing Apple of Texas, for example, from competing with Apple of New York and Apple of Alaska. Though technically correct, we do not usually think that there is anything objectionable in an Apple Store in Texas not competing against an Apple Store in New York. After all, these are stores of the same company.

This restriction on self-competition is the crime for which Standard Oil would be broken up. The accusation was that in combining different corporations under the Standard Oil umbrella, Rockefeller was suppressing competition. There was, however, no other mechanism for founding a corporation the size of Standard Oil within the confines of the legal system of that time. Rockefeller could not have created Standard Oil through the same legal mechanisms that Steve Jobs used to create Apple, because these did not exist. Rockefeller had to approach Standard Oil by combining legally separate corporations and structuring them so that they would act as though they were a single corporation. The problem here was not Rockefeller's actions, but the antiquated legal system under which he was operating.

Before the antitrust case against Standard Oil, Rockefeller was criticized for taking advantage of Standard Oil's size to obtain preferential railroad rates. Owner-operators were not in a bargaining position to obtain similar rates, which put them at a competitive disadvantage. At the time, preferential railroad rates were not illegal. Rockefeller's critics (in particular, Standard Oil's first biographer, Ida Tarbell), however, argued that this practice was ethically suspect.

Rockefeller saw nothing wrong. He pointed out that everyone understood that the listed railroad rates were just a starting point for negotiations and that some of Standard Oil's rivals obtained superior rates from certain railroads.[83] Rockefeller told one person, "I deny that it was regarded as a dishonorable practice for a merchant or manufacturer to obtain the best rates possible for his goods."[84]

The moral case against preferential railroad rates was based on the assumption that railroads are common carriers and are, therefore, obliged to offer everyone the same rates. This assumption would eventually be relied on to justify laws making it a punishable offense for railroads to charge customers different rates.[85] Though Standard Oil was not accused of violating these laws, the criminalization of preferential rates cast a shadow on the practice, legitimizing earlier criticisms.

In a free market, a railroad is a private business. It is, therefore, legally free to charge its customers whatever it wishes, including charging different customers different prices. Morally speaking, this practice is not wrong, so long as there is an objective basis for the different rates. Market forces prevent railroads from setting prices capriciously. Rockefeller was able to obtain preferential rates from railroads because the scale of Standard Oil's operations meant that the railroads made more profit from the preferential rates charged to Standard Oil than the higher rates charged to independent owner-operators. Standard Oil could have shipped its oil by trucks or by barge, and the preferential rates were a way for the railroads to keep a valued customer.

The railroads, however, did not operate in a free market. Railroads were established under state charters so that they could obtain the right of eminent domain. The railroads traded their independence for the right to compel owners to sell their land. There *is* a moral problem here. The problem, though, was not with Standard Oil and its preferential rates, but with the mixed economy within which Standard Oil was forced to operate.

A common theme behind these criticisms is that *economic* power is the equivalent of *political* power.[86] John Sherman, the Republican senator behind the Sherman Antitrust Act, asserts that businessmen like Morgan and Rockefeller exercise "a kingly prerogative inconsistent with our form of government. . . . If we will not endure a king as a political power we should not endure a king over the production, transportation, and sale of any of the necessities of life. If we would not submit to an emperor, we should not submit to an autocrat of trade."[87]

Consider Rockefeller's dominance in the oil industry. Did Rockefeller exercise a "kingly prerogative" over oil? Rockefeller formed Standard Oil by purchasing other companies' stock. If their owners refused to sell, Rockefeller could do nothing except increase his offer. That was Rockefeller's power—the power to offer an incentive. Rockefeller did not have the power to send in the police or the armed services to confiscate the refineries of those owner-operators who refused to sell. He could not have recalcitrant sellers shot, hanged, or guillotined. *These* would have been kingly prerogatives.

Contrary to Rockefeller's critics, it was not Rockefeller who exercised kingly prerogatives, but his opponents. Owner-operators who declined to sell their stock formed a "Petroleum Parliament," which generated several resolutions, including a free-pipeline bill and the prohibition of preferential railroad rates.[88] Though the legislature did not adopt these resolutions, they are an attempt to exercise the prerogatives of kings. Consider the free-pipeline bill. Pipelines do not grow in nature. These pipelines would have been "free" in the sense that they are free to the owner-operators advocating for the law. The pipelines would have been built at taxpayers' expense, and the right to build the pipelines across private land would, presumably, have been obtained through the government's powers of eminent domain. The powers of taxation and eminent domain were once kingly prerogatives, inherited by modern forms of government.

Did Rockefeller exploit the ignorance of the owner-operators who sold Standard Oil their stock? Here is the deal that Rockefeller offered: "Take payment for your stock in cash or stock in Standard Oil." Those who opted for Standard Oil stock made a fortune; their descendants would populate twentieth-century American high society.[89] These sellers did not complain. Most of the companies that Rockefeller bought were failing under incompetent management. Those who opted for cash thought they were the ones exploiting Rockefeller's ignorance, and snickered at his imbecility. After their companies were incorporated into Standard Oil and brought under the control of Standard Oil's management team, the companies began to make money. The former owners then turned around and accused Rockefeller of having taken advantage of them, overlooking the fact that they could never have made this profit themselves.

The evidence that Rockefeller was not exercising a "kingly prerogative" is that many owner-operators refused to sell their failing businesses. These refiners condemned Rockefeller when their failing businesses failed. Consider Franklin Tarbell. He set up a barrel shop at a time when iron tanks were replacing wooden barrels. When this business failed, he turned to oil production and refining, just as Rockefeller was consolidating the industry.[90] He refused to sell, and never forgave Rockefeller for achieving a success he could not. Franklin's daughter, Ida, would go on to write the history of the Standard Oil Company, a vitriolic hit piece masquerading as journalism, which would taint assessments of Rockefeller's character for decades to come.[91]

EDISON AS A BUSINESSMAN

Edison's status as an inventor immunized him against the character assassinations faced by Morgan and Rockefeller. As an inventor, the popular prejudices against businessmen were not thought applicable. Nevertheless, criticism is implicit in the claim that Edison was not a businessman. Edison *was* a businessman, and in insisting that he was too good to be one, critics were condemning him in the form of praise.

Edison was an inventor-businessman. Throughout his life, Edison demonstrated a consistent interest in invention and in making money. At age eleven, Edison and a friend laid out a vegetable garden. They hired a horse and cart, and Edison drove around the town selling onions, lettuce, cabbages, and peas. The first summer, they made two or three hundred dollars.[92]

While working as a train-boy, Edison maintained a laboratory in the baggage car, so that he could carry on his experiments, and a press so that he could publish a local newspaper, which he edited, printed, and sold. Edison's *Weekly Herald* was the first newspaper in the world to be published on a train.[93]

When Edison became a professional inventor, he recognized that he would need to invent products that would be in "commercial demand" if he was to make a living.[94] Edison once declared, proudly: "I measure everything I do by the size of the silver dollar. If it don't come up to that standard then I know it's no good."[95] Not the words of a man who would reject the honorable title of *businessman*.

MIXED CHARACTERS

Though many of the criticisms of these businessmen are unjust, reflecting the anti-business bias of their critics, they had genuine shortcomings. Morgan was a man of integrity in his business dealings and valued integrity in his business partners. Nevertheless, Morgan was a serial adulterer. Morgan's view of the ideal wife clashed with the type of woman he found sexually attractive. He believed that an ideal wife should be happy at home taking care of her husband and their children. He was, however, sexually attracted to women who were intelligent and self-possessed, that is, women who were his spiritual equal.[96] Morgan's view of the ideal wife reflected the assumptions of his time. Sadly, Morgan did not bring the intellectual independence he demonstrated in his business to challenging conventional views on the role of a wife.

Rockefeller was a devout Northern Baptist. His religious beliefs sabotaged the value of his wealth in his family's life. Rockefeller and his wife adopted a frugal lifestyle on moral principle, denying themselves and their children the benefits of Rockefeller's fortune. When the children asked for bicycles, Rockefeller and his wife bought them one bicycle to share among all five. Though they could easily have afforded to buy the children a bicycle each, the Rockefellers wanted their children to learn to sacrifice for one another.[97]

Rockefeller accepted the doctrine of Christian stewardship, which means that he could not take pride in the wealth he created, or accept that his wealth was available for his benefit. As one author explains, "the Christian doctrine of stewardship is the most radical of all doctrines concerning property. It maintains that a man owns *nothing*; what he has he holds in stewardship under God" (emphasis in original).[98] Rockefeller believed that God placed the oil in the ground, and that he was merely the instrument through which God worked to get oil into people's homes. Rockefeller interpreted his wealth as a sign of God's favor for a job well done. This wealth was not his to do as he pleased. Rockefeller believed that he held this wealth in trust on behalf of God, and was under an obligation to distribute this wealth to those in need.[99] When Rockefeller donated buildings to a school, the school, in a statement that Rockefeller would have approved of, did not thank Rockefeller but thanked God for having given them the buildings through Rockefeller.[100]

Edison was not a good husband or father. He worked in his laboratory eighteen or more hours a day, and when he came home for meals would say little to his family, his mind still in his laboratory.[101] Romantic love and children are important values. Edison's mistake was not to bring the intelligence he applied to his inventions to reflecting on the roles of a wife and children in his life. A value is that which one acts to gain and/or keep. Edison did not treat his wives and children as values. Edison could have decided to forgo this aspect of life, given the demands of his work. Had Edison reflected on these issues before marrying and having children, he would have realized that this choice entails investing the time needed to nourish these relationships.

ROLE MODELS

Morgan, Rockefeller, and Edison are role models because these men possess character traits that we should want our children to emulate.

We should want our children to grow up to be *thinkers*. We should want our children to ask themselves, "What is the evidence for this?" We should want them to consider the implications of ideas. We should want them to compare what they are hearing or reading with other ideas that they have heard or read. If a religious classmate tells our daughter that God is omnipotent and benevolent, we would want her to think back to a newspaper report she read the week before about children starving in Sudan, and to grasp that if God is omnipotent he could have prevented these children from starving, in which case he cannot be benevolent. We would want our daughter to do so, because she would be raising, in her own terms, what philosophers call the problem of evil.[102]

We should want our children to recognize that *facts are absolute*. We should want our children to recognize that assertions need to be tested against the evidence. If our child's grandparents tell him that there is a Santa Claus who delivers presents to children every year on Christmas Eve, we would want him to ask a few questions, such as, "How can Santa deliver toys to every child in the world in a single night?" "Does Santa deliver toys to the children in Sudan?" "Why do my parents return defective toys to the local toy store instead of Santa's office in the South Pole?"

We should want our children to act on their *own judgment*. We should want them to chart their own course in life, even when their decisions are not the ones we would have made. Independent children are responsible children because when we assume the responsibility of choice, we assume responsibility for the consequences that follow logically from that choice. For this reason, independent children do not steal, because their friends steal; do not cheat on exams, because "everyone does"; do not take drugs, because it will make them popular; and do not drink to excess, because it will impress someone they just met.

We should want our children to be *selfish* in the sense that they possess an identity of their own. We should recognize that our children are not extensions of us, that they are not a second chance for us to make choices for them, which we wished we had made for ourselves. We should want our children to choose which sports they will play (if any), the types of clothes they like to wear, their friends, the books they enjoy, and their political views.

Wanting our children to develop these character traits is wanting them to live the life of a Morgan, Rockefeller, and Edison, at least in these respects.

PROFIT MAXIMIZATION'S MORALITY

The case for the morality of profit maximization has been made. Chapter 1 established that the debate over the morality of profit maximization is a debate over the value of *what* businessmen produce and *how* they produce it. Chapter 2 established the theoretical basis for concluding that businessmen produce goods and services that are of objective value (so profit meets the "*what* condition") and that businessmen must do so virtuously (so profit meets the "*how* condition"). Chapter 3 provided evidence that profit meets the *what* condition by examining historical examples of how businessmen conceptualize facts and integrate these facts to conceptualize ends and the means to these ends. This chapter has provided evidence that profit meets the *how* condition by demonstrating that historical businessmen possess the virtues needed to conceptualize objective value.

The last three chapters shall clarify our thinking about the morality of profit maximization in light of the foregoing argument.

NOTES

1. As one example of the difficulties in discussing the life of a contemporary businessman, see the conflicting accounts of Steve Jobs's life in Walter Isaacson, *Steve Jobs* (London: Little, Brown, 2011) and Brent Schlender and Rick Tetzeli, *Becoming Steve Jobs: The Evolution of a Reckless Upstart into a Visionary Leader* (New York: Crown Business, 2015).
2. For a history of the word "entrepreneur," see Bill Bolton and John Thompson, *Entrepreneurs: Talent, Temperament and Opportunity*, 3rd ed. (Oxon: Routledge, 2013), 71–72.
3. Rand's description of Midas Mulligan's investment strategy in *Atlas Shrugged* mirrors Morgan's. Ayn Rand, *Atlas Shrugged* (New York: Signet, 1992), 294–95. I have seen no other evidence that Rand based Mulligan on Morgan.
4. Jean Strouse, *Morgan: American Financier* (New York: Random House, 1999), x and 367 n.
5. Ibid., 251–53.
6. Ron Chernow, *Titan: The Life of John D. Rockefeller, Sr.* (New York: Vintage Books, 1998), 73–74.
7. Quoted in ibid., 230.
8. Ibid., 116.
9. Ibid.
10. Ibid., 285.
11. Ibid., 180–81.
12. Ibid., 558–59.
13. Esteban Buch, *Beethoven's Ninth: A Political History*, trans. Richard Miller (Chicago: University of Chicago Press, 2004), 1; Janet B. Pascal, *Arthur Conan Doyle: Beyond Baker Street* (New York: Oxford University Press, 2000), 71; Michael A. Cusumano, *The Business of Software: What Every Manager, Programmer, and Entrepreneur Must Know to Thrive and Survive in Good Times and Bad* (New York: Free Press, 2004), 12.
14. Matthew Josephson, *Edison: A Biography* (New York: History Book Club, 1959), 163–64. Watch an episode of the 1982 television series *Knight Rider*, which features a car named KITT that can talk and drive itself. When KITT speaks, onlookers search for the human being who is talking because it does not occur to them that a car could talk. Today's children would likely find the onlookers' confusion perplexing because they are used to having conversations with inanimate objects.
15. Ibid., 159.
16. Ibid., 159–60.
17. Ibid., 160.
18. Ibid.
19. Quoted in ibid., 137.
20. Ibid., 133–34.
21. Ibid., 133.
22. Strouse, *Morgan*, xii.
23. Ibid., 13.
24. For a discussion of the metaphysical status of a man's character, see Ayn Rand, "The Metaphysical Versus the Man-Made," in *Philosophy: Who Needs It* (New York: Signet, 1984), 31.
25. Strouse, *Morgan*, 58.
26. Ibid., 65.

27. Quoted in Chernow, *Titan*, 46.
28. Ibid., 178–79.
29. Josephson, *Edison*, 21.
30. Ibid., 33.
31. Ibid., 440.
32. Ibid., 47.
33. Ibid., 65.
34. For a discussion of the primacy of existence, see Leonard Peikoff, *Objectivism: The Philosophy of Ayn Rand* (New York: Meridian, 1993), 17–23.
35. Strouse, *Morgan*, 250.
36. Ibid., 160 and 217–18.
37. Ibid., 218.
38. Chernow, *Titan*, 492.
39. Ibid., 405.
40. Josephson, *Edison*, 349 n.
41. Ayn Rand, *The Fountainhead* (London: HarperCollins, 1994), 665.
42. For a discussion of the meaning of independence, see Peikoff, *Objectivism*, 251–59; Tara Smith, *Ayn Rand's Normative Ethics: The Virtuous Egoist* (New York: Cambridge University Press, 2006), 106–34; Smith, "Unborrowed Vision: Independence and Egoism in *The Fountainhead*," in *Essays on Ayn Rand's* The Fountainhead, ed. Robert Mayhew (Lanham, MD: Lexington Books, 2007).
43. Quoted in Strouse, *Morgan*, 39.
44. Ibid., 183.
45. Ibid., 230. For further background on Morgan's support for Edison's electrical distribution system, see Josephson, *Edison*, 291–93.
46. Chernow, *Titan*, 190.
47. Quoted in ibid., 284.
48. Quoted in ibid., 285. Rand had Dagny Taggart make a similar offer for the building of the John Galt Line. Rand, *Atlas Shrugged*, 183.
49. Josephson, *Edison*, 20.
50. Ibid., 440.
51. Ibid., 132.
52. Ibid., 176–77.
53. Ibid., 177.
54. Ibid., 180.
55. Ibid., 186.
56. Quoted in ibid., 196. Cf. Strouse, *Morgan*, 183.
57. Josephson, *Edison*, 206.
58. Ibid., 195.
59. Ibid., 224.
60. Nathaniel Branden, "Alienation," in *Capitalism: The Unknown Ideal*, ed. Ayn Rand (New York: Signet, 1967), 289–90.
61. For an explanation of why narcissists are not egoists, see Edwin A. Locke and Ellen Kenner, *The Selfish Path to Romance: How to Love with Passion and Reason* (Doylestown, PA: Platform Press, 2011), 20–23.
62. Quoted in Patrice Debré, *Louis Pasteur*, trans. Elborg Forster (Baltimore: The Johns Hopkins University Press, 1998), 231.
63. Ibid., 250–51.
64. Ibid., 251.
65. Ibid., 255.
66. Ibid., 235 and 238.
67. F. Dawtry Drewitt, *The Life of Edward Jenner: Naturalist, and Discoverer of Vaccination* (Cambridge: Cambridge University Press, 2013).
68. Debré, *Louis Pasteur*, 380.
69. Ibid., 378–79.
70. Ibid., 417.

71. Ibid., 425.
72. Ibid., 438–41 and 496.
73. Ibid., 97.
74. Ibid., 105.
75. Quoted in ibid., 411.
76. Ibid., 410.
77. Quoted in ibid., 433.
78. Strouse, *Morgan*, 410. For a discussion of the morality of finance, see Yaron Brook and Don Watkins, eds., *In Pursuit of Wealth: The Moral Case for Finance* (Irvine, CA: Ayn Rand Institute Press, 2017).
79. Quoted in Strouse, *Morgan*, 354.
80. Francis, *Apostolic Exhortation: Evangelii Gaudium of the Holy Father Francis to the Bishops, Clergy, Consecrated Persons and the Lay Faithful on the Proclamation of the Gospel in Today's World* (Vatican City: Vatican Press, 2013), 49.
81. Eric Daniels, "Reversing Course: American Attitudes about Monopolies, 1607–1890," in *The Abolition of Antitrust*, ed. Gary Hull (New Brunswick, NJ: Transaction Publishers, 2006), 88.
82. Thomas A. Bowden, "Antitrust: The War against Contract," in *The Abolition of Antitrust*, ed. Gary Hull (New Brunswick, NJ: Transaction Publishers, 2006), 96. For a discussion of the problems with the Sherman Antitrust Act, see Ayn Rand, "Antitrust: The Rule of Unreason," in *The Voice of Reason: Essays in Objectivist Thought*, ed. Leonard Peikoff (New York: Meridian, 1990); Alan Greenspan, "Antitrust," in *Capitalism: The Unknown Ideal*, ed. Ayn Rand (New York: Signet, 1967); Gary Hull, ed., *The Abolition of Antitrust* (New Brunswick, NJ: Transaction Publishers, 2006); Dominick T. Armentano, *Antitrust and Monopoly: Anatomy of a Policy Failure*, second ed. (Oakland, CA: The Independent Institute, 1990); Armentano, *Antitrust: The Case for Repeal*, revised 2nd ed. (Auburn: Ludwig von Mises Institute, 2007).
83. Chernow, *Titan*, 115.
84. Quoted in ibid., 117.
85. Ibid., 116.
86. For a discussion of the distinction between economic and political power, see Ayn Rand, "America's Persecuted Minority: Big Business," in *Capitalism: The Unknown Ideal* (New York: Signet, 1967), 46–48.
87. Quoted in Strouse, *Morgan*, 302–303.
88. Chernow, *Titan*, 206–207.
89. Ibid., 168.
90. Ibid., 436.
91. Ida M. Tarbell, *The History of the Standard Oil Company*, 2 vols. (New York: Cosimo Classics, 2009).
92. Josephson, *Edison*, 26.
93. Ibid., 37–38.
94. Ibid., 66.
95. Quoted in ibid., 283.
96. Strouse, *Morgan*, 293.
97. Chernow, *Titan*, 125.
98. F. Ernest Johnson, "Commentary on the Ethical Implications of the Study," in *Social Responsibilities of the Businessman*, by Howard R. Bowen (New York: Harper & Brothers, 1953), 244.
99. Chernow, *Titan*, 55 and 76.
100. Ibid., 482.
101. Josephson, *Edison*, 285 and 87.
102. Steve Jobs raised this question as a child in his Sunday school class. See Isaacson, *Steve Jobs*, 14–15. Cf. Robert White, "Two Sides of Think Different," in *Steve Jobs and Philosophy: For Those Who Think Different*, ed. Shawn E. Klein (Chicago: Open Court, 2015), 129.

Chapter Five

Clarifying Confusions about Profit Maximization

A moral case for profit maximization is controversial because critics assume that such a case must defend a range of suspect practices, if not explicitly then at least by implication. This book argues that profit maximization is moral when businessmen maximize profit by selling goods or services that are of objective value. These suspect practices do not follow when businessmen meet the conditions required for profit maximization to be moral.

This chapter is titled "Clarifying Confusions about Profit Maximization" because clarifying why these suspect practices do not follow from the moral case for profit maximization clarifies our understanding of the relationship between profit and ethics. The title has a double meaning. We are clarifying confusions about profit maximization, and by so doing we are clarifying our understanding of the moral basis of profit maximization.

This chapter explains why the moral case for profit maximization does *not* imply that businessmen must set aside non-profit considerations, that businessmen must prioritize profit above all other values, that a "market mentality" should be extended to every aspect of human life, that businessmen must be moral by definition, or that everyone has a moral duty to maximize profit.

This chapter concludes by considering the implications of the moral case for profit maximization for business education.

GOOGLE AUTOCOMPLETE

Even readers sympathetic to this book's argument might mistakenly infer that a moral case for profit maximization provides a moral sanction to suspect business practices. The human mind works like Google autocomplete.[1] You start a thought, and your mind completes the thought based on your past thinking. Your personal Google autocomplete cannot be more accurate than your mental filing system. Cognitive work is needed to keep your mental file folders tidy. Reading a book is insufficient. Until you tidy your mental file folders, your Google autocomplete will continue to throw up implications that follow from false assumptions that you previously integrated with the concept of "profit," even when you no longer formally accept them.

The implications that we shall consider are not unreasonable. The goal here is not to preempt objections but to further clarify the relationship between ethics and profit by considering why specific implications do not follow when profit is grounded in the conceptualization of objective value.

PROFIT MAXIMIZATION IS *NOT* THE STANDARD OF THE GOOD

The *first* implication that may be mistakenly read into the moral case for profit maximization is that profit maximization requires businessmen to make business decisions solely by the standard of profit maximization, setting aside non-profit considerations. If profit maximization is moral, then that which maximizes profit is good, and that which diminishes profit is bad or evil.

This implication suggests

—that a businessman contemplating whether to invest in a company that streams hardcore pornography should squelch his moral concerns and make the investment decision solely based on the company's bottom line;[2]

—that a music company executive contemplating whether to sign a black metal band whose songs are littered with misogynist and racist lyrics should squelch his moral concerns and make the decision based solely on whether there is a market for such music;[3]

—that the head of a movie distribution company that distributes movies made by a production company whose CEO is notorious for sexually harassing actresses should squelch his moral concerns and think only of the revenue these movies will bring;[4]

—that the owner of a company which has received an order for aircraft parts from the North Korean government should squelch his moral concerns about this government's human rights violations and think solely about the revenue this deal will bring;[5] and,

—that the CEO of an international chocolate company contemplating whether to close a plant that has been operating in a small town for over eighty years should squelch his concerns about the hundreds of employees who will be put out of work and think solely about the cost savings.[6]

A CORPORATE EXECUTIVE'S FIDUCIARY DUTY

Critics allege that these implications follow from a corporate executive's fiduciary duty to maximize profit for shareholders.

When Henry Ford wanted to reinvest Ford Motor Company's profits instead of paying dividends to its shareholders, he appealed to the public good. Two shareholders sued, arguing that Ford should be serving the interests of his company's shareholders, not the interests of the public. The judge agreed, ruling that a "business corporation is organized and carried on primarily for the profit of the stockholders" and, therefore, the "powers of the directors are to be employed for that end."[7] This case is notorious in the field of business ethics for establishing that a corporate executive's primary obligation is to maximize profits.[8]

Critics of the corporate form argue that this fiduciary duty corrupts the characters of corporate executives by requiring them to banish moral considerations and to think solely in terms of profit maximization.[9] A corporate executive who allowed non-profit considerations to enter his thinking would be labeled a lousy executive by his company's board and shareholders and may even open himself to legal sanctions for breach of his fiduciary duties.

A young woman with ambitions to become a corporate executive needs to train herself to think in terms of profit maximization because boards seek this quality. Though boards today are prepared to consider candidates who care about non-profit factors, they only do so because critics have successfully convinced generations of business students that they should not focus on profit maximization.

The fiduciary duty to maximize profit is allegedly the root of all that is wrong with corporations. In making a moral case for profit maximization, this book may seem to provide a moral sanction to corporate malfeasance. If correct, this book would need to be placed next to Niccolò Machiavelli's *The Prince* and Bernard Mandeville's *The Fable of the Bees* as one of the most corrupt books in the history of ethics.[10]

Critics focus on corporations because corporate executives have a fiduciary duty to maximize profit. Sole proprietorships and partnerships are not subject to the same criticism because the owners of these organizations are not subject to the same fiduciary duties. Sole proprietors and partners are legally free to take into account moral considerations. In making a moral case for profit maximization, this book seems to be extending the requirement to maximize profit to sole proprietors and business partners, thereby encouraging their moral characters to be similarly corrupted.

In chapter 1, we saw that business ethics developed as an academic discipline in response to the perception of incessant corporate irresponsibility. The source of corporate malfeasance was thought to be something peculiar to the corporate form, namely that a corporation is an artificial entity without a body to kick or a soul to be dammed. We expect sole proprietors to put people before profit because sole proprietors are flesh-and-blood human beings with ties to the local community. The moral case for profit maximization seems to encourage sole proprietors to act like corporations. If profit maximization is moral, then it seems that sole proprietors must brush aside their community ties and think only about the bottom line.

THE *WHAT* OF PROFIT MAXIMIZATION

These implications do not follow from the moral case for profit maximization. In chapter 2, we saw that profit is a businessman's reward for successfully conceptualizing facts and integrating these facts to form values. Profit is the market mechanism by which businessmen learn whether or not they have successfully formed objective values. In a free market, profit maximization requires businessmen to think about the objective value of the goods and services they sell. A businessman *solely* concerned with profit maximization needs to consider the objective value of his or her goods or services.

A businessman can maximize profit in a regulated economy by producing goods and services that are not of objective value. These implications may follow from profit maximization in economies that have corrupted the market system's communication channels and reality's feedback mechanism. These implications do not follow when businessmen seek to maximize profit under those conditions that morally justify its pursuit, namely creating objective value for their customers.

A profit-maximizing businessman contemplating whether to invest in a company that streams hardcore pornography must consider whether this service is of objective value. This businessman must consider whether there is evidence that hardcore pornography redounds to human life; otherwise, he or she cannot morally justify maximizing profit this way. Though a discussion of pornography's value is outside of this book's scope, the value status of pornography is relevant to a businessman wanting to justify his or her profits morally.[11]

Critics do not grasp the ethical implications of profit because they think of profit in strict accounting terms. They observe that a businessman streaming hardcore pornography has a balance sheet on which revenue exceeds expenses and concludes that he or she is maximizing profit. The mere fact that non-profit organizations can have an identical looking balance sheet should give pause for thought. The moral status of a businessman's profits depends on what his or her profits signify. If the businessman's profits signify the successful conceptualization of objective value, then the profits are moral. If the businessman's profits signify something else, such as his or her success at wooing politicians, then the profits are immoral.

A businessman who invests in a streaming service for hardcore pornography may find that his or her revenues exceed expenses. Nevertheless, if hardcore pornography is not of objective value to its viewers, then this businessman cannot morally justify his or her profits. The moral case for profit maximization is not a moral case for profits that arise from the sale of an immoral good or service.

The music company executive is in the same position. An executive who refuses to sign a black metal band because misogynism and racism are anti-values is the executive who acts in accordance with the moral basis of profit maximization. He or she has correctly grasped the objective value of this music.

This conclusion may seem counterintuitive. The moral case *for* profit maximization is a moral case *against* a businessman bringing in significant revenue that will bolster the company's bottom line. This conclusion only seems counterintuitive because we have trained our minds to think of profit solely in terms of the difference between revenue and expenses, without considering what the profit signifies. Our Google autocomplete pushes against this conclusion because it is functioning based on an impoverished understanding of what profit maximization requires. We must integrate the need for businessmen to conceptualize objective value with the concept of "profit" before this conclusion will seem obvious.

An analogy may be helpful. Many university students are grade maximizers in the sense that their goal is to maximize the number of "A" grades on their academic transcript. Can a moral case for being an "A student" justify plagiarism? No. Grades are not merely letters on a transcript. These letters are grades because they signify students' mastery of the subjects as evaluated by their professors. An "A" signifies that, in the professor's judgment, the student has mastered the subject. An "A" awarded as the result of undetected plagiarism does not have the same signification. This pseudo "A" is not a genuine grade. It is a fraud committed against anyone who reads the transcript. A moral case *for* being an "A student" is a moral case *against* obtaining an "A" through plagiarism. The moral case for being an "A student" is a moral case for "A" grades that signify the student's mastery of the subject, not for "A" grades that signify the student's ability to deceive his or her professor.

THE *HOW* OF PROFIT MAXIMIZATION

The first chapter demonstrated that a profit-maximizing businessman needs to consider *what* he is maximizing and *how* he maximizes it. Profit maximization is morally demanding because businessmen must cultivate the virtues to conceptualize objective values.

There is another, personal reason why businessmen need to consider how they maximize profit. A businessman undermines the contribution that profit makes to his life when he maximizes profit in a manner that corrupts his character. In a regulated economy, a businessman can maximize profit through vicious means. So doing is not to the businessman's benefit, however.

Profit's *raison d'être* is the furtherance of human life. Profit is of value as a means to an end. Profit furthers the life of a businessman because his goods or services express his values and further his ends. Profit also furthers the lives of a businessman's customers through the goods or services that they purchase. These goods and services express the customer's values and further his or her ends.

A businessman who corrupts his character when maximizing profit acts contrary to profit's *raison d'être*. He may be enhancing his purchasing power. He is doing so in a way that sabotages his ability to find value in these goods and services, however. He has severed the connection between profit and the end that profit serves.

Consider the head of a movie distribution company who turns a blind eye to sexual harassment. This businessman is maximizing profit. The movies are of objective value in moviegoers' lives. This businessman, however, is maximizing profit in a way that violates the principle of justice.[12] He or she is colluding with a harasser to maintain the position of power that the harasser holds over vulnerable actresses.

PROFIT HAS ETHICAL IMPLICATIONS

Morality is not a constraint on profit maximization. Profit requires businessmen to consider *what* they produce and *how* they produce it. Profit and ethics cannot be separated because the moral case for profit maximization is the moral case for profit that signifies the creation of objective *value*.

Consider the manufacturing company that received an order for aircraft parts from the North Korean government. The owner is conspiring with this government to violate its citizens' rights. So doing corrupts his character. Consequently, his profit will not serve the end that justifies its pursuit. This businessman would be acting contrary to profit's *raison d'être*.

A businessman who refuses to maximize profit when so doing would corrupt his moral character is not necessarily failing to *maximize* profit. The refusal to maximize profit *this way* leaves open all of the other ways in which a moral businessman can maximize profit. Profit is an abstraction. The concept of profit subsumes all of the particular ways in which a businessman can make a profit. A businessman can refuse to maximize profit *this way* while still aiming at profit maximization.

A bodybuilder who refuses to eat broccoli because he despises the taste is not refusing to eat nutritious food. He is refusing to eat this particular instantiation. He can still choose from all the other instantiations.

When ABC canceled Roseanne Barr's sitcom after she posted a racist tweet, some newspapers celebrated ABC's willingness to place people before profit.[13] These newspapers listed the revenue that Barr's show brought in and inferred from the show's cancellation that ABC would now miss out on this revenue. For our purposes, let us accept that ABC was morally correct to cancel Barr's show. Is ABC failing to maximize profit? Not necessarily. ABC is forgoing the revenue that this particular show would have brought. ABC, however, will be expecting this show's replacement to bring in comparable revenues. It is not as though ABC canceled Barr's show intending to shut down its broadcast during her former timeslot.[14]

Similarly, if the head of a movie distribution company refused to work with this particular production company, there are plenty of other production companies he or she could work with instead.

Of course, if these businessmen have to choose between maximizing profit and refusing to work with Barr or a sleazy movie producer, then they should *not* maximize profit. The moral case for profit maximization is not a case for maximizing profit under these circumstances.

PROFIT VERSUS ALTRUISM

The moral case for profit maximization is grounded in the human need to pursue objective values. Profit maximization is not compatible with an ethics that demands self-sacrifice. Consequently, a moral commitment to profit maximization will require businessmen to make decisions that are incompatible with altruism.

The CEO of an international chocolate company is justified in closing a long-standing factory, even though so doing will put hundreds of employees out of work. A businessman does not owe his employees their jobs. An employment relationship is a trade. An employee exchanges his knowledge, skills, and time for wages or a salary. Like all trades, both parties expect to benefit from the exchange. They should only continue to trade so long as they expect to benefit. An employer is not obligated to employ someone when so doing is no longer to his advantage any more than an employee is obligated to stay with an employer when he can find a better offer elsewhere.[15]

Losing a job is painful. For many workers, the job has been so thoroughly integrated into their lives that it has become part of their personal identity. They might socialize with their coworkers. Their children might play with their coworkers' children. Their lives may have been organized around this particular job for decades. Nevertheless, responsible workers recognize that a job is not guaranteed for life. A market economy is a dynamic system in which the job market is in constant flux. Responsible workers plan for the possibility that they may have to transition to a new job, perhaps by setting money aside so that they can support themselves while temporarily unemployed, or by ensuring that their skills meet the needs of the current market.

In the immediate aftermath of a job loss, a worker may experience the news as a threat to his or her interests. Over the long term, however, a flexible job market is more critical to the worker's well-being than holding onto a particular job. One must be careful not to commit what the French economist Frédéric Bastiat calls the broken window fallacy.[16] When a chocolate factory closes, we observe the employees on the evening news being shut out of the factory and watch interviews of them expressing their fears about not being able to support their families. We do not see the wealth that has been freed for new investments, investments which will create value for everyone, including the redundant employees.

PROFIT MAXIMIZATION VERSUS PROFIT PRIORITIZATION

The *second* implication that may be mistakenly read into the moral case for profit maximization is that profit maximization requires businessmen to prioritize profit above all other values. For the reasons that we saw in the first two chapters, this book defends the morality of profit *maximization*, not the morality of profit *satisfaction*. Profit maximization does not oblige a businessman to make a profit but to make as much profit as possible. A businessman who runs his or her business at a profit but could have made more would seem to be morally deficient by the standards of profit maximization.

Critics object to profit *prioritization*, not to the making of profit as such. Critics find profit maximization objectionable because they think that it requires businessmen to prioritize profit above other values.[17] Business ethicists typically discuss two cases in their classes to demonstrate the moral hazards of profit maximization. The first case concerns alleged flaws in the design of the Ford Pinto. Early tests showed that the Pinto was vulnerable to the fuel tank exploding in rear-end collisions. Ford allegedly performed a cost-benefit analysis, which concluded that it was cheaper for Ford to compensate families for the deaths of the cars' occupants than to amend the car's design. In pushing ahead with production, Ford seemingly prioritized profits over the lives of its customers.[18]

The second case concerns Nestlé allegedly marketing baby formula to mothers in third-world countries. Since these mothers did not have access to safe drinking water, they mixed the formula with contaminated water, endangering their children's lives. A pamphlet titled *The Baby Killer* first exposed this case. In Switzerland, this pamphlet was published under the title *Nestlé Kills Babies*. In marketing baby formula to ignorant mothers, Nestlé seemingly prioritized profits over the well-being of third-world children.[19]

The examples that business ethicists cite of moral businessmen typically consist of businessmen who prioritize other values above profit. A classic example is Aaron Feuerstein, CEO of Malden Mills. When Feuerstein's synthetic textile and upholstery plant burned to the ground, workers expected him to shift the jobs to a country with cheaper production costs, as similar companies were doing. The factory's closure would have devastated the local economy, which centered around the mills. Instead, Feuerstein committed to rebuild the factory and pay his employees their full salary and benefits during the reconstruction.[20] Roger L. Martin, writing for the *Harvard Business Review*, praises Feuerstein for prioritizing his employees' well-being above profits.[21]

Dan Price, CEO of Gravity Payments, is a recent example. In 2015, Price made national headlines when he announced that he would slash his salary and raise the minimum wage of his employees to $70,000.[22] Though this decision does not appear to have harmed the company's bottom line, a company-created web page celebrates Price's policy by selling a T-shirt with the slogan "Purpose Over Profit."[23]

As we saw in chapter 1, profit *maximization*'s opponents do not necessarily oppose *profit*. They can recognize that a business needs to make a profit in order to stay in business. The opposition to profit maximization is opposition to a businessman elevating profit above what the critics believe should be higher values, like employee or customer well-being.

PROFIT *PRIORITIZATION* IS NOT SELF-INTERESTED

If profit *maximization* implies profit *prioritization*, then this book's argument is self-contradictory. The moral case for profit maximization consists in demonstrating that businessmen maximize profit by making new value integrations, and they must do so by conceptualizing the relationship between goods and services and the ultimate end of human survival. Profit is a means to an end. If profit *maximization* implies profit *prioritization*, however, then profit must be the final end, the *summum bonum*, and cannot be a means to an end.

Furthermore, profit prioritization clashes with the morality of self-interest. Self-interest is about the pursuit of objective values. Profit prioritization would require a businessman to sacrifice values in the name of profit. Egoistically, some things should be more important than profit. If a businessman has to choose between a business meeting and his daughter's piano recital, his hierarchy of values would require him to prioritize the latter. Profit prioritization, however, would seem to require him to prioritize the former, calling upon him to act against his values.

VALUE MAXIMIZATION

This implication does not follow from the moral case for profit maximization. This book does not defend the maximization of goods and services as such. Instead, this book defends the maximization of goods and services in so far as they have the status of objective values. Goods and services should not be maximized when they are not of objective value.

Profit *maximization* is not the value on a businessman's value hierarchy. The value is *profit*. The goal of a businessman should be to maximize his *values*, and he should be maximizing profit in so far as profit signifies the creation of objective values.

Talk of prioritization only makes sense when we are discussing the relationship between two values. Profit is a value within a specific context. Outside of this context, there is no value in profit. Profit should not appear on a businessman's hierarchy of values when it is achieved under those conditions in which it is not a value. So there is no issue here of which has priority.

Profit is a businessman's reward for correctly conceptualizing objective value. Profit is also of objective value to businessmen. Profit does not possess intrinsic value. Profit is a value to a businessman under specific conditions. When profit meets these conditions, profit is a value that a businessman should pursue greedily, like all of his other values. When profit does not meet these conditions, profit is not a value and should not be pursued. Profit is not a value to a businessman who would prioritize a business meeting above his daughter's piano recital. Such a businessman is not elevating one value above another. Profit ceases to be of value when prioritized above his daughter's piano recital. Similarly, profit is not a value to a businessman who maximizes profit at the cost of his health. The morality of profit maximization cannot be invoked to justify a businessman missing his daughter's piano recital or harming his health because maximizing profit is not moral under these conditions.

Critics misframe the issue because they are not thinking in terms of objective values. The first question to ask is not, which has priority, but whether profit is a value in the particular context. If we establish that profit is a value in this context, then we should maximize profit, as we should with all of our values. If profit is not a value in this context, then profit should not appear on our hierarchy of values, and so the prioritization issue is mute.

FORD AND NESTLÉ

The moral case for profit maximization recognizes that businessmen should maximize profit by integrating facts to form values. The cases typically cited in business ethics classes are not about businessmen conceptualizing values. These cases concern businessmen who deliberately produce goods or services that are *not* of objective value.

In the Ford Pinto case, the problem is not that Ford ranked profit above people but that an exploding car is not of objective value to its customers. Ford presented the Pinto as a product that it expected its customers to benefit from when it knew that the Pinto is a potential deathtrap. The cash that Ford accumulated from selling the Pinto is a measure of its success at defrauding customers, not a measure of value creation. The problem here is not that Ford prioritized profit but that it sought to make a profit in a way that violated the *what* and *how* conditions.

Similarly, with the Nestlé case, the problem is not that Nestlé sought to maximize profit, but that Nestlé sold a product in conditions where that product is not of objective value. Baby formula is a value in countries where mothers have access to safe drinking water. Baby formula is not of value when mixed with contaminated water. The problem was not that Nestlé prioritized profit but that Nestlé sought to profit from selling a good that they should have realized would not be of objective value to their customers under these conditions.

These cases are presented in the business ethics literature as though the facts are uncontroversial. The cases have been presented here at face value, for the purposes of this chapter. Nevertheless, we must acknowledge that the cases against Ford and Nestlé are not as clear-cut as presented here. The Ford case is presented as though the Pinto was a death trap. Ford looked at subcompact fatality rates from 1975 to 1980 and found that the rate of a rear-fire fatal accident in the Pinto was 2.74 annually per million cars in operation compared with 2.24 for other subcompacts. The rate of rear-fire fatalities for other subcompacts was lowered during this period by the VW Beetle, whose fuel tank was located at the front.[24] Purchasing a Pinto was, thus, not significantly more risky than other subcompacts.

Similarly, the Nestlé case is presented as though Nestlé's baby formula was a poison inflicted on third-world babies by a greedy corporation. Actually, there is no evidence that any children died from being fed Nestlé's baby formula. The pamphlet, *Nestlé Kills Babies*, relies on a 1970 study by Fernando Monckeberg of the University of Chile. Monckeberg rejects the use of his study to indict Nestlé. He writes: "The entire controversy has been blown out of proportion, and the guilt of the companies exaggerated." Monckeberg notes that the Chilean government distributed the baby formula as part of a free milk program, not the formula companies. Monckeberg also notes that as a result of this program, the mortality rate of babies declined from 150 babies out of 1,000 births to 46 per 1,000.[25] The myth of the Nestlé baby formula case arose because mothers fed critically ill infants artificially, and so the death rate among artificially fed infants was higher than among breast-fed babies. Proponents of breastfeeding observed the statistical correlation between artificial feeding and infant deaths and concluded that baby formula was the cause, overlooking the fact that these infants were already at a high risk of dying.[26]

THE VIRTUE OF JUSTICE

We must identify the relevant moral principle before considering the Feuerstein and Price cases. These cases are concerned with the virtue of *justice.* The law of supply and demand is the mechanism through which an employee's labor is priced. CEOs are paid significantly more than janitors because significantly fewer people possess the qualities needed to be successful CEOs. Jeff Bezos can do a janitor's job. A janitor cannot do Jeff Bezos's job.

Profit maximization requires employees to be compensated justly. People who think that just compensation conflicts with profit maximization reveal that they are thinking of profit in strict accounting terms. They imagine two columns, one labeled "revenue" and the other "expenses." Employee compensation increases the total of the expense column, so they conclude that higher expenses mean less profit. They miss that these employees help produce the wealth signified by the revenue column. Justly compensating employees furthers profit maximization because these employees help create wealth.

When Henry Ford significantly increased his employees' salaries, he was criticized by other businessmen for his charity. There was no charity involved, however. The Ford Motor Company had a high staff turnover, and the higher salaries reflected the fact that few people were prepared to stay in a monotonous job long at the lower wage rate. The additional expense furthered the goal of profit maximization by reducing employee turnover.[27]

ALMS ARE NOT WAGES

Feuerstein's commitment to continue paying his employees' "wages" during the reconstruction was not an act of *justice* but *charity.* Feuerstein's payments to his employees were not *wages* but *alms.* A wage is a payment in exchange for work. Feuerstein's employees were not working. To the extent that this money was Feuerstein's, he is legally entitled to donate his profits to his former employees. Feuerstein cannot be praised or criticized for placing people before profits because he was not making a profit. The business was temporarily shut down. There is a moral issue of whether Feuerstein is placing his former employees' well-being ahead of his own. That, however, is a different issue from profit prioritization.

A businessman supporting his workers during reconstruction is not necessarily alms. The businessman could be investing in valued employees by paying them a retainer while the factory is rebuilt. So doing prevents the employees from taking a job elsewhere. Under these circumstances, a businessman supporting his employees maximizes profit over the long term. Feuerstein was not in this position, however. The profit-maximizing strategy would have been to keep the factory closed and move production offshore, where the production costs are significantly cheaper.

Feuerstein's commitment to rebuilding the plant instead of offshoring the jobs diminishes his profits. Feuerstein's rebuilt plant may produce the same number of goods as before. If Feuerstein is spending more on creating these goods than he needs, however, then he is undermining the creation of value, which makes everyone worse off, including his employees and the town in which the factory operates.

Feuerstein's commitment to rebuilding the plant is a commitment to diminishing the value created by his company. Though Feuerstein and his supporters frame this commitment in terms of placing people before profits, no one is better off when a company deliberately suppresses its ability to produce value. Like the case of the chocolate factory, we must not commit the broken window fallacy. We can observe the plant being rebuilt, the former employees being put back to work and shopping at local stores, and the smiling faces of the employees' families. We do not see the opportunities lost because Feuerstein chose to channel this wealth into creating make-believe work for his employees instead of creating genuine value.[28]

Of course, making the transition to new jobs would have been trying for Feuerstein's former employees and for local businesses, which depended on the factory for their customers. Still, Feuerstein's workers knew that similar jobs were being offshored and so should have been prepared for the likelihood of losing their jobs well before the factory burned down. Responsible people do not treat their jobs as guaranteed for life and recognize that they need to be prepared for market changes that may render their jobs unprofitable.

One cannot make a trade-off between profit and people because profit signifies the creation of value that furthers human life. Businessmen like Feuerstein should not be criticized for misguidingly placing people first, but for acting contrary to the requirements of profit maximization. They do not really place people first because they are acting contrary to the requirements of human life, including the lives of the people they pretend to help.

ANTI-PROFIT IS ANTI-PEOPLE

In the Price case, we must differentiate between Price's *explanation* for raising his employees' salaries and an objective *assessment* of his actions. Price and Gravity Payments have spun a narrative that fails to recognize that profit is concerned with value creation. This narrative is morally objectionable because Price and Gravity Payments are providing an ideological challenge to the system upon which all of our lives depend.

An objective assessment, however, requires us to consider whether Price's actions, in fact, violate the requirements of justice. We must allow for the possibility that Gravity Payments had been underpaying its employees and that the new "minimum wage" accurately reflects the employees' value to the company. If so, the "minimum wage" is consistent with the requirements of profit maximization.

We are not in a position to make this assessment. Regardless of whether Price's actions were justifiable in terms of justice, there is nothing admirable about someone critical of profit. Price's assertion that he places people before profit is unsustainable. Profit serves human life. Thus, to be anti-profit is to be anti-people.

THE MARKET MENTALITY

The *third* implication that may be mistakenly read into the moral case for profit maximization is that a moral sanction of profit maximization promotes a culture in which a "market mentality" is extended to every aspect of human life. If profit maximization is moral, then it might seem that no area of life should be off-limits when profit is to be made.

The BBC sitcom *Absolutely Fabulous* dramatizes this complaint. Edina Monsoon decides to adopt a Romanian orphan. She asks for a selection to be sent over so that she can pick one. A few minutes later, she changes her mind. When she realizes that the "merchandise" is on its way, she begins to fret. Edina asks her friend, Patsy, for assurance that she will be able to return the babies. Patsy suggests that Edina mark the babies up and sell them on.[29] Edina's attitude is obnoxious because babies are not merchandise to be bought and sold.[30]

Though an extreme example of the market mentality, there are plenty of mundane ones. Anyone who works in a university is familiar with businesses that help students to cheat on assignments. Typically, these businesses hire financially strapped PhD candidates to write bespoke essays. Since these essays are tailored to specific assignments, plagiarism detection services do not catch them. Some of these businesses even offer a guarantee—an "A" or your money back.

Alternatively, consider a businessman who establishes a website advertising Russian brides. Russia has a shortage of potential husbands, with women outnumbering men. Moreover, a foreign husband represents an opportunity to leave Russia and immigrate to a more prosperous country. The people visiting these websites are stereotypically older men who struggle to find wives in their own countries. An entrepreneurial businessman may see an opportunity to create an online marketplace that puts potential wives in contact with potential husbands.[31]

SOME VALUES CANNOT BE PURCHASED

This implication does not follow from the moral case for profit maximization. The problem with these types of cases is that such values cannot be purchased through the marketplace. The value of handing in an "A" assignment is to be found in doing the work oneself, not in paying someone else to do the work for you. The value of marriage is to be found in creating a shared life with another human being, not in obtaining a visa to immigrate to another country. These are not the type of values that can be bought and sold.

Profit signifies the value created by goods and services that can be bought and sold. Not all values can be traded in a marketplace. A consumer can find value in purchasing a refrigerator. A lonely person cannot find value in renting a friend. A person willing to be his "friend" for an hour in exchange for cash is not a friend.

Friendship is a trade, and there is a sense in which a person pays for another's friendship. Virtue is the appropriate currency for a friendship, not cash.[32] Profit signifies the creation of values that can be monetarized. Friendship is outside the scope of profit because money cannot measure the value of a friendship.

The point is not that it would be immoral or inappropriate to rent a friend. The point is that friendship is not the type of value that can be bought and sold. Profit, therefore, is incapable of measuring the creation of a friendship in the same way as it can measure the value created by a wheelset, a refrigerator, or a shipping container.

Michael Sandel is the market mentality's leading critic. He authored a book titled *What Money Can't Buy: The Moral Limits of Markets*.[33] Though Sandel agrees that certain things are off-limits to the market, he elevates so-called non-market values above market values. Sandel thinks that certain things, like friendship, are of superior value because they cannot be bought and sold. He does not recognize the value of the goods and services that businessmen produce.

Friendship is a significant value. So are wheels, refrigerators, and shipping containers. Friends provide us with a value that wheels, refrigerators, and shipping containers cannot. Wheels, refrigerators, and shipping containers provide us with values that friends cannot. These values are not mutually exclusive. The meal that we enjoy with a friend was preserved in a refrigerator. We traveled to our friend's house in a car made possible by wheels revolving on a stationary axle. We bought our friend a present made possible by containerization.

The elevating of non-material above material values is a relic of the mind-body split that we rejected in the third chapter. All values are important in virtue of being *values*.

A VALUE MENTALITY

The moral case for profit maximization encourages a *value* mentality, not a *market* mentality. Businessmen maximize profit by being concerned with the conceptualization of value. A value mentality is appropriate in every area of our lives. We should be value-prospectors. We should look for new opportunities to find value, whether this takes the form of a new friendship, the discovery of an inspiring movie, or a tennis match between two extraordinary players. Profit-maximizing businessmen look for opportunities to create value in the form of goods and services.

The focus on value creation explains why there is no contradiction between a person being for-profit and working for a non-profit organization. A non-profit is non-*profit*, not non-*value*. Usually, organizations are non-profit because they create value that cannot be monetarized. A non-profit organization that advocates for free markets acts on behalf of its supporters to promote ideas that its supporters do not have the time, the skill, or necessarily the interest in promoting themselves. The organization is not selling a good or service.

IMMORAL BUSINESSMEN

The *fourth* implication that may be mistakenly read into the moral case for profit maximization is that if profit is moral, then businessmen must be moral by definition. Profit maximization is the defining activity of business. A businessman is a *business*-man because he or she aims at the maximization of profit. Since profit maximization requires businessmen to make value integrations, to be concerned with profit is to be concerned with values, at least in a free market. Thus, it may seem as though businessmen can do no wrong because as soon as they do wrong, they cease to be *business*-men.

For critics, this objection is the *reductio ad absurdum* of the moral case for profit maximization. Immoral people can be found in every profession. There are immoral professors, immoral doctors, immoral policemen, and immoral priests. Business, however, allegedly attracts people who possess psychopathic tendencies. Psychopaths are not necessarily violent. The psychopath's defining characteristic is that he treats other people as objects to be manipulated for his own ends.

Even if a person is not naturally psychopathic, business seems to reward psychopathic qualities. A person must develop these qualities to advance up the corporate ladder. After all, boards of directors want to hire hardnosed businessmen as CEOs, not humanitarians. A person who can fire thousands of workers to boost the bottom line would make a good CEO. A person who would empathize with these workers and their families would not.

BUSINESSMEN CAN BE IGNORANT OF PROFIT'S MORALITY

This implication does not follow from the moral case for profit maximization. Businessmen do not necessarily understand the morality of profit maximization. As John A. Allison observes, "business education tends to be primarily technical."[34] Business schools teach students the basics of accounting, finance, marketing, and management. Business students are not usually expected to reflect on the nature of the profession to which they intend to devote the rest of their lives.

This problem is not unique to business. A person can become a teacher, thinking that his job is to train students to rote learn the state-mandated curriculum so that the students can regurgitate the answers in an exam. He does not understand that a teacher's job is to teach students how to think.

A person can become a defense attorney, believing that her job is to exonerate her clients, regardless of their guilt. She judges her success by the number of cases won. She does not understand that the job of a defense attorney is to ensure that a trial serves the end of justice by holding the prosecution to the highest standard of evidence.

A person can become a television news reporter believing that appearing on the evening news allows him to propagandize his political views. He does not understand that his job is to report the news not to advocate for a political position.

This book argues that the moral basis of profit maximization is not well understood. We cannot expect businessmen to have a better grasp of profit's morality than anyone else.

Profit is an abstraction. Businessmen are experts on particular instantiations of profit, not on the nature of profit as such. Steve Jobs, for instance, was an expert in creating value through consumer electronics. This expertise did not make Jobs an expert on profit in the abstract.

Businessmen may be expected to possess psychopathic tendencies. Profit maximization is not the source of this problem. The source is the failure of business schools to teach generations of business students the moral basis of profit maximization. Across their business classes, students receive a consistent message that there is no ethics in profit maximization. Courses on business *ethics* are really courses on business *taming* or business *bashing*. Students come away from these courses with the message that maximizing profit is the root of all wrong in business.[35]

Businessmen have learned their lessons well. They have been taught that it is either-or, profit maximization or ethics, and some choose profit maximization. The result is that generations of businessmen have been well trained in the technical skills needed to maximize profit without understanding the moral status of the end that these technical skills are expected to serve.

THE *WHAT* OF BUSINESS IMMORALITY

There are two types of immorality in business. The first concerns *what* a businessman produces and sells. The second concerns *how* a businessman goes about maximizing profit.

A moral businessman aims at the creation of objective values. He may not conceptualize his aim in these terms. Still, the moral businessman expects his goods or services to benefit his customers. A businessman who sells goods or services when he has no grounds for thinking that they will be of objective value is not moral. He is offering a good or service for trade on the implicit representation that his customers will benefit from the exchange when he does not expect them to benefit. The Ford and Nestlé cases allege this type of dishonesty.

A variation of this type of immorality is con men who pass themselves off as businessmen. These con men claim to be selling a good or service that is of objective value when the good or service is a fraud. Bernard Madoff is a notorious example. Madoff was not actually a businessman. He used the cloak of business to trick his clients into handing over their life's savings. He promised to invest his clients' money when he kept the money for himself.

Con men don different disguises to fool their victims. Frank Abagnale would dress like a pilot to fool bank tellers into cashing fraudulent checks. Some con men dress like businessmen.

THE *HOW* OF BUSINESS IMMORALITY

In large corporations, the workplace psychopath can appear successful. Profit maximization depends on a businessman having the character needed to conceptualize value. The workplace psychopath lacks the requisite character.

The corporation may still be profitable because the corporation's success does not depend on this particular person but on all of the other people in the organization who are not psychopaths.

The workplace psychopath appears successful because he successfully advances up the corporate ladder—at least until his superiors grasp his real character. To the extent that the workplace psychopath disrupts his colleagues' work, he is a threat to profit maximization.

Critics might think that all businessmen are secret psychopaths. This expectation reveals their prejudices and shows no appreciation of the character strengths needed to maximize profit.

NO DUTY TO MAXIMIZE PROFIT

The *fifth* implication that may be mistakenly read into the moral case for profit maximization is that this case imposes on everyone a duty to maximize profit. Anyone who is not maximizing profit is morally deficient. If there were a hierarchy of morally legitimate careers, business would be at the top, and non-profit careers on the bottom or omitted entirely.

Consider a young man contemplating what career to pursue. He is a good introspecter and has noticed that he loves reading English literature and talking with others about the books he has read. He decides to become a professor of English literature. His parents, concerned about his career choice, recommend that he read this book. He agrees with the book's thesis. Despondent at the thought of giving up on his dreams, he tells himself that he needs to do the right thing and enrolls in a business administration degree. By the standard of this book, it might seem that this young man is doing the right thing.

I have witnessed this attitude from a person who believes in the morality of profit maximization. In the late 1990s, I attended the anniversary celebration of a free-market periodical for which I was a regular contributor. I sat across the dinner table from a property developer who had provided the magazine's initial funding. He chided me for being a "sell-out" in wanting to pursue an academic career instead of becoming a profit-maximizing businessman like him.

Profit maximization is moral when profit signifies the creation of objective value. We should want businessmen to create objective value because so doing enhances our lives. We should also seek to create objective value in the context of our lives. A person does not have to become a businessman to create value, however. The life of a profit-maximizing businessman is one option on the smorgasbord of lives from which we can choose.

"Life" is an abstraction. What exists are particular lives. When a person decides on a career, he must consider the particularities of his own life.

Establishing the morality of profit maximization demonstrates that the life of a Rockefeller, a Morgan, or an Edison should be on the smorgasbord of lives from which a person can choose. A moral defense of profit maximization does not restrict the smorgasbord to those lives that maximize profit, however. The smorgasbord includes the entire range of moral lives, including the life of a Pasteur and an English professor.

Profit is an abstraction. Within this abstraction, there are countless particularities, some of which are of value to particular people and some which are not. Steve Jobs found value in creating new consumer products because he recognized that his customers found value in these products. Producing soft drinks is also a legitimate instantiation of profit maximization. Jobs, however, once dismissed Pepsi as "sugared water," so it is unlikely that he would have found value in maximizing profit this way.[36]

Profit is an abstraction that is subsumed by a higher abstraction, namely the human need to produce objective values in order to survive. Profit maximization is one way in which human beings create value in the world. There are other ways. Just as a businessman can find value in maximizing profit *this* way but not *that* way, so a person can create value in his or her life through becoming a professor of English literature instead of a profit-maximizing businessman.

In specific contexts, it would be immoral for a person to become a profit-maximizing businessman. The young man above, whose interests are pointing toward a career as an English literature professor, should pursue this goal, even though so doing means forgoing the wealth that he could have earned as a businessman. Wealth is not of value when it comes at the price of the career that one loves.

A SUCCESSFUL LIFE

Do not equate self-interest with money. Self-interest is about the achievement of values, and what is of value for one person is not necessarily of value for another. Thus, a billionaire businessman who sacrificed his or her passion for English literature to pursue a business career may be miserable, while a modestly paid professor of English literature may be gloriously happy.

Wealth is not the standard of a successful life. Wealth is often employed as a proxy to gauge the success of someone's life, even by people who purport to reject the morality of profit maximization. A successful life consists in the achievement of one's values. For some people, a successful life will consist of obtaining great wealth. For others, of obtaining non-material values, such as raising a child or advocating for specific ideas.[37]

For a dramatization of genuinely self-interested happiness, read the final scene of Nevil Shute's novel *Trustee from the Toolroom*. Keith Stewart is a man who takes the trolley bus, dresses in a shabby raincoat, runs a little fat, and has just enough money invested to do the things he enjoys: spending afternoons in the Library of the Patent Office and evenings in his workshop. As Shute describes Stewart, "He has achieved the type of life that he desires; he wants no other. He is perfectly, supremely happy."[38]

PROFIT DOES NOT POSSESS INTRINSIC VALUE

The unidentified assumption behind this confusion is that profit possesses *intrinsic value*. The moral case for profit maximization is interpreted to mean that profit possesses the attribute of value in the same way as a baby's eyes might possess the attribute of blue. Anyone who maximizes profit, therefore, brings more value to the world, even when pursuing profit makes him or her miserable.

In chapter 2, we saw that value is *objective*, not *intrinsic* or *subjective*. Objective value is relative because, as a matter of fact, certain things further a particular individual's life but not someone else's.[39] Value does not adhere in profit maximization. Profit maximization can, therefore, be moral, in specific contexts, even though it would be immoral for some people to maximize profit.

RETHINKING BUSINESS EDUCATION

The above implications do not follow from the moral case for profit maximization. Let us conclude by considering an implication that does follow, namely the urgent need for business students to reflect on the moral basis of profit maximization.

Business students need to be taught that if their concern is to maximize profit, then they need to think about whether the goods or services that they produce will be of objective value in their customers' lives.

A moral problem arises when businessmen focus on *revenue maximization* instead of *value creation*. An issue in Australia and New Zealand has been bank staff selling products to customers merely to meet their sales targets. As a consequence, retirees have been sold income protection insurance, from which they will never be able to benefit.

Toyota New Zealand has recognized the need for its business model to focus on value creation. Traditionally, car salespeople worked on a commission, and would-be purchasers were expected to negotiate the selling price. Toyota New Zealand introduced a new business model in which it pays its salespeople a salary, and prices its cars at a lower, non-negotiable rate, which includes on-road costs. When a customer enters a Toyota store, they know how much they must pay to take the car home, and the salesperson will not pressure them into purchasing a car they do not need to get a commission.

Among other things, a focus on value creation means that business students need to think carefully about what companies they will work for after graduation. There was a time when a business graduate would need to decide whether to work for a tobacco company. A business student *only* concerned with profit maximization must take the time to consider whether tobacco products are of objective value to the company's customers. Today, business students thinking about working for companies such as Google or Facebook might need to consider whether the privacy practices of these companies undermine the value that they would otherwise create for their users.

Business students must also be taught that if their concern is to maximize profit, then they need to think about the type of character they must cultivate. Business students need to be taught that, to conceptualize value, they need to cultivate a character that is concerned with grasping the facts of reality. Business students also need to be taught that they need to cultivate a moral character to derive value from profit. They need to understand that there is no value in maximizing profit when the profit comes at the cost of a psychopathic character.

Profit is morally demanding. The ethical implications of profit maximization are not usually grasped because the relationship between value creation and profit is not well understood. Only when we understand that profit signifies the conceptualization of value can we see that profit is pregnant with ethical implications.

NOTES

1. Harry Binswanger used this analogy in a Meeting of the Minds conference call. Any shortcomings are mine, not his.
2. See, for example, MindGeek, which owns several pornographic video sharing services, including Pornhub, RedTube, and YouPorn.
3. See, for example, the controversy surrounding Slayer's lyrics, which allegedly inspired a group of teenage boys to murder a fifteen-year-old girl as a virgin sacrifice. Michael Hammer, "Violent Music: Sony, Slayer, and Self-Regulation," in *Case Studies in Business, Society, and Ethics*, ed. Tom L. Beauchamp (Upper Saddle River, NJ: Pearson Education, 2004).
4. See, for example, the allegations against Harvey Weinstein.
5. In June 2018, Pacific Aerospace, from Hamilton, New Zealand, was fined for supplying North Korea with aircraft parts.
6. In March 2018, Cadbury closed its factory in Dunedin, New Zealand. Cadbury had made chocolate at this factory since 1930. I toured the factory three months before its closure. The tour guide explained that the factory needs to be closed to reduce production costs.
7. Geoffrey Heal, *When Principles Pay: Corporate Social Responsibility and the Bottom Line* (New York: Columbia University Press, 2008), 15–16. Henry Ford criticized his own company's profits as "awful." He told the *Detroit News* that a "reasonable profit is right, but not too much." Quoted in J. Mark Ramseyer, *Business Organizations*, second ed. (New York: Wolters Kluwer, 2017), 112.

8. Joel Bakan, *The Corporation: The Pathological Pursuit of Profit and Power* (New York: Free Press, 2004), 37.

9. Louis P. Pojman and James Fieser, *Ethics: Discovering Right and Wrong*, 7th ed. (Boston, MA: Wadsworth, 2012), 81; Wanda Teays, *Business Ethics through Movies: A Case Study Approach* (Chichester, West Sussex: John Wiley & Sons, 2015), 121. For a response to the claim that markets economize on virtue, see Jason Brennan, "Do Markets Corrupt?" in *Economics and the Virtues: Building a New Moral Foundation*, ed. Jennifer Baker and Mark D. White (Oxford: Oxford University Press, 2016).

10. Niccolò Machiavelli, *The Prince*, trans. Peter Bondanella and Mark Musa (Oxford: Oxford University Press, 1998); Bernard Mandeville, "'The Grumbling Hive,' in *Fable of the Bees*," in *Economic Morality: Ancient to Modern Readings*, ed. Henry C. Clark and Eric Allison (Lanham, MD: Lexington Books, 2015).

11. For an introduction to the issues in the debate over pornography, see Katherine Smits, *Applying Political Theory: Issues and Debates* (New York: Palgrave Macmillan, 2009), 86–108.

12. For a discussion of the virtue of justice, see Leonard Peikoff, *Objectivism: The Philosophy of Ayn Rand* (New York: Meridian, 1993), 276–91; Tara Smith, *Ayn Rand's Normative Ethics: The Virtuous Egoist* (New York: Cambridge University Press, 2006), 135–75. For a discussion of the application of justice in business, see Jaana Woiceshyn, *How to Be Profitable and Moral: A Rational Egoist Approach to Business* (Lanham, MD: Hamilton Books, 2012), 69–80; John A. Allison, *The Leadership Crisis and the Free Market Cure: Why the Future of Business Depends on the Return to Life, Liberty, and the Pursuit of Happiness* (New York: McGraw Hill, 2015), 71–79.

13. See, for example, Kate Hawkesby, "Roseanne, Racism and Choosing Values over Profit," *New Zealand Herald* (31 May 2018).

14. ABC continued Barr's show without her. Though the ratings for this timeslot declined, ABC aimed at profit maximization.

15. For a discussion of the morality of offshoring jobs, see the example of Bob Miller in Woiceshyn, *How to Be Profitable and Moral*, 1–9.

16. For an explanation of the broken window fallacy and its application to contemporary economic issues, see Henry Hazlitt, *Economics in One Lesson*, 50th anniversary ed. (San Francisco: Laissez Faire Books, 1996).

17. Robert White, "Profit Maximization Does Not Necessitate Profit Prioritization," *The Journal of Ayn Rand Studies* 17, no. 2 (December 2017): 202–204.

18. For a summary of the Ford Pinto case, see Teays, *Business Ethics Through Movies*, 120–22. The accuracy of this case has been called into question by Gary T. Schwartz, "The Myth of the Ford Pinto Case," *Rutgers Law Review* 43 (1990).

19. For a summary of the Nestlé case, see Marianne M. Jennings, *Business Ethics: Case Studies and Selected Readings*, 8th ed. (Stamford, CT: Cengage Learning, 2015), 409–11. The accuracy of this case has been called into question by Fred D. Miller Jr., *Out of the Mouths of Babes: The Infant Formula Controversy* (Bowling Green, OH: The Social Philosophy and Policy Center, 1983). I discuss the Ford Pinto and Nestlé cases in White, "Profit Maximization Does Not Necessitate Profit Prioritization."

20. For a summary of the Malden Mills case, see Jennings, *Business Ethics*, 439–41.

21. Roger L. Martin, "The Virtue Matrix: Calculating the Return on Corporate Responsibility," in *Harvard Business Review on Corporate Responsibility* (Boston, MA: Harvard Business School Press, 2003), 86.

22. Leonard J. Brooks and Paul Dunn, *Business and Professional Ethics for Directors, Executives & Accountants*, 8th ed. (Boston, MA: Cengage Learning, 2017), 297–98.

23. https://gravitypayments.com/thegravityof70k/

24. Schwartz, "The Myth of the Ford Pinto Case," 1032–33n77.

25. Miller Jr., *Out of the Mouths of Babes*, 47–48.

26. Ibid., 46. These critically ill infants were not necessarily fed commercial baby formula. Artificial feeding included milk from goats, cows, and water buffalo, and water mixed with honey or sugar.

27. Yaron Brook and Don Watkins, *Equal Is Unfair: America's Misguided Fight Against Income Inequality* (New York: St. Martin's Press, 2016), 106–107.

28. Search YouTube for videos of Feuerstein. You will see crowds cheering and clapping as Feuerstein walks past. A news segment or a YouTube video cannot similarly record the value *not* created because of Feuerstein.

29. Jennifer Saunders, "Iso Tank," in *Absolutely Fabulous* (BBC, 1992).

30. The attitude dramatized in this scene has been interpreted as paradigmatic of consumer culture. See Chantal Cornut-Gentille d'Arcy, "*Absolutely Fabulous*: 'Money Makes the World Go Round' or a Politicised Notion of Fulfilment," in *Culture and Power: Challenging Discourses*, ed. María José Coperías Aguilar (València: Universitat de València, 2000), 66.

31. For a discussion of the Russian mail-order bride phenomenon, see Ericka Johnson, *Dreaming of a Mail-Order Husband: Russian-American Internet Romance* (Durham, NC: Duke University Press, 2007). Curiously, Johnson blames this phenomenon on the hardships created by Russia's transition from communism to capitalism. See pp. 4–5.

32. Marlene Podritske and Peter Schwartz, *Objectively Speaking: Ayn Rand Interviewed* (Lanham, MD: Lexington Books, 2009), 171.

33. Michael Sandel, *What Money Can't Buy: The Moral Limits of Markets* (London: Allen Lane, 2012).

34. John A. Allison, "Foreword," in *Perspectives on Ayn Rand's Contributions to Economic and Business Thought*, ed. Edward W. Younkins (Lanham, MD: Lexington Books, 2018), xiii.

35. Tibor R. Machan tells the story of a professor from George Washington University who taught a term of business ethics at Harvard Business School. The professor complained to *Newsweek* that he failed to convince his MBA students "that there is more to life than money, power, fame and self-interest." The professor is Amitai Etzioni, whose lionization of European culture was cited in chapter 3. Tibor R. Machan, "Business Ethics in a New Key," *Journal of Private Enterprise* 21, no. 2 (Spring 2006): 1–2.

36. Walter Isaacson, *Steve Jobs* (London: Little, Brown, 2011), 154. Cf. White, "Profit Maximization Does Not Necessitate Profit Prioritization," 214.

37. For a discussion of the contribution that money makes to a happy life, see Tara Smith, "Money *Can* Buy Happiness," *Reason Papers* 26 (Summer 2003). Smith's argument does not suggest that money is the *gauge* of a happy life but (consistent with this book's argument) that money *serves* an individual's values.

38. Nevil Shute, *Trustee from the Toolroom* (London: Vintage, 2009), 311.

39. For a discussion of the relativity of objective value, see Tara Smith, *Viable Values: A Study of Life as the Root and Reward of Morality* (Lanham, MD: Rowman & Littlefield Publishers, 2000), 97–101.

Chapter Six

Incomplete Defenses of Profit Maximization

Milton Friedman and Elaine Sternberg are prominent defenders of profit maximization. Friedman's defense is one of the most cited articles in business ethics.[1] Friedman and Sternberg make substantive contributions to the defense of profit maximization. Nevertheless, their defenses are incomplete because they do not make a *moral* case. Considering the strengths and limitations of their arguments helps us to appreciate the indispensable role of morality in the defense of profit maximization.

Proponents of CSR vilify Friedman and Sternberg.[2] They are not discussed in the business ethics literature because ethicists sympathize with their arguments, but because their arguments are used as foils to represent a position that these ethicists vigorously oppose. Though this chapter identifies problems with Friedman's and Sternberg's arguments, both thinkers make valuable contributions to the defense of profit maximization and, therefore, deserve to be treated with respect. This chapter's criticisms should not be read as an endorsement of their many critics.

We shall examine Sternberg's argument first. Friedman's argument appeared several decades before Sternberg's and is more widely discussed. Nevertheless, Sternberg's argument must be discussed first because she addresses a fundamental issue that Friedman does not, namely the defining function of business.

This chapter considers how Sternberg appeals to the defining function of business to justify profit maximization. This chapter then considers why Friedman's classic article should be read as a defense of shareholder prerogatives, not profit maximization. This chapter then considers why ethics must trump economics in debates over the propriety of profit maximization. Finally, this chapter explains why profit maximization is a cause worthy of a moral crusade.

WHAT BUSINESS IS

Sternberg begins by asking a question that business ethicists rarely ask: *What is business?* CSR's proponents assume that business is what businesses do. If a business raises funds for breast cancer research, then so doing is a business activity, no less than the sale of goods or services. The assumption is that a business is an entity, and anything that this entity can do must be a business activity.

Sternberg argues that business is something specific. A businessman is *politically* free to direct his company to any end that he chooses. He is not *epistemologically* free to assert that he is doing *business*.[3] Ben and Jerry are politically free to turn their ice-cream parlor into an advocacy organization for environmental causes. They are not epistemologically free to claim that environmental advocacy is a business activity.

Sternberg argues that the "*defining purpose of business is maximising owner value over the long term by selling goods or services*" (emphasis in original).[4]

BUSINESS IS AN ACTIVITY

Sternberg points out that business is not an *entity* but an *activity*. She warns against equating business with a corporation.[5] Some corporations are businesses. Some are not. Amazon is a business. Greenpeace is not. Corporations can be directed to non-business ends. Businesses cannot be directed to non-business ends and still be businesses. A corporation is only a business when the corporation aims at the end that defines the activity of business.

Business is something that human beings *do*. In this respect, business is like any other human activity. Business is like walking, running, swimming, reading, juggling, horse riding, and so forth. Business is unlocking a store in the morning, stocking shelves, greeting customers, ringing up a sale, ordering new stock, evaluating employees, banking the day's receipts, resolving customer complaints, conducting stock takes, and preparing a profit and loss statement.

Most businessmen incorporate because there are few legal barriers to incorporation today, and incorporation comes with certain legal advantages, such as limited liability. A business, however, could also be a partnership or a sole proprietorship. The legal form does not make an organization a business. Corporations, partnerships, and sole proprietorships are *businesses* because of the end to which the legal form is directed.

A sole proprietor who operates a corner grocery store is engaged in business when he is at the store selling groceries. When this proprietor takes a lunch break or finishes work for the day, he is no longer engaged in business. Whether the proprietor is engaged in business or not depends on what he is *doing*, not on the legal status of his operation.

Sternberg brings objectivity into business ethics by establishing that a business cannot be directed to any end that the business ethicist desires and still be a business. "Business" classifies activities directed towards a specific end. When a businessman pursues a different end, he or she is no longer a *business*-man.

A PRECISE DEFINITION

Sternberg words her definition of business precisely. A person who maximizes owner value over the long term but does not do so by selling goods or services is not engaged in business. A homeowner is not engaged in business when he installs a new kitchen, thereby increasing his home's value. A car enthusiast is not engaged in business when she replaces the rims on her car's wheels, thereby increasing its value.

A person who sells goods or services but does not do so in order to maximize long-term owner value is not engaged in business. Trade Aid is not engaged in business when it sells goods produced in developing countries. Girl Guides (or Girl Scouts) is not engaged in business when it sends its members door to door selling cookies.

Sternberg writes of "maximising owner value" instead of "profit maximization." She avoids talk of profit because she fears that "profit" implies a focus on the short term.[6] A business can be maximizing profit within a given financial year while sabotaging long-term owner value—think Blockbuster.[7] A business can be maximizing long-term owner value while operating at a loss within a given financial year—think Amazon in its early years.[8] There is no necessary connection between profit within a given financial year and the maximization of long-term owner value.

Sternberg does not assert that her definition exhausts all of business's characteristics. Businessmen do many things in conducting a business, from marketing their products to training new employees. Sternberg's point is that these activities are only *business* activities when they are directed to the end that defines business.

Sternberg states that business's defining purpose is the maximization of long-term owner value by selling goods or services. Henceforth, the phrase "maximization of long-term owner value" shall be used as a shorthand for the defining purpose.

BUSINESS ETHICS'S PROPER SCOPE

Sternberg makes a significant contribution to the business ethics literature by identifying business ethics's proper scope. She points out that "only a *business* can be an ethical business" (emphasis in original).[9] Sternberg objects to corporate social responsibility because CSR expects businesses to be ethical by refraining from business.[10] Sternberg argues that *business* ethics is appropriately concerned with ethics in business, just as medical ethics is concerned with ethics in medicine, legal ethics with ethics in the law, and sports ethics with ethics in sport.[11]

Consider Avon's support for breast cancer research. Sternberg's argument implies that Avon is not an ethical *business* because it supports breast cancer research. *Charitable* activities are not *business* activities. Avon's status as an ethical business must be established by the ethics of how Avon sells cosmetics, not by the moral status of Avon's side activities.

Consider a sole proprietor who operates a corner grocery store. This man is not a lousy *business*-man if he cheats on his wife, because his moral status as a businessman depends on how he conducts his business, not on how he treats his wife. Similarly, we could not cite the fact that this man alters the expiration date on expired products to establish that he is a lousy *husband* because his moral status as a husband depends on how he treats his wife, not on how he conducts his business.

Business ethics should be about how a person conducts his or her *business* activities.

THE PUBLIC GOOD DOES NOT DEFINE BUSINESS

David W. Lutz questions Sternberg's claim that the public good is not business's purpose. He writes: "From the fact that activities other than business promote the public good, it does not follow that the purpose of business is not to promote the public good. It is possible that organizations of two or more different categories have the same purpose."[12]

Sternberg does not deny that businesses promote the public good. She denies that promoting the public good *defines* business. A business that promotes the public good has to do so through the maximization of long-term owner value to be a business. A "business" that promotes the public good *instead of* maximizing long-term owner value is not a business. A business that promotes the public good *alongside* the maximization of long-term owner value cannot be evaluated as a moral *business* based on these non-business activities. So doing would be like evaluating a grocer based on how he treats his wife.

Lutz is wrong to think that two *different* organizations can have the same *defining* purpose. Two organizations with the same *defining* purpose are not different and belong in the same category.

PROFIT'S ETHICAL IMPLICATIONS

Sternberg mistakenly rejects talk of profit maximization. "Profit" does not imply a focus on the short term, as she suggests. On the contrary, profit requires businessmen to conceptualize facts and to integrate these facts to form values. A businessman who can do so successfully is someone concerned with the long term. In chapter 4, we saw that Rockefeller invested in scientific research because he wanted to find new ways to create value from oil. The owner-operators who were out to make a quick profit did not invest in scientific research because a person focused on a quick profit is not the type of person to take an interest in science. A businessman fixated on yearly profits wants the cash and is not concerned with whether his profits signify objective value.

"Owner value" does not signify the same facts as "profit." Sternberg notes that by "value," she means *financial* value.[13] This definition suggests that Sternberg understands the maximization of long-term owner value in terms of maximizing *cash* over the long term and does not consider what profit signifies. Little wonder then that Sternberg felt the need to reject the term "profit" to bring in a focus on the long term.

Profit is a businessman's reward for maximizing objective value, at least in a free market. Consequently, the maximization of profit is brimming with ethical implications, as we saw in the previous chapter.

BUSINESS ETHICS'S REQUIREMENTS

After Sternberg defines the proper subject of business ethics, she turns to a discussion of its content. According to Sternberg, business ethics consists of *distributive justice* and *ordinary decency*. She argues that *distributive justice* consists of rewarding contributions to the maximization of long-term owner value and that *ordinary decency* "consists of fairness and honesty and refraining from coercion and physical violence."[14]

Sternberg concludes that if "an organisation is not directed at maximising long-term owner value, it is not a business; if it does not pursue that purpose while satisfying Distributive Justice and Ordinary Decency, it is not ethical."[15]

Sternberg justifies distributive justice and ordinary decency as the ethical requirements of doing business on the basis that these are *preconditions* for maximizing long-term owner value.[16] In so doing, Sternberg treats the defining purpose of business as though it were a moral standard.

A DEFINING PURPOSE IS NOT A MORAL STANDARD

We can accept the first part of Sternberg's argument without accepting the second. One can accept that business has a specific function and that the scope of business ethics needs to be constrained by business's defining function without accepting that this function establishes business's ethical requirements.

The problem with the second part of Sternberg's argument is that the defining purpose of business cannot be an ultimate end in ethics. Business is an activity, and like all human activities, the ethics of business must be established by reference to the ultimate end of human survival.

In chapter 2, we saw that most of our values are instrumental because they are part of a series of value chains that end with the ultimate value of human life. This ultimate value is a final end that justifies all of the subordinate means-end relationships. Business's moral status depends on business forming part of this value chain.

Business's defining purpose is a standard of moral evaluation within the context of this value chain. Starting a hair salon is a moral business activity because this activity redounds to human life. The defining purpose of business does not establish the morality of starting a hair salon. What does so is business's defining purpose *as a means to the ultimate end of human survival*. Furthermore, this ultimate end establishes the conditions under which business's defining purpose is moral. Business is moral under those conditions where business furthers human life. Business is not moral outside of this context.

Consider the moral status of a business that sells pornography. The first part of Sternberg's argument implies that the moral status of selling pornography is a legitimate question for business ethics. The second part implies that we must establish the morality of selling pornography by appealing to the maximization of long-term owner value. We can accept the legitimacy of questioning the moral status of a pornography business while refusing to accept that the maximization of long-term owner value, on its own, provides a standard for moral evaluation.

STERNBERG DOES NOT EXPLAIN WHY BUSINESS IS MORAL

Sternberg invokes the language of Aristotelian ethics, which gives the impression that she is making a moral argument. She does not make a moral case for business, however.

Sternberg claims that the defining purpose of business is a business's *telos* and that when a business is directed to another end, the business is being *teleopathological.*[17] In Aristotelian ethics, the concept "*telos*" is rich with ethical implications when used to denote the relationship between what a living organism *is* and what that living organism has the *potential* to become.[18]

A tadpole's *telos* is to become a frog. A frog is the fulfillment (or perfection) of the tadpole's natural end. Therefore, that which furthers the tadpole's maturity toward this end is *good*, and that which impedes the tadpole's maturity is *bad.*[19]

The tadpole's *telos* provides an ethical standard because the tadpole's potential is inherent in its nature as a tadpole. Written into the tadpole's DNA is the potential to become a frog.[20]

A business does not have a *telos* in this sense. A business has a defining end. Not every end is a *telos*, however.

Sternberg notes that we evaluate artifacts and activities by reference to their ends. She writes: "The criteria of a good handkerchief are different than those of a good razor, because the purposes of handkerchiefs and razors are different."[21]

Sternberg is equivocating between two senses of "good." When we say that a razor is good, we mean that the razor can fulfill a razor's functions, not that we approve of the uses to which someone may put the razor. A good razor possesses a sharp edge because the razor's function is to cut. We can recognize that a razor is good, in this sense, and still disapprove of a serial killer using a razor to mutilate his or her victims. The razor's function is not a standard by which to evaluate its use.

A business that fulfills business's defining purpose is a good business in the sense that the business is good at being a business. The defining purpose provides a standard for evaluating a businessman's success as a *businessman*. The defining purpose, however, does not provide a standard of *ethical* evaluation except in relation to an ultimate end that justifies the pursuit of that purpose.

Sternberg acknowledges, at one point, that accepting "a definition is not the same as approving of what is defined; precise definition is equally a precondition for criticising and rejecting a subject."[22] Nevertheless, Sternberg proceeds to treat the defining purpose of business as though it could do the work that she claims we cannot expect of a definition.

STERNBERG'S CASE IS INCOMPLETE

Sternberg's argument is incomplete because she has not made a moral case for the maximization of long-term owner value. Sternberg has made a substantive contribution to the defense of profit maximization. In establishing what is and is not a business, Sternberg clarifies the proper scope of business ethics. Nevertheless, business's defining function needs to be evaluated by the ultimate end of human life for Sternberg to make a moral case for the maximization of long-term owner value.

Business critics reject profit maximization because they have embraced the morality of altruism not because they are confused about business's defining function. Sternberg correctly points out that CSR's proponents want to direct businesses to non-business purposes. They want to do so, however, because they are altruists, not because they are confused about the defining purpose of business. (We discuss the relationship between CSR and altruism in the next chapter.)

Being convinced by Sternberg's argument would only further condemn business in the eyes of altruism's apostolates, not morally legitimize business, as Sternberg assumes.

FRIEDMAN'S *NEW YORK TIMES* ARTICLE

Friedman's article "The Social Responsibility of Business Is to Increase Its Profits" is one of the most extensively cited articles in business ethics. The article is widely cited not because those citing the article agree with Friedman's conclusions, but because they want to use Friedman's arguments to highlight what they see as the defects in the case for profit maximization.

The *New York Times* published Friedman's article in 1970. At the time, CSR talk was entering the mainstream, thanks, in part, to anti-corporate activists such as Ralph Nader.[23]

PARAPHRASIS

Friedman observes that CSR talk is notable for its "analytical looseness and lack of rigor."[24] Friedman wants to impose rigor by translating the question, "What are the social responsibilities of corporations?" into a question with an empirical reference.

Friedman engages in *paraphrasis*, a method of analysis that Jeremy Bentham originated. Bentham believed that intellectual rigor could be brought to bear on controversial issues by translating abstract claims into claims with an empirical reference.[25] Paraphrasis consists of substituting what Bentham regarded as fictional entities with real entities. "Furniture" is a fictional entity, for example, because there is no such *thing* as furniture. The real entities are chairs, tables, beds, wardrobes, and so forth. We impose intellectual rigor on talk about furniture by translating furniture talk into talk about these physical objects.

Friedman notes that a corporation is not a physical entity.[26] As we saw in chapter 1, business ethicists think that the corporate form poses special moral issues because a corporation does not have a body to kick or a soul to be damned. Tim Cook can be hit or kicked. Apple cannot. The claim is not that Tim Cook deserves to be hit or kicked, only that it is physically possible to do so. People can be hit or kicked. Corporations cannot be. So the real entity in CSR talk is not the corporation but the corporate executives who run it.

Thus, the question "What are the social responsibilities of corporations?" becomes "What are the social responsibilities of corporate executives?" Translated into terms with an empirical reference, the question, for Friedman, is easy to answer. Corporate executives are agents of the shareholders, so their social responsibility is to follow the shareholders' desires. Friedman writes: A "corporate executive is an employee of the owners of the business. He has direct responsibility to his employers. That responsibility is to conduct the business in accordance with their desires."[27]

SHAREHOLDERS' DESIRES

Friedman grounds his argument in the right to private property. According to Friedman, the shareholders own the corporation, and as the owners, they get to decide the corporation's purpose. Corporate executives have a fiduciary duty to follow shareholders' instructions because the corporate executives are spending the shareholders' money, not their own.[28]

Friedman assumes that shareholders want their corporate executives to maximize profit. To complete the above quote: A "corporate executive is an employee of the owners of the business. He has direct responsibility to his employers. That responsibility is to conduct the business in accordance with their desires, *which generally will be to make as much money as possible*" (emphasis mine).[29]

Friedman's critics assign to him the view that corporate executives *should* maximize profit. The imperative, in Friedman's argument, pertains to following shareholders' desires not to profit maximization.

Observe that Friedman acknowledges that if the shareholders desire a corporation to be directed to non-profit purposes, the corporate executives must obey. He writes: "A group of persons might establish a corporation for an eleemosynary purpose—for example, a hospital or a school. The manager of such a corporation will not have money profit as his objective but the rendering of certain services."[30]

Later in the article, Friedman acknowledges that he has no objections to sole proprietors being socially responsible because the sole proprietor "is spending his own money, not someone else's." He explains: "If [the sole proprietor] wishes to spend his money on such purposes, that is his right, and I cannot see that there is any objection to his doing so."[31]

Friedman is defending the right of a property owner to determine how his property is used. Friedman does not take a position on what a property owner should do. For Friedman, profit maximization and social responsibility are equally legitimate purposes, so long as the end represents shareholders' desires.

FRIEDMAN DOES NOT DEFEND PROFIT MAXIMIZATION

Friedman does not make a case for profit maximization in his *New York Times* article. Friedman appears to defend profit maximization in an earlier work, *Capitalism and Freedom*. In this book, Friedman states that "there is one and only one social responsibility of business—to use its resources and engage in activities designed to increase its profits so long as it stays within the rules of the game, which is to say, engages in open and free competition, without deception or fraud."[32] Friedman quotes this passage at the end of the *New York Times* article.[33] Stating that the "one social responsibility of business . . . [is] to increase its profits" suggests that Friedman believes that shareholders should desire profit maximization.

In private correspondence, Thomas L. Carson points out to Friedman the contradiction between the arguments in his two works. Friedman acknowledges the contradiction and states that he agrees with the formulation in *Capitalism and Freedom*, with one exception: He would replace "increase its profits" with "in accordance with the wishes of the owners."[34]

Again, we see that Friedman is not arguing for profit maximization, but for the rights of shareholders to determine a corporation's direction.

Unlike Sternberg, Friedman seems to allow that a business firm can be directed to any end that the shareholders desire without losing its identity as a business. Friedman's concern is to defend the prerogatives of shareholders. He does not address himself to the function of business or the moral status of profit maximization.

FRIEDMAN CHALLENGES STAKEHOLDER THEORY

Friedman's argument works as a challenge to stakeholder theory. This theory's proponents allege that corporate executives should take into account the interests of everyone with a stake in the corporation, and should not privilege the interests of shareholders above other stakeholders.[35]

Friedman points out that the shareholders have a special stake in the corporation, in the same sense that a homeowner has a special stake in his or her house—the shareholders *own* the corporation; it is their *property*. Ownership designates a relationship between a person (or persons) and a thing (or things). To own a thing means that you get to decide what happens to that thing. If you do not have that prerogative, then you are the owner in name only.

Shareholders' desires should be privileged above the desires of other stakeholders because the shareholders own the corporation.[36]

FRIEDMAN'S TITLE IS MISLEADING

Friedman does not defend profit maximization. Friedman defends profit maximization *as an expression of shareholders' desires*. The *title* of Friedman's *New York Times* article indicates that he defends profit maximization. If one looks past the title to the article's content, however, one will not find an argument for profit maximization. As José Salazar and Bryan W. Husted recognize, "the title of the essay was more provocative than its actual content."[37]

When discussing Friedman's article in my business ethics class, at a certain point, I would ask students to find the passage where Friedman claims that corporate executives *should* maximize profit. Over ten years of teaching this course, not one student could find this passage—because it is not there.

FRIEDMAN'S ARGUMENT SUPPORTS CSR

CSR's proponents like to posit Friedman as their primary opponent. In fact, Friedman's argument supports CSR. Friedman wrote at a time when shareholders wanted their corporate executives to focus on profit maximization. Today, shareholders want their corporate executives to be socially responsible. Salazar and Husted point out that, since Friedman's article was published, "many stockholders have in fact decided that they do want corporations to make expenditures on social programs."[38] By the logic of Friedman's argument, corporate executives must obey.

Friedman defends the prerogatives of shareholders. He does not defend the morality of shareholders having a preference for profit maximization. Consequently, Friedman has not defended profit maximization, despite his article being held up by critics as *the* argument for profit maximization.

ETHICS HAS PRIMACY OVER ECONOMICS

Critics vilify Friedman and Sternberg because they believe that only a loathsome person could defend profit maximization. Profit maximization cannot be defended on economic grounds alone because people who are convinced that profit maximization is immoral are closed to the economic arguments.

Given a choice between an economic argument that points to one conclusion and an ethical argument that points to an opposing conclusion, most people choose the ethical argument. Those who do not resolve the conflict by dismissing the field of ethics.

People do not evaluate ethical conclusions by economic standards. They evaluate economic conclusions by ethical standards. Observe the history of free-market economics. The economic case for capitalism was made more than 240 years ago when Adam Smith published *The Wealth of Nations*. Nevertheless, people continue to reject capitalism because capitalism clashes with their moral sensibilities.[39]

People do not reject the morality of altruism because it clashes with free-market economics. They reject free-market economics because it clashes with the morality of altruism. Of course, not everyone who embraces altruism rejects free-market economics. Some people compartmentalize the two fields to stop the contradiction coming to conscious awareness. Others twist their arguments into pretzel-like contortions to reconcile the contradiction. The result is never convincing, as we shall see.

For evidence, observe the history of socialism. Failure after failure has proved the economic theories of socialism to be flawed. The Soviet Union—failed. Communist China—failed. Cuba—failed. North Korea—failed. Khmer Rouge—failed. Economics explains why any country that adopts socialism must result in death and destruction.[40] Still, Venezuela embraced socialism. Why? Socialism is a moral ideal, so its proponents felt the need to set aside economic conclusions and try to make the unworkable work.[41]

Intellectuals continue to look for ways to make the moral ideal of socialism practical. John E. Roemer and Richard Wolff independently proposed forms of market socialism that allegedly reconcile the ends of socialism with the means of capitalism.[42]

Young people party in nightclubs named after the KGB and wear T-shirts featuring the face of the Marxist guerrilla fighter Che Guevara.[43]

Imagine the outrage if professors at reputable universities proposed market *Nazism* or democratic *Nazism* as a solution for making Nazism work. Imagine the outrage if a nightclub were named after the SS or if young people thought it cool to dress in T-shirts featuring Joseph Goebbels.

Why the double-standard? People support the ends of socialism, not of Nazism. They may not support the secret police, dictatorships, or gulags, all of which are entailed by socialism's ideals. Still, they maintain that socialism is ideal because socialism accords with their moral assumptions.

More people died at the hands of communist regimes than the Nazis.[44] Still, these deaths do not lead people to reject socialism as evil because these deaths were in the service of an end that they regard as moral. The Nazis are rightly condemned as mass murderers, not because of the number of innocent people killed but primarily because the atrocities were carried out in the service of an evil end. The communists are not similarly condemned because people's moral premises wipe the bloodstains from *The Communist Manifesto.*

OUR ENDS ESTABLISH OUR STANDARD OF EVALUATION

People typically choose ethical over economic conclusions because ethics establishes the ends by which economic conclusions should be judged. There is nothing wrong with means-end evaluations. We *should* evaluate our economic conclusions by the standard of our moral ends. Problems arise when people adopt indefensible ethics that lead them to hold unjustifiable ends.

Consider the economic case against minimum wage laws. Economics demonstrates that raising the minimum wage above the market rate results in unemployment. Economists have identified a fact of reality. Mandating a minimum wage does not alter a person's economic contribution to a business. A businessman will not pay a $15 wage to employ someone who makes a $10 contribution, any more than he or she will spend $15,000 to purchase a car that is worth $10,000.

Still, certain intellectuals clamor for raises to the minimum wage even though they know that there will be job losses. Sean McElwee, for example, states that if "some businesses [were] to fail, unemployment rose and prices increased, a higher minimum wage could still be an acceptable policy."[45] McElwee is not concerned by the job losses because he regards these losses as justified in the service of a noble end—the achievement of economic equality.

ETHICS DETERMINES OUR SELF-WORTH

Our ethics establishes the standard by which we evaluate economic conclusions. This conflict is not an intellectual curiosity. When we act contrary to economic conclusions, we are bad *economists*. When we act contrary to ethical conclusions, we are bad *people*.

Imagine that you could face yourself, as though you were looking at a mirror, and what you saw reflected back was a morally crooked, sordid, bespotted, and loathsome beast.[46] We turn ourselves into such a person—*in our own eyes*—when we act contrary to our ethical conclusions.

If your moral standards imply that profit maximization is immoral, then embracing the economic arguments condemns yourself.

THE EVIL THAT "GOOD MEN" DO

Do not underestimate morality's power. People were willing to do evil in Nazi Germany because they did not regard what they were doing as evil. Their flawed sense of morality led them to believe that only a loathsome person would refuse to turn his or her Jewish neighbors into the authorities or would refuse to be a party to genocide.[47]

The Amazon television series *The Man in the High Castle* illustrates this point. Reichsmarschall John Smith's teenage son realizes that he suffers from a genetic disorder. The son voluntarily submits himself to the authorities to be euthanized because he accepts genetic hygiene as a moral ideal.[48]

Of course, not every Nazi party member believed in Nazi ideals. Some Nazis spouted Nazi slogans to rationalize their brutality. Nevertheless, these brutes needed to spout *moral* rationalizations because only a moral rationalization could justify their actions. They could not have similarly justified their brutality with *economic* rationalizations alone.

The Japanese Kamikaze pilots committed suicide out of a commitment to Shintoism, a religion that held the emperor of Japan to be a living god.[49] Today, Islamic terrorists commit similar atrocities out of similar motives.[50] A person does not fly a plane into a building or blow himself and others up out of a commitment to an *economic* theory but a flawed *moral* ideal.

Similar examples can be found in Western countries. A white nationalist murdered fifty innocent men, women, and children at a mosque in Christchurch, New Zealand. He would have killed more had he not been stopped. This man published a manifesto explaining why he believed that his atrocity was *morally* justified.

The movie *Oranges and Sunshine* tells the true story of children forcibly relocated by the British government from the United Kingdom to Australia and Canada. The British authorities told the children that their parents had died. The parents were not told that their children had been shipped to other countries. The children were promised oranges and sunshine. They found hard labor and sexual abuse. Some of the children were as young as three. The British authorities facilitated the systematic abuse of children out of a commitment to doing the right thing. They believed that they were combating child poverty.[51]

The opponents of profit maximization are not would-be Nazis or Kamikaze pilots. These examples illustrate how the wrong moral premises can lead a person to crusade for atrocities. In the case of profit maximization, the wrong moral premises led to the tragic spectacle of the Occupy Wall Street movement, where idealistic young people passionately fought against the system that made their lives possible.

PROFIT MAXIMIZATION CONFLICTS WITH ALTRUISM

Profit maximization cannot be reconciled with the altruist morality. Profit is about the *achievement* of objective values. Altruism is about the *sacrifice* of values. Altruism does not mean caring for loved ones or helping a friend in times of need. Altruism means benefiting others at a cost to one's own life. C. S. Lewis argues that "the only safe rule" in establishing how much we ought to give to those in need is to "give more than we can spare. . . . If our charities do not at all pinch or hamper us, I should say they are too small. There ought to be things we should like to do and cannot do because our charitable expenditure excludes them."[52] For Lewis, moral charity must hurt.

Anyone who accepts the morality of altruism and wants to defend profit maximization must confront this conflict. One tactic has been to deny that profit-maximizing businessmen are really self-interested. George Gilder, for example, claims that businessmen are altruists, like Mother Teresa, in a business suit. He writes: "In a world always divided in part between the givers and the takers, businessmen are among the most persistent and ingenious of donors and all of us who benefit should be thankful."[53]

Businessmen are not *donors*. They charge us for this benefit. Steve Jobs did not *donate* iPhones to his customers. He expected them to pay.

The world is not divided into givers and takers. Altruism divides the world this way, and then asserts that the moral ideal is to be a "giver." We do not have to be a giver or a taker, however. We can reject this alternative and choose to be a *trader*—exchanging value for value.

Another tactic is to divide the world into the *private* and *public* spheres. Profit maximization countenances self-interest, which is a *private vice*, but market mechanisms channel this vice to the social good, which is a *public virtue*.

Adam Smith popularized this idea. He observed that when the butcher, the brewer, and the baker pursue their self-love, the result is the public good, even though this was not their intention.[54] Bernard Mandeville's book *The Fable of the Bees* contains a similar idea.[55]

Michael Novak invokes this idea in attempting to reconcile his support of profit maximization with his Catholicism. According to Novak, the market system channels our "sinful tendencies" toward the social good.[56]

ALTRUISM GIVES ETHICS A BAD REPUTATION

The need to make a moral case for profit maximization is not often recognized because the importance of ethics in life is not often recognized. When ethics is equated with altruism, it is rendered irrelevant to life. Economists, thereby, come to think of ethics as dispensable. Friedman, for instance, expressed disdain for ethics, claiming, in private correspondence with one of his critics, that ethical discussions "lend themselves to an excessive amount of bull."[57]

Altruism is the ethics that most people accept, handed down unthinkingly from previous generations. Altruism, however, is not treated as one moral theory among many but as the equivalent of ethics. Until recently, moral philosophers did not even recognize an alternative to altruism, treating egoism not as the opposite of *altruism* but as the opposite of *morality.*[58]

People can live without altruism, so if altruism is the same thing as morality, then people can live without morality.

This last point can be stated in stronger terms. Altruism is the morality of self-sacrifice, so it necessarily threatens the practitioner's life. If altruism is morality, then *morality* is a threat.

Consistent altruism means death. Consider the following passage from Jean de la Bruyere: "That man is good who does good to others; if he suffers on account of the good he does, he is very good; if he suffers at the hands of those to whom he has done good, then his goodness is so great that it could be enhanced only by greater sufferings; and if he should die at their hands, his virtue can go no further: it is heroic, it is perfect."[59] If altruism is the same thing as morality, then being *morally* consistent means death.

Consequently, people protect their lives from altruism by siloing it to one aspect of their life. Morality, for them, becomes volunteering in the soup kitchen at the weekend or writing a check to help starving orphans in Africa, not a necessary tool for everyday living, as in an egoist ethics.

For economists raised to think of morality in altruistic terms, the *moral* case for profit maximization is interpreted as the *altruist* case. Since altruism and profit maximization are incompatible, bringing moral arguments into the discussion is seen as a threat to profit maximization. Profit's proponents, therefore, conclude that they should avoid talk of ethics altogether.

PARETO EFFICIENCY AS A PROXY FOR ETHICS

Even those economists who reject the realm of ethics and attempt to erect an intellectual firewall between their ethics and their economics need to justify their economic conclusions by appealing to an end. Their solution is an economic end that acts as a proxy for ethics in economic thought—Pareto efficiency. As Robin Cowan and Mario J. Rizzo explain in their economic case for profit maximization, "Pareto efficient allocations are considered to be good, and the closer to Pareto efficiency, the better."[60] An outcome is Pareto optimal if, in Cowan and Rizzo's words, "no one's utility can be increased without decreasing someone else's."[61] For Cowan and Rizzo, the efficient allocation of economic resources is the end that justifies their economic conclusions.

Pareto efficiency is not a substitute for a moral standard because it is itself based on a moral standard—the ethics of collectivism. Pareto efficiency assumes that resources are a collective asset and that the question is how to allocate them to maximize the utility of the whole. The resources to be allocated (or perhaps, more accurately, *reallocated*) are individuals and their property.

Human beings are not resources to be allocated. Economists cannot move people around like pieces on a chessboard. Human beings are entities with thoughts of their own. Each one of us makes an economic plan within the context of our own lives. Our plans are coordinated with the plans of billions of others through the market system. The result is an allocation of resources that is not determined by a single mind but by the minds of billions of individuals through the countless decisions that we make in our day-to-day lives.[62]

An economy is not a mechanism to be managed by a benevolent dictator acting for the common good.[63] In a free market, different people produce different amounts of wealth and make different judgments about what to purchase. The result can be expressed mathematically in the form of a pie chart.[64] In this mathematical sense, we can talk about the allocation of resources.

The efficient allocation of resources is not the end by which we should judge profit maximization. Profit maximization is moral because through the pursuit of profit individuals achieve the objective values upon which all of our lives depend.

ECONOMICS CANNOT CLASH WITH ETHICS

Ethical conclusions that are grounded in the facts of reality cannot clash with economic conclusions that are also grounded in the facts of reality. There is one reality. Reality is not divided into zones, one reserved for ethical facts and another for economic facts. Ethics and economics study the same reality, so if our ethical and economic conclusions clash, one must be wrong.[65]

The moral case for profit maximization is not an optional add-on to the economic case. The moral case is *the* case for profit maximization. The economic case *integrates* with the moral case and provides support. Without moral arguments, however, there is no case.

NEUTRALITY IS NOT AN OPTION

We cannot be morally neutral toward profit. We need to recognize that profit is for our life because conceptualizing values is for our life. We cannot be morally neutral toward profit because we cannot be morally neutral toward the businessmen who have conceptualized values and, in so doing, created goods and services that have enhanced our lives in incalculable ways.

Some people are moral crusaders *for* profit. Some people are moral crusaders *against* profit. Some people do not care. On hearing that the United States Department of Justice is prosecuting Amazon or Facebook, they yawn. For them, this news has no more considerable significance than hearing a weather report for a far-off country.

The opponents of profit are wrong. People who are indifferent to profit are also wrong. Profit's opponents mistakenly believe that profit is against their life. People who are indifferent to profit do not grasp the contribution that profit makes to their life. Facts do not depend on someone grasping them. The failure to grasp profit's value does not erase the fact that profit is for their life. In a world where profit is routinely attacked, neutrality is not an option.

We cannot be neutral toward the great profit maximizers of history—people like Morgan, Rockefeller, and Edison, or their modern counterparts such as Bill Gates, Steve Jobs, and Jeff Bezos. Whatever these men's shortcomings, their high profits signify the contribution that they have made to human life on earth. Even when we do not benefit directly from their achievements, we benefit indirectly from living in a world shaped by their minds. We should, therefore, honor their achievements in the same way as we honor the achievements of people like Sir Edmund Hillary and Stephen Hawking.

We also cannot be neutral toward the opponents of profit maximization—people like Annie Leonard, Michael Moore, and Ralph Nader. People who take a stand against profit are taking a stand against our lives and deserve to be treated accordingly. Many of the participants in the Occupy Wall Street movement have the excuse of youth. They do not comprehend the issues involved, and their high school teachers and university professors have misled them. Professional opponents of profit do not have this excuse. They have a moral responsibility to know the nature of that against which they crusade.

The opponents of profit maximization attempt to live a series of contradictions. Profit maximization, in fact, furthers their life. So they spend some of their time acting for their life while engaging in a moral crusade against their life. This contradiction has not gone unnoticed. Some commentators on the Occupy Wall Street movement noted that the participants coordinated their nefarious activities on their smartphones and through Facebook and Twitter, the very companies against which they were protesting.[66]

TRANSFORMING HUMAN LIFE

Once we recognize businessmen's contribution to our lives, we must recognize the need to crusade for profit maximization. To appreciate the contribution that profit-maximizing businessmen have made to human life on Earth, consider what life was like before businessmen were free to pursue profit.

People lived on the verge of death. Movies and television shows set in the pre-industrial era do not capture the reality of pre-industrial life. Well-fed actors dressed in period clothes enjoy a hearty meal with friends. Such presentations have as much in common with the pre-industrial world as *Hogan's Heroes* has with life as a prisoner of war in Nazi Germany.

Before the Industrial Revolution, famine was the normal state of affairs in Europe's wealthy countries. Three years of harvests were typically followed by one year of famine. To hold off starvation, people would sell all of their meager possessions, including their clothes. Strangers and travelers were routinely killed for the dinner plate. Gallows would be torn down by men frantic for the taste of warm flesh.[67]

Few people lived beyond their thirtieth birthday, most dying from disease. The few men who reached the grand old age of forty looked like a centurion today, with white hair, bent back, and knurled face. A woman in her thirties might be referred to as Old Gretel.[68]

Parents regularly abandoned newborn babies, unable to cope with another mouth to feed. In sixteenth-century Vienna, 8 to 10 percent of newborns were abandoned.[69]

There was no awareness of time. People did not own watches, clocks, or calendars. Since there was little difference between everyday life in one year and the next, a person had no reason to know the time or year.[70]

Few libraries possessed more than three hundred books. The Duke of Gloucester owned five hundred. The King of France, nine hundred. So valuable were books that each volume was chained to a desk or lectern.[71]

Most people were ignorant of the world outside of their village. They took seriously stories of griffins, and of men with dog heads who barked and snarled. They believed in imaginary lands, such as Atlantis.[72]

Businessmen have opened up to us a world inconceivable to even our recent ancestors. Though books have existed since ancient times, technological advances have made books affordable for the masses. A six-year-old child today can own a library that would be unfathomable to medieval children.[73]

Television enables us to perceive other times and places. We can see and hear events from World War I, even though we were not born at the time. Peter Jackson's 2018 movie *They Shall Not Grow Old* restores old footage, bringing a war from one hundred years ago alive for current generations.[74] Streaming services, such as Netflix and Amazon Prime, have made the world's television and movie libraries accessible to people around the planet. Medieval people barely knew a world outside of their village. Today, a young man in a remote town can experience many different cultures.[75]

Google Street View enables us to walk the streets of cities in which we have never stepped foot. Already, Google allows us to dial back time and explore cities as they existed several years ago. Imagine centuries from now future historians walking virtually through the streets of twenty-first-century Earth, thanks to Google.

Intellectual evils such as racism and homophobia are challenging to pass down the generations in the modern world. Parents who attempt to instill racist or homophobic ideas in their children will find that their children have access to books and television programs that challenge their prejudices. A young child told by his parents that black people are intellectually inferior to white men can covertly download to his Kindle a book by a black woman more intelligent than the white men around him.[76]

CRUSADING FOR PROFIT MAXIMIZATION

Friedman's and Sternberg's defenses of profit maximization are incomplete because they do not make a moral case. Without the moral case, people will reject profit maximization even when they acknowledge the validity of the economic arguments. Moreover, the moral case explains why we need to crusade for profit maximization.

Taking a moral stand in defense of profit maximization means taking a stand for the objective values upon which our lives depend. We are standing up for the supermarkets that supply us with food, for the streaming services that entertain us, for the whiteware companies that free our time, for the clothing companies that protect us from the elements, for the toy companies that entertain and educate our children, and for the transportation companies that enable us to traverse great distances. Few causes have been so great or misunderstood.

NOTES

1. Jeremy Moon, *Corporate Social Responsibility: A Very Short Introduction* (Oxford: Oxford University Press, 2014), 102. Friedman's article has been cited more than seventeen thousand times.

2. In the second edition of *Just Business*, Sternberg notes that most "reviewers seem to have been so surprised or offended by [the book's] challenging of received wisdom, that they have not dealt with the text that was published. Even relatively lengthy examinations, by academics and others, have been directed instead at views that their authors have simply attributed to me—independent of, and often contrary to, what was published in the text." Elaine Sternberg, *Just Business: Business Ethics in Action*, 2nd ed. (Oxford: Oxford University Press, 2000), xii.

3. Ibid., 45.

4. Ibid., 32. Cf. Elaine Sternberg, "The Need for Realism in Business Ethics," *Reason Papers* 31 (Fall 2009): 33.

5. Sternberg, "The Need for Realism in Business Ethics," 33.

6. Sternberg, *Just Business*, 46.

7. Blockbuster was more profitable than Netflix in a given financial year when streaming video services were first introduced. Still, Netflix was the one maximizing long-term owner value. For a history of Blockbuster and its downfall, see Henry C. Lucas Jr., *The Search for Survival: Lessons from Disruptive Technologies* (Santa Barbara, CA: Praeger, 2012), 45–59.

8. Amazon was founded in 1994 and did not make its first quarterly profit until 2001. Even then, Amazon had accumulated losses of $2.3 billion. Bill Bolton and John Thompson, *Entrepreneurs: Talent, Temperament and Opportunity*, 3rd ed. (Oxon: Routledge, 2013), 252.

9. Sternberg, "The Need for Realism in Business Ethics," 34. Cf. Sternberg, *Just Business*, 67.

10. Sternberg, "The Need for Realism in Business Ethics," 34.

11. Sternberg, *Just Business*, 67–68.

12. David W. Lutz, "Beyond Business Ethics," *Oikonomia: Journal of Ethics and Social Sciences* 2 (2003): 6. The phrase "public good" is of dubious authenticity since the "good" is always the good of individuals. If there is such a thing as a "public good," it is a good that is common to all individuals, such as the protection of individual rights. This phrase is used here only for explication.

13. Sternberg, *Just Business*, 44.

14. Ibid., 80 and 82.

15. Sternberg, "The Need for Realism in Business Ethics," 46.

16. Sternberg, *Just Business*, 79–80. Cf. Sternberg, "The Need for Realism in Business Ethics," 45.

17. Sternberg, *Just Business*, 4 and 111.

18. Henry B. Veatch, "Might 'Objectivism' Ever Become Academically Respectable?" *Liberty* 5, no. 3 (January 1992): 64.

19. Henry B. Veatch, *Human Rights: Fact or Fancy?* (Baton Rouge: Louisiana State University Press, 1985), 69.

20. For a discussion of how DNA seems to confirm Aristotle's account of potentiality, see Allan Gotthelf, *Teleology, First Principles, and Scientific Method in Aristotle's Biology* (Oxford: Oxford University Press, 2012), 88; Douglas J. Den Uyl and Douglas B. Rasmussen, *Liberty and Nature: An Aristotelian Defense of Liberal Order* (La Salle, IL: Open Court, 1991), 43–44; Robert Pasnau, *Thomas Aquinas on Human Nature: A Philosophical Study of* Summa Theologiae Ia 75–89 (Cambridge: Cambridge University Press, 2002), 103.

21. Sternberg, "The Need for Realism in Business Ethics," 34. Cf. Sternberg, *Just Business*, 4.

22. Sternberg, *Just Business*, 33.

23. Archie B. Carroll et al., *Corporate Responsibility: The American Experience* (Cambridge: Cambridge University Press, 2012), 240–42.

24. Milton Friedman, “The Social Responsibility of Business Is to Increase Its Profits,” in *Economic Morality: Ancient to Modern Readings*, ed. Henry C. Clark and Eric Allison (Lanham, MD: Lexington Books, 2015), 321.

25. Allison Dube, “In Defence of a Utilitarian University Education,” in *Liberal Education and the Idea of the University: Arguments and Reflections on Theory and Practice*, ed. Karim Dharamsi and James Zimmer (Wilmington, DE: Vernon Press, 2019), 81.

26. Friedman, “The Social Responsibility of Business Is to Increase Its Profits,” 321.

27. Ibid.

28. Ibid., 322.

29. Ibid., 321. Though Friedman frames the issue in terms of *money*, he presumably means *profit*.

30. Ibid.

31. Ibid., 325.

32. Milton Friedman, *Capitalism and Freedom*, fortieth anniversary ed. (Chicago: University of Chicago Press, 2002), 133.

33. Friedman, “The Social Responsibility of Business Is to Increase Its Profits,” 327.

34. Quoted in Thomas L. Carson, “My Correspondence with Milton Friedman about the Social Responsibilities of Business,” *Business and Society Review* 123, no. 2 (2018): 223. Carson misquotes Friedman. He alleges that Friedman claims, in *Capitalism and Freedom*, that “the one and only obligation of business is to *maximize* its profits while engaging in open and free competition without deception or fraud” (emphasis mine). Ibid., 218. Carson cites his own summary of Friedman from an earlier article. Thomas L. Carson, “Friedman’s Theory of Corporate Social Responsibility,” *Business and Professional Ethics Journal* 12, no. 1 (1993): 3. The misquotation is not necessarily innocuous, since Friedman-in-*Capitalism-and-Freedom* defends the *increasing* of profits, while Friedman-as-misquoted-by-Carson defends the *maximization* of profits.

35. For an explanation of stakeholder theory, see Domènec Melé, “Corporate Social Responsibility Theories,” in *The Oxford Handbook of Corporate Social Responsibility*, ed. Andrew Crane et al. (Oxford: Oxford University Press, 2009), 62–68. For a critique of stakeholder theory, see Sternberg, *Just Business*, 49–53.

36. The proponents of stakeholder theory allege that shareholders do not really own the corporation because the prerogatives of ownership are exercised by a board of directors, not by the shareholders, who may have little or no say in the day-to-day running of the corporation. Shareholders as a total own the corporation. A particular shareholder owns a *share* of the corporation and can exercise all the prerogatives of ownership over that share.

37. José Salazar and Bryan W. Husted, “Principals and Agents: Further Thoughts on the Friedmanite Critique of Corporate Social Responsibility,” in *The Oxford Handbook of Corporate Social Responsibility*, ed. Andrew Crane et al. (Oxford: Oxford University Press, 2009), 137.

38. Ibid., 138.

39. For a discussion of why bad ethics leads to bad economics, see Michael S. Berliner, ed., *Letters of Ayn Rand* (New York: Dutton, 1995), 257–59.

40. For an explanation of why socialism *must* result in economic chaos and a totalitarian dictatorship, see George Reisman, *Capitalism: A Treatise on Economics* (Ottawa, IL: Jameson Books, 1998), 268–95.

41. The Nordic model is not an example of successful socialism. On the 2019 Index of Economic Freedom, Iceland is ranked 11; Denmark, 14; Sweden, 19; Finland, 20; and Norway, 26. In comparison, the United States is ranked 12; Luxembourg, 17; Chile, 18; Germany, 24; and Japan, 30. The Nordic countries have a more extensive welfare system than other Western countries, but the economic system is predominately capitalist.

42. John E. Roemer, *A Future for Socialism* (Cambridge, MA: Harvard University Press, 1994); Richard Wolff, *Democracy at Work: A Cure for Capitalism* (Chicago: Haymarket Books, 2012). For a debate on market socialism among socialists, see Bertell Ollman, ed., *Market Socialism: The Debate among Socialists* (New York: Routledge, 1998). For an explanation of why market socialism must suffer from the same problems as regular socialism, see Reisman, *Capitalism*, 279–82.

43. There is a KGB Café and Bar in Belgrade, Serbia. The logo incorporates the red star worn by uniformed members of the KGB.
44. For a catalog of the horrors of communism, see Stéphane Courtois et al., *The Black Book of Communism: Crimes, Terror, Repression*, trans. Jonathan Murphy and Mark Kramer (Cambridge, MA: Harvard University Press, 1999).
45. Quoted in Yaron Brook and Don Watkins, *Equal Is Unfair: America's Misguided Fight Against Income Inequality* (New York: St. Martin's Press, 2016), 125.
46. Cf. St. Augustine's self-description after being converted to Christianity. Geoffrey P. Dobson, *A Chaos of Delight: Science, Religion and Myth and the Shaping of Western Thought* (Oxon: Routledge, 2014), 215.
47. For an explanation of why the Nazis (wrongly) believed their atrocities to be moral, see Leonard Peikoff, *The Ominous Parallels: The End of Freedom in America* (New York: Meridian, 1993), 68–99.
48. Erik Oleson, "Fallout," in *The Man in the High Castle* (Amazon Studios, 16 December 2016).
49. John David Lewis, *Nothing Less Than Victory: Decisive Wars and the Lessons of History* (Princeton, NJ: Princeton University Press, 2010), 238–43 and 252–54.
50. Elan Journo, "What Motivates the Jihad on America," in *Winning the Unwinnable War: America's Self-Crippled Response to Islamic Totalitarianism*, ed. Elan Journo (Lanham, MD: Lexington Books, 2009).
51. Roana Munro, *Oranges and Sunshine* (See-Saw Films, 2010).
52. C. S. Lewis, *Mere Christianity*, revised and amplified ed. ([London]: Collins, 1958), 77–78.
53. Quoted in Yaron Brook and Don Watkins, *Free Market Revolution: How Ayn Rand's Ideas Can End Big Government* (New York: Palgrave Macmillan, 2012), 43.
54. Adam Smith, *The Wealth of Nations* (London: David Campbell Publishers, 1910), 13 and 399. For a discussion of why Smith believes that self-love can be channeled to the public interest, see Robert White, "Ayn Rand Versus Adam Smith," *The Journal of Ayn Rand Studies* 7, no. 1 (Fall 2005): 141–43 and 56–58.
55. Bernard Mandeville, "'The Grumbling Hive,' in *Fable of the Bees*," in *Economic Morality: Ancient to Modern Readings*, ed. Henry C. Clark and Eric Allison (Lanham, MD: Lexington Books, 2015). For a discussion of Mandeville's argument, see M. M. Goldsmith, *Private Vices, Public Benefits: Bernard Mandeville's Social and Political Thought* (Cambridge: Cambridge University Press, 1985).
56. Michael Novak, *The Spirit of Democratic Capitalism* (Lanham, MD: Madison Books, 1991), 353.
57. Quoted in Carson, "My Correspondence with Milton Friedman about the Social Responsibilities of Business," 226.
58. Jan Österberg, *Self and Others: A Study of Ethical Egoism* (Dordrecht: Kluwer Academic Publishers, 1988), 82–83; Kurt Baier, "Egoism," in *A Companion to Ethics*, ed. Peter Singer (Oxford: Blackwell Reference, 1991), 201–202; Kai Nielsen, *Why Be Moral?* (Buffalo, NY: Prometheus Books, 1989), 169–70.
59. Quoted in Jeffrey A. Kottler, *Doing Good: Passion and Commitment for Helping Others* (Philadelphia: Brunner-Routledge, 2000), 74.
60. Robin Cowan and Mario J. Rizzo, "Fundamental Issues in the Justification of Profits," in *Profits and Morality*, ed. Robin Cowan and Mario J. Rizzo (Chicago: University of Chicago Press, 1995), 6.
61. Ibid., 2.
62. Cf. F. A. Hayek, "The Pretence of Knowledge," *The American Economic Review* 79, no. 6 (December 1989).
63. Reisman, *Capitalism*, 426.
64. Ibid., 327.
65. For an explanation of why knowledge must be a total, see Leonard Peikoff, *Objectivism: The Philosophy of Ayn Rand* (New York: Meridian, 1993), 123.
66. William Cohen, "Occupy Wall St Movement an Exercise in Contradictions," *New Zealand Herald* (18 October 2011).

67. William Manchester, *A World Lit Only by Fire: The Medieval Mind and the Renaissance—Portrait of an Age* (New York: Hachette Book Group, 1992), 54.

68. Ibid., 55. Manchester notes that a person in his or her forties would look like an eighty year old today. He was writing in 1992. With medical advances in the last twenty-eight years, an eighty year old today could pass for a young person in the medieval period. In Ayn Rand's novel *Atlas Shrugged*, one of the effects of industrial civilization's collapse is that people age earlier. Hank Rearden and Dagny Taggart meet an old woman in a town where there had once been a great factory. When Dagny realizes that the woman is pregnant, she asks the woman's age—she is thirty-seven. As they leave town, Dagny asks Hank how these people came to such a state. The next paragraph notes that Dagny and Hank see a decrepit billboard advertising a washing machine. Rand is dramatizing the connection between the goods and services of industrial civilization and quality of life. Ayn Rand, *Atlas Shrugged* (New York: Signet, 1992), 267–68.

69. Carlo M. Cipolla, *Before the Industrial Revolution: European Society and Economy, 1000–1700*, 3rd ed. (New York: W. W. Norton, 1984), 57.

70. Manchester, *A World Lit Only by Fire*, 22–23.

71. Ibid., 95.

72. Ibid., 233.

73. My son owns hundreds of books in English and Bulgarian.

74. Peter Jackson, director, *They Shall Not Grow Old* (WingNut Films, 2018).

75. Growing up in New Zealand, we had two television channels, both state-owned. One channel showed British programs. The other, American. Non-English programs were rare. A child growing up in New Zealand today can watch programs from Britain, the United States, Holland, France, Mexico, Spain, Germany, Canada, Korea, and almost every other country on the planet, expanding his or her world in a way never before possible, thanks to streaming services like Netflix and Amazon Prime.

76. The internet can reinforce preexisting prejudices by enabling a person to curate an online world that confirms his or her preexisting beliefs. Nevertheless, the internet makes alternative views accessible in a way that was not possible previously, if one chooses to look.

Chapter Seven

The Inconvenient Truth about Corporate Social Responsibility

CSR is posited as a businessman's leading alternative to profit maximization. CSR's proponents do not necessarily oppose profit. Some claim that CSR redounds to the bottom line. Nevertheless, all variants of CSR oppose the *morality* of profit maximization. CSR is based on the premise that businessmen do *well* by producing goods and services and must do something else to do *good*.

In chapter 1, we saw that the *raison d'être* of business ethics is the problem of how to subject corporations to the expectations of morality. CSR's proponents believe that amoral corporations aim at profit maximization and that CSR brings ethics into business by encouraging business leaders to be socially responsible. They are mistaken. CSR sabotages business ethics. Business ethics must be grounded in the recognition that profit maximization requires businessmen to cultivate the virtues needed to conceptualize objective values.

This chapter explains why many of the practices advocated in CSR's name, such as philanthropy and cause marketing, are consonant with profit maximization. We then consider how CSR was conceived as a strategy for advancing an altruist and collectivist agenda. We then consider why a corporation's legal status does not open the door to corporate social responsibility, as CSR's proponents assume.

This chapter then considers why CSR is an invalid concept. We argue that responsibilities are individual, not social. We consider why CSR fails to promote genuine responsibility in business. We consider a businessman's legitimate responsibilities to his or her investors, customers, and employees.

This chapter then explains how CSR undermines business ethics by sidelining ethics to a business's side activities.

This chapter concludes that businessmen do not need to engage in nonprofit activities to do good, because businessmen already do good by producing goods and services that further human life.

BUSINESS'S FINAL END

Let us first consider whether profit maximization is consonant with several practices advocated in CSR's name. Corporate philanthropy, cause marketing, and volunteerism are the three most widely adopted practices advocated in the CSR literature. Opposition to CSR does not mean opposition to these practices. On the contrary, the same values that motivate profit maximization can also motivate these practices. A profit-maximizing businessman is a lover of values, and the same love of values that inspires a businessman to produce the goods or services that he sells can also inspire him to be philanthropic, to promote specific causes, and maybe also to volunteer in the local community.

A business's final end justifies all of the activities within the business. Whether businessmen should engage in these practices alongside their business activities depends on whether the practices are consonant with this end.

A *businessman*'s final end is his or her flourishing, not profit maximization. Within the context of business, however, a businessman's ultimate goal is to maximize profit. The end of profit maximization provides the standard by which a businessman should make *business* decisions.

Cash is not a businessman's final end. The final end is profit-*that-signifies-the-creation-of-objective-values*. One cannot separate profit from the values that it signifies. The final end is profit *and* the values signified by profit.

Abstractly, a businessman's final end, within the context of the business, is profit maximization. Concretely, a businessman's ultimate goal is to produce particular goods and services. Businessmen typically articulate their particular final end in their company's mission statement. Microsoft's final end, under Bill Gates, was to put a computer on every desk and in every home. Google's—to organize the world's information and make it universally accessible and useful. Walmart's—to save people money so that they can live better. LinkedIn's—to connect the world's professionals to make them more productive and successful.

MEANS-END REASONING

In chapter 2, we saw that a final end is a cognitive integrator that justifies all of its subservient ends. We first establish our end, and then our end determines the steps that we must take. Aristotle calls this process *final causa-*

tion.[1] Means-end reasoning enables us to select among alternatives. If we live in London and our goal is to drive to Glasgow, then this end establishes the range of routes from which we can legitimately choose.[2]

University students are familiar with means-end reasoning, at least implicitly. If a student's goal is to graduate with a major in art history, then this end establishes the range of courses from which the student must choose. Majoring in art history requires this student to select from *this* range but not *that* range. Of course, this student can take a course unrelated to his major, but when he makes this decision, he needs to know that so doing will not undermine his goal.

When we abandon the means to an end, we abandon the end. If our goal is to drive to Glasgow, but at the first fork, we take the road to Cardiff, then we are no longer driving to Glasgow. If our stated goal is to major in art history, but given a choice we choose courses in finance, then we are no longer pursuing this goal.

When a businessman engages in activities that do not serve the business's ultimate goal, he or she is, to this extent, no longer pursuing this goal. If Microsoft's CEO decides to diversify its product line by introducing concrete mixers (not *smart* concrete mixers just regular ones), then, to this extent, Microsoft is no longer pursuing the goal of putting a computer on every desk and in every home.

Microsoft would be abandoning its ultimate goal, even if it were to find that concrete mixers are more profitable than software. A business's ultimate goal is not profit in the abstract but the particular values that a company creates through the production of its goods and services.

A businessman can change his or her business's final end. The new end may no longer justify choices that were justified by the previous end. This decision would, therefore, cascade through the business, changing its operations in numerous ways. Microsoft could decide to produce industrial machines instead of software. So doing would spark a complete reorganization of Microsoft's activities, with Microsoft needing to drop its entire product range, letting current employees go, hiring new staff, and introducing a range of new products.

A business's ultimate goal—the values that it aims at creating—is the standard by which we must judge whether a business should embrace corporate philanthropy, cause marketing, and volunteerism.

PHILANTHROPY

Philanthropy is when a businessman donates money or goods to a person or a group of people, such as the Red Cross, the State Opera House in Vienna, or Georgetown University. Avon, for example, donates a percentage of the sales of its "pink ribbon" products to organizations researching a cure for breast cancer.[3]

Philanthropy can express a businessman's commitment to the same values served by his goods or services. Avon markets itself as *the* company for women. Though men can develop breast cancer, women are disproportionally affected. Avon aims at the well-being of women when it sells cosmetics *and* when it raises funds for breast cancer research.

Supporting prostate cancer research would also have been a worthy cause. Avon's directors would not have been justified in running a campaign to support prostate research, however. The well-being of women is not an end that can justify supporting such research.

CSR's proponents recognize that philanthropy needs to align with the business's corporate mission.[4] This alignment is justified as a tactic to convince recalcitrant executives to be philanthropic. CSR's proponents do not recognize the moral legitimacy of a businessman justifying philanthropy by appealing to the same values that motivate the business's mission. A businessman, they assume, has a moral obligation to be philanthropic even when so doing does not further his or her ultimate end.

Philanthropy seems opposed to profit maximization when one thinks of profit in strict accounting terms. Philanthropy represents an additional expense, which, intuitively, would seem to reduce a company's profit. The accounting mentality misses the value signified by a company's bottom line. Regardless of the marketing benefits, philanthropy is justified out of a commitment to this value.

Of course, philanthropy needs to be engaged in a way that does not undermine the value that a businessman creates through production. A businessman is a *business*-man because he produces goods or services. When a businessman decides to promote his values in other ways, he must not undermine the business's ultimate goal, which is to create value *through the production of goods or services*.

The value created through philanthropy need not conflict with the value created through production because philanthropy signals the company's values to its customers. Avon demonstrates to its customers that it values the well-being of women through its support of breast cancer research.

Philanthropy is not a morally superior means for businessmen to promote their values. Trading wealth for wealth is morally superior to giving wealth away. Furthermore, businessmen create significantly more value by producing goods and services than redistributing the wealth that they have created. John D. Rockefeller was one of the first great philanthropists in business. Nevertheless, Rockefeller maintained that he did more good through creating Standard Oil than he ever did through giving away his wealth.[5]

CAUSE MARKETING

Cause marketing is another way in which a businessman can further the same values he furthers through his business. Cause marketing is when a businessman uses his or her business to market a cause. Pampers, for example, support a campaign to encourage parents to place their infants on their backs to sleep. Sometimes infants stop breathing and die while asleep. The cause is unknown. These deaths are classified as Sudden Infant Death Syndrome (SIDS), or "cot death." Though the cause is unknown, doctors know that infants are less likely to die when they sleep on their back. The purpose of the "Back to Sleep" campaign is to reduce infant deaths.[6]

Pampers produce disposable diapers, a product that has improved the well-being of young children and their parents. In marketing the Back to Sleep campaign, Pampers is promoting the same value that it promotes through its disposable diapers, and is doing so in a way that does not undermine its bottom line. Pampers is marketing its disposable diapers and the Back to Sleep campaign simultaneously.

A campaign warning of the dangers of drunk driving would also have been a worthy cause. This cause would not necessarily have been appropriate for Pampers, however. The well-being of young children would not justify such a campaign unless the campaign focuses on how drunk driving impacts children.

A student's first introduction to business ethics is often in his or her marketing course. The implication being that ethics is good marketing. Marketing does not morally justify philanthropy and cause marketing. These activities market the company's products. The moral justification, however, is that these activities promote the businessman's values, the same values that led him or her to create the company in the first place. A profit-maximizing businessman does not have to make a marketing case for these activities. A case formulated in terms of values *is* sufficient because profit is about conceptualizing values.

UNJUSTIFIED PHILANTHROPY AND CAUSE MARKETING

Philanthropy and cause marketing is not justified when these activities promote values that are irrelevant to the business's end. The Product Red campaign raised money to fight the spread of AIDS in Africa. Bono convinced Steve Jobs to support the campaign by creating a red iPod. Jobs did not believe that Apple needs to be philanthropic to do good. He recognized that Apple was already doing good by creating great consumer products. Nevertheless, Bono was Jobs's friend, and Jobs agreed to support the campaign.[7] A red iPod was not justified because fighting AIDS has nothing to do with the value created by Apple's products.

The Product Red campaign was a worthy cause. Nothing would have been morally wrong with Jobs or any of Apple's employees or investors personally supporting this campaign, assuming that so doing would not have been self-sacrificial. Nevertheless, Apple's ultimate goal cannot justify the Product Red campaign, and so it was wrong of them to support the campaign *through the business*. Apple's support was like Avon raising funds for prostate cancer research or Pampers campaigning against drunk driving.

Similarly, Ben and Jerry's use of their ice-cream chain to raise awareness of climate change does not serve the same end as the production of ice cream.[8] Let us set aside the issue of whether this cause is worthy.[9] Climate change awareness has nothing to do with the value of ice cream. The ultimate goal of satiating people's hunger for a cold dessert does not justify promoting climate change awareness.[10]

Ben and Jerry are notorious for their left-wing sympathies, so climate change awareness is consistent with their personal values.[11] A business, however, is not a pulpit for a businessman to promote whatever values he or she happens to support. For cause marketing to be morally justified *within the context of the business*, the cause has to further the same values that the businessman is pursuing through the business.

In chapter 6, we saw that an ethical business activity must first be a *business* activity. Business ethics is the application of ethical principles to the end of business. A morally justified cause must be consonant with a business's final end to fall within the scope of business ethics. A businessman who promotes an irrelevant cause as part of his or her business activities does not earn any moral credit as a *business*-man.

VOLUNTEERISM

Volunteerism usually consists of expecting employees to take time away from work to serve the community, such as volunteering in a soup kitchen or cleaning rubbish from a beach. When Timberland sends its salespeople and executives on a retreat, they are expected to spend their extracurricular time on service projects, such as building affordable housing for the poor or a playground for a school.[12]

Volunteerism is not morally justified within the context of business because community service has nothing to do with business's ultimate goal. Maybe there are ways to align volunteerism. A talk on finance to high school students, for instance, may align with a bank's ultimate goal. Volunteerism's proponents do not usually have such cases in mind, however. Volunteerism is typically interpreted to mean volunteering for a *service* project.

Volunteerism is an imposition on employees. A businessman hires an employee to do a job. This relationship is a trade. The employee provides his or her services in exchange for a wage or salary. An employee should be expected to do the job for which he or she was hired. The employer has no right to determine how an employee spends his or her time outside of work. Expecting employees to serve the community is overstepping the employer's prerogatives. It is like expecting employees to attend religious ceremonies or political rallies. Volunteerism falls outside the scope of the employer-employee relationship.

PROFIT MAXIMIZATION IS MORALLY SUFFICIENT

A businessman does not have to be philanthropic or promote worthy causes to be moral. Avon is a moral company not because it raises funds for breast cancer research, but because it sells cosmetics. Pampers is a moral company not because it promotes the Back to Sleep campaign, but because it sells disposable diapers. Avon and Pampers are moral companies because the people running them successfully created goods and services that serve their customers' values.

Businessmen committed to realizing their values in the world are likely to want to be philanthropic or promote particular causes. When John Allison was BB&T's CEO, he promoted his values by using BB&T to support the education of capitalism in American universities.[13] Since BB&T is a bank, educating young people about the nature of capitalism supports BB&T's ultimate goal. Allison did not need to support the education of capitalism to be moral, however. Allison was already moral because he was running a principled and successful bank.[14]

Businessmen who engage in philanthropy and cause marketing may be doing good. They are not doing good while doing well, however. Businessmen do not need to engage in these activities to do good because they are already doing good by creating objective value through the production of goods and services.

PHILANTHROPY AND CAUSE MARKETING IS NOT CSR

Philanthropy and cause marketing is moral under certain circumstances. This conclusion does not imply that CSR is moral under certain circumstances. CSR's proponents try to equate philanthropy and cause marketing with CSR when these are not equivalents. One can morally endorse the former while opposing the latter.

CSR'S IDEOLOGICAL ORIGINS

We shall consider the moral assumptions that led to the coining of CSR. We shall then consider CSR's legitimacy as a concept.

CSR stands for *corporate* social responsibility. CSR is directed at corporations for a reason, which we shall explain shortly. For now, we shall ignore this distinction and treat CSR as though it were directed at all businessmen, not only those businessmen who choose to incorporate.

CSR is a strategy for advancing the moral-political agenda of altruism and collectivism among businessmen. Howard R. Bowen has been described as the father of CSR.[15] Bowen wrote a book in 1953 that was part of a series applying Christian ethics to economic life. In this book, Bowen argues that the "businessman should be actuated by the motive of serving society rather than maximizing profit."[16] The book's title: *Social Responsibilities of the Businessman.*

THE CALL TO SERVICE

The call to service is central to CSR. In *Compassionate Capitalism: How Corporations Can Make Doing Good an Integral Part of Doing Well*, Marc Benioff and Karen Southwick explain that their purpose is to show businessmen how they can "dare to be great by integrating community service" into their companies.[17] Benioff and Southwick praise Salesforce because its CSR program means that employees are not merely given a job but "a path to service in their community."[18] They describe "the need to serve" as "one of the most meaningful, important, *human* callings" (emphasis in original).[19]

The call to service is not novel to the CSR movement. We can find this call throughout Western culture.

When Michelle Obama was First Lady, she gave a commencement address at the University of California, Merced, in which she endorsed the following quote from activist Marian Wright Edelman: "Service is the rent we pay for living. . . . It is the true measure, the only measure of our success."[20]

When George H. W. Bush was president, he called on Americans to serve their communities, the nation, and the world. Bush's call to service led to the creation of Learn and Serve America, an organization that promotes service-learning programs in schools.[21] As a result of this program, over one million American children, from kindergarten to college, have engaged in community service.[22]

Note the phrase "from *kindergarten* to college." Consider the implications. Children who have yet to learn to read or write are taught that good children serve their communities.

Socially active parents establish websites to share ideas on how toddlers can volunteer in the community. Kidworldcitizen.org suggests that young children decorate placemats for Meals on Wheels or fill a backpack with school supplies to donate to a local child in need.

Some universities require community service as a condition of graduation. Tulane University in New Orleans requires all students to take a class with a service-learning component in their first two years and to complete a second service-learning requirement in their last two.[23]

When Johnny attends kindergarten, he is taught that good children serve the community. He receives the same message in primary school, high school, and college. He hears this message from politicians and his parents. He watches movies and television programs honoring people who serve their communities. CSR's proponents are merely showing the adult Johnny how he can continue to do at the office the same thing he has been expected to do all of his life.

ALTRUISM

The call to service is grounded in the morality of altruism. The French philosopher Auguste Comte coined the term. Comte wanted to found a new religion that would sweep away what he called the "fictitious" gods of the past. The gods of Judaism, Christianity, and Islam were to be replaced by a new deity—Society. The moral precept of this religion was *live for others*, which is the literal meaning of altruism.[24]

Though Comte opposed past religions, altruism secularizes the teachings of prior religions, banishing the pretense of a reward in the next life. Jesus reportedly kneeled on the floor and washed the feet of his disciples, an act customarily reserved to a servant.[25] In having Jesus model the role of a servant, the Bible's authors dramatize the message that the moral ideal is to serve others. Comte preserved the religious belief in the morality of service for a post-religious age.

BUSINESSMEN AS TRUSTEES OF SOCIETY'S RESOURCES

The call to service provides the foundation for collectivism. Bowen argues that there is no right to property. According to Bowen, property owners are the trustees of society's resources. They must, therefore, use the property that they nominally own to serve their communities. He writes: "Those who own property have the duty of using and administering it, not exclusively for their own purposes, but in ways that will serve the needs of the whole society. . . . The owner is a trustee accountable to God and society."[26]

Bowen was not an ambassador of the Soviet Union. He was a right-wing conservative who advocated CSR as a strategy for defending the free-enterprise system against the encroachment of communism.

Bowen's book was published in 1953. The major political conflict, at the time, was between the Soviet Union and the United States of America. F. Ernest Johnson, in an appendix to Bowen's book, argues that the essential difference between communism and capitalism is that under communism society entrusts its resources to the state on the condition that the state will use society's resources to serve society, whereas under capitalism society entrusts its resources to businessmen on the condition that businessmen will use society's resources to serve society. Johnson warns that if businessmen fail to demonstrate that they are using society's resources to society's satisfaction, society will reclaim its resources and reassign trusteeship to the state.[27]

BUSINESSMEN OPERATE BY SOCIETY'S PERMISSION

CSR is based on the collectivist assumption that businessmen operate their businesses by permission of society. If businessmen do not demonstrate that they are serving society, then society may withdraw a businessman's permission to operate. Domènec Melé observes that many authors writing about CSR emphasize that "society gives license to business to operate and, consequently, business must serve society not only by creating wealth, but also by contributing to social needs and satisfying social expectations towards business."[28] The Committee for Economic Development states that "business functions by public consent and its basic purpose is to serve constructively the needs of society—to the satisfaction of society."[29] Norman E. Bowie, one of the most respected scholars in the field of business ethics today, states: "The corporation must not only benefit those who create it, it must benefit those who permit it (namely society as a whole)."[30]

Keith Davis and Robert L. Blomstrom formulated this assumption as an uncontestable law: "In the long run those who do not use [economic] power in a manner which society considers responsible will tend to lose it."[31]

There are examples of where "society"—as represented by the United States Department of Justice—has withdrawn a businessman's permission to operate. We saw in chapter 4 that society withdrew Standard Oil's permission to operate. Society attempted to withdraw Microsoft's permission to operate because society's representatives objected to Microsoft bundling Internet Explorer with its Windows operating system.[32] There are indications that society may attempt to revoke Facebook's permission to operate.

These examples do not evidence the Davis-Blomstrom law at work. These cases are based on the United States antitrust legislation, which rests on the same ideological assumption as CSR.

THE BUSINESS CASE FOR CSR

CSR dresses collectivism up in the language of business. Few businessmen would find CSR's moral-political agenda digestible in its naked form. Instead, CSR's proponents dress collectivism in the language of marketing and management, so that CSR is made to appear as just another business tool that any hardnosed businessman would be foolish to ignore. Thus, Dyanne Crompton, then senior manager of worldwide community relations at Adobe, frames Adobe's adoption of CSR in terms of advancing the company's corporate objectives. Crompton claims that CSR is a "vehicle to enhance Adobe's reputation as a socially responsible corporation and to attract and retain employees."[33] No wonder Friedman dismissed CSR talk as "hypocritical window-dressing."[34]

The so-called "business case" for CSR consists of CSR improving a business's reputation, promoting employee morale, and gaining favor with politicians.[35] The implication is that CSR's proponents and the businessmen who adopt it do not think that a business can cultivate a good reputation and boost employee morale by educating its employees and the public on the value of the goods or services it produces.

The so-called "business case" for CSR is a confession by CSR's proponents that they do not recognize the value that businessmen create. Do not be shocked. Altruism does not recognize the value in the *production* of goods and services. Altruism only grants value to the *sacrifice* of wealth. CSR's proponents, being committed altruists, believe that businessmen need to sacrifice wealth in order to cultivate a good reputation and boost employee morale.

Consider the website of Z Energy, a New Zealand fuel distributor.[36] Z Energy's website transmits to its customers the message that the company does not believe in the value of its product. The page listing Z Energy's leadership team shows photos of the team members dressed in casual clothes outside in nature, half with young children strategically placed next to them. The CEO, for example, is dressed in hiking clothes and is standing next to the sign for Mackinnon Pass in New Zealand's Fiordland National Park. Z Energy's general manager for its commercial operations is shown sitting next to a bay window reading his young children a book. The website focuses on Z Energy's philanthropic activities, through its "Good in the Hood" fundraising program, and their support for specific causes, such as diversity, Maori language week, and the phasing out of plastic bags. Their foundation document states that "Z will move from being a part of the climate change problem to the heart of the solution."[37]

Ponder the last sentence. According to Z Energy's website, its product is a "problem." Not surprising then that the website does not mention the value of its product and instead stresses its commitment to social responsibility.

COURTING POLITICIANS' FAVOR

CSR might help businessmen to court the favor of politicians. Though businessmen should not have to do so, businesses today operate in a mixed economy in which politicians can change economic conditions on a whim. CSR's proponents think that it is an advantage that businessmen can use CSR as a strategy for placating politicians or even convincing politicians to favor them.[38]

This strategy must fail in the long run. The CSR strategy is for businessmen to convince politicians that they, the businessmen, are the politicians' willing servants. Rarely mentioned in the CSR literature is that the correlative of a servant is a master. When businessmen reduce themselves to servants, they elevate politicians to the status of their masters. The result is that politicians assume the right to exercise a master's prerogatives.

A businessman might find that this strategy "works" today because politicians in power favor his or her company or industry. Tomorrow, the same businessman will find that these politicians have changed their minds or have been replaced by different politicians. Granting arbitrary power to politicians is not a good business strategy.

A CONCEPTUAL HODGEPODGE

Not everything advocated under CSR's banner is grounded in altruism and collectivism. As we have seen, philanthropy and cause marketing can be consonant with profit maximization. Furthermore, selling safe products, treating one's employees well, all of which are often advocated in CSR's name, redound to a company's bottom line.

Nevertheless, CSR's proponents are advancing an altruist-collectivist agenda that, in the long run, undermines profit maximization, even when they advocate practices consonant with profit maximization.

Imagine that CSR is a conceptual file folder. CSR's proponents throw into this folder diverse activities, some of which are self-sacrificial, and some of which are means to profit maximization. As Yaron Brook and Don Watkins observe, "corporate 'social responsibility' is a hodgepodge. . . . It labels as 'socially responsible' both legitimate concerns of profit-seeking businesses . . . and concerns that aren't relevant to a business."[39]

A CONCEPTUAL SLEIGHT-OF-HAND

The conceptual hodgepodge that is CSR advances the altruist-collectivist agenda by enabling CSR's proponents to engage in a conceptual sleight-of-hand. If you oppose CSR because you do not think that businessmen operate their businesses by society's permission, its proponents can retaliate by accusing you of being opposed to product safety. Of course, you have not said anything about product safety. CSR's proponents, however, have conceptually united the ideological assumption that businessmen operate by society's permission with the obligation of businessmen to sell safe products.

This conceptual sleight-of-hand leads decent people to swallow the ideological assumption that businessmen operate by society's permission. This conceptual sleight-of-hand also intimidates decent people from opposing CSR out of fear that they will be accused of endorsing all sorts of corporate maleficence.[40]

CSR's proponents can point to activities promoted in CSR's name that are not altruistic or collectivist. These examples do not contradict this chapter's thesis. CSR's proponents created a concept that combines such activities with activities that are altruistic and collectivist in order to convince businessmen to swallow CSR.

CORPORATIONS

Bowen wrote about the social responsibilities of *businessmen*. CSR's proponents write about the social responsibilities of *corporations*. CSR is *corporate* social responsibility because the claim that businessmen operate by society's permission seems plausible when framed in terms of corporations.

In chapter 1, we saw that business ethicists believe that the special legal status of a corporation gives rise to the need to explain how corporations can be subject to the requirements of morality. CSR's proponents allege that corporations are creatures of the state, and therefore the state brings corporations into existence. The state, they argue, is only justified in granting existence to a corporation and permitting a corporation to continue to exist when so doing serves the public interest. Thus, Bowie writes, "The operation of a business, particularly when the business is a corporation, is not a matter of right. . . . In return for the permission to do business, the society places certain obligations and duties on the business. The corporation is created by society for a specific purpose or purposes."[41]

CSR's proponents are wrong. The state does not create corporations. The United States government did not create Microsoft, Apple, or Amazon. A corporation is a group of individuals who act as though they were a single entity, like a family or a social club. The state does not create these individuals or the relationships between them. These individuals and these relationships exist. The state merely grants legal standing to these individuals to act as though they were a single entity.[42]

Alternatively, CSR's proponents claim that society grants businessmen certain privileges when they incorporate, such as limited liability. When a corporation is liquidated, the investors are not personally liable for the corporation's debts. Social responsibilities, CSR's proponents claim, should be imposed in exchange for such privileges. Robert Hessen demonstrates that these "privileges" preceded the practice of incorporation and were already being achieved through contract. The corporate form was popular with businessmen as a convenient legal mechanism for achieving what was already possible through other means.[43]

The claim that corporations operate by society's permission is not substantially different from the claim that John Smith, the local greengrocer, operates his business by society's permission. CSR's proponents like to equivocate between corporations and businesses, appealing to the *corporate* form to explain why *businessmen* operate by permission of society. To avoid this equivocation, we discuss CSR strictly in terms of businessmen throughout this chapter.

EITHER-OR

A businessman must choose between profit maximization or CSR. He or she cannot embrace the morality of self-interest and the morality of altruism too.

Leonard Peikoff employs a skyscraper analogy to explain how ideas depend on other ideas.[44] If profit maximization were the upper level of a skyscraper, one of the levels below would be the morality of self-interest. If CSR were one of the upper levels, below would be the morality of altruism. Profit maximization and CSR cannot be levels on the same philosophical skyscraper because they depend on contradictory foundations.

Altruism is not a foundation for profit maximization. Businessmen benefit other people in a way that also furthers their own life. Profit maximization is a win-win. When you purchase a milk bottle from a grocer, you win, because you get the milk, and the grocer wins, because he or she makes a profit. Altruism is not about *benefiting* others; it is about *sacrifice*.

Consider the parable of the widow's offering. According to the Bible, Jesus watched a crowd put money into the temple treasury. Rich people threw in large amounts. A poor widow put in two small coins worth a fraction of a penny. Jesus called his disciples to him and said, "Truly I tell you, this poor widow has put more into the treasury than all the others. They all gave out of their wealth; but she, out of her poverty, put in everything—all she had to live on."[45] The offerings of the rich were of greater *benefit* to the treasury because they gave more. The widow's offering is morally superior, according to Jesus, because she *sacrificed.*

Profit maximization has no moral standing in altruism because profit maximization is about achieving values, not sacrificing them.

An examination of these competing moralities is outside this book's scope. A complete defense of self-interest and a complete critique of altruism require book-length treatments. For our purposes, the critical point is that CSR and profit maximization are irreconcilable.

THE RIGHT TO LIFE

CSR is premised on the assumption that businessmen operate their businesses by permission of society. This assumption denies the right to life. Business is an activity. It is something that *human beings* do. When CSR's proponents assert that businessmen operate their businesses by permission of society, the exact meaning of this claim is that human beings act by permission of society.

Recall the quote endorsed by Michelle Obama: "Service is the rent we pay for living."[46] If we must rent our lives, then we have no right to life and must, instead, live by permission of the person to whom we are expected to pay rent. The denial of a right to life is inherent in the call to service.

Profit maximization is grounded in the assumption that human beings have a right to life. Businessmen do not have to justify the existence of their businesses to anyone. Businessmen operate their businesses by right. The resources that businessmen command belong to them, not to "society." Businessmen, therefore, have no obligation to demonstrate that they are serving the public interest. Businessmen have to establish, to *their* satisfaction, that operating the business is in their interests. A businessman's customers have to establish, to *their* satisfaction, that purchasing the businessman's goods or services is in their interests. Otherwise, whether a business continues to operate is no one else's concern.

AN INVALID CONCEPT

We have considered the motivation of CSR's proponents for creating the concept of CSR. Suspect motivation is the least of CSR's problems. The inconvenient truth is that CSR is not a valid concept.

Its proponents concede the problem. The authors of *Corporate Responsibility: The American Experience* state that "corporate responsibility is, somewhat like beauty, in the eye of the beholder."[47] The authors quote Dow Votaw: "The term [CSR] is a brilliant one; it means something, but not always the same thing, to everybody."[48] Geoffrey P. Lantos states that "the concept of corporate social responsibility (CSR) is a fuzzy one with unclear boundaries and debatable legitimacy."[49]

Some proponents defend CSR's conceptual wooziness by claiming that CSR is what they call a "contested concept." Jeremy Moon, for instance, asserts that CSR is part of what William Gallie called a "class of *essentially contested concepts*," like "democracy" and "justice" (emphasis in original).[50] Duane Windsor asserts that "CSR conceptualization" is still in an "embryonic and contestable condition."[51]

Some proponents claim that CSR should not be considered a concept at all. Andrew Crane et al., for example, suggest that the problem with conceptualizing CSR can be overcome if CSR is not understood as "a concept, a construct, or a theory but as a *field of scholarship*" (emphasis in original).[52]

These are astonishing concessions that, in any other field, would have led CSR to be dismissed from serious consideration without further discussion. CSR has not been abandoned because its proponents did not create the concept to understand the world but to advance their moral-political agenda.

VALID CONCEPTS

Harry Binswanger observes that to "validate a concept and establish its proper definition, one should ask oneself: *What facts of reality give rise to the need for such a concept?*" (emphasis in original).[53] No facts give rise to CSR.

The history of ideas is littered with concepts that turned out to have no basis in reality. "Phlogiston," for instance, was thought to identify an element in combustible bodies that is released during the process of combustion. For almost one hundred years, scientists believed that phlogisticated substances dephlogisticate when burned. This concept was replaced by "oxidation" in the late 1700s once the causal mechanisms were understood.

The difference between phlogiston and CSR is that scientists mistakenly believed that there were facts that gave rise to the concept. Legitimate philanthropy and cause marketing give CSR credence, suggesting a factual basis for the concept. Nevertheless, CSR's proponents do not care whether there are such facts, as witness the above quotes.

MISCLASSIFICATION

Rejecting the concept of CSR does not mean that we have to reject everything that its proponents have classified under this heading. Philanthropy, for instance, can be a valid concept even if CSR is not. We can reject CSR while still supporting philanthropy. Rejecting the concept of CSR means rejecting a particular way of classifying things. It does not mean rejecting the things misclassified.

"RESPONSIBILITY"

To grasp CSR's problem, let us analyze its antecedent concepts, as we did with the concept of profit in the first chapter. The main antecedent concepts are *responsibility* and *society*. We shall set aside *corporation* for the reasons explained above.

What facts give rise to the concept of "responsibility"? The fact that we possess the capacity to deliberate about our voluntary actions.

"Responsibility" presupposes that *actions are voluntary*. Aristotle argues that actions are voluntary when "the moving principle is in the agent himself."[54] A person voluntarily acts when he possesses the power to act or not to act.[55] A person who hits someone over the head with a baseball bat voluntarily acts because he moves the arm holding the bat and could have chosen not to. A person who is carried by the wind acts involuntarily because the moving principle is outside of himself. He is the subject of the action, not the cause.[56]

Aristotle argues that to act voluntarily, a person must understand the concrete facts of the situation in which he acts. A person who acts out of ignorance of the facts involuntarily acts because he does not know what he is doing.[57] You shoot at what you believe to be a deer. The deer turns out to be another hunter. You did not voluntarily shoot the man because you did not know that it was a man at which you were shooting. Had you known, you would not have fired the shot.

"Responsibility" also presupposes *deliberation*. Aristotle believes that animals and young children act voluntarily. Still, Aristotle does not think them responsible for their voluntary actions because they cannot deliberate.[58] Animals and young children are subject to their passions and appetites. Adult human beings do not have to act on their desires. We can deliberate about our actions, and this capacity to do so makes us responsible for the consequences of our voluntary actions.[59] A five-year-old boy throws a toy at his father in anger, striking the father's forehead. This boy is not responsible because he is still developing the capacity to deliberate. A father who throws the toy back at the child, striking him, would be responsible because he can deliberate.

An adult does not have to deliberate to be responsible. Adults are responsible because they have the *capacity* to deliberate although they may choose not to do so.

A book-length critique of CSR would require an analysis of the competing theories of responsibility.[60] For this chapter, we just need to observe that one factor is fundamental to any account of responsibility—the capacity to reason. Only a rational being can have responsibilities because deliberation is an act of reason. We are responsible for our actions because we are rational animals.

Responsibility is individual because reason is an attribute of the individual, like the functioning of a person's heart and lungs. As Rand explains, the connections of reason "must be performed by each man alone. . . . No man can use his brain to think for another. All the functions of body and spirit are private. They cannot be shared or transferred."[61]

"SOCIETY"

What facts give rise to the concept of "society"? The fact that individuals live within a definable geographical area and are united by a common political system and cultural heritage. Society is not a physical entity. The individuals and the relationships between them are nonetheless real. "Society" conceptualizes real relationships between real people.[62]

The facts that give rise to the concepts of *responsibility* and *society* do not justify the idea of *social responsibility*. Individuals deliberate. Societies do not. Group decisions are an extension of the deliberations of the individuals who compose the group. Groups can be responsible only because the individuals who constitute the group are responsible.

A COLLECTIVE BRAIN

Michael Muthukrishna and Joseph Henrich argue for the existence of a "collective brain."[63] The discovery of such a brain would provide the factual grounds for the concept of "social responsibility"—with far-reaching implications. Muthukrishna and Henrich argue, for example, that if there is a collective brain, then great innovators like Rockefeller, Morgan, Edison, and Pasteur deserve no more credit than a firing neuron.[64]

They argue that "societies and social networks act as *collective brains*" with the "social networks of the collective brain" having "underlying structures" like "the neural networks of the biological brain" (emphasis in original).[65] This structure evidences Muthukrishna and Henrich's ability to analogize, not the existence of a collective brain. Social networks are networks of individuals, each with a brain of his or her own. Our *individual* rational faculty gives us the ability to transmit our thoughts to others through the spoken and written word. One of the many advantages of living in society is our ability to benefit from the thinking of others. Still, knowledge transmission presupposes individual thought. A young physicist must direct her own thought processes to grasp the discoveries of Galileo, Newton, Einstein, and

Hawking, and to take their insights further. Any original conclusions that she reaches will be *her* achievement, not an achievement of the great minds who went before her.

Responsibilities are *individual*. Social responsibilities are fiction. Social responsibility, therefore, cannot provide a standard for classifying things under the heading of CSR.

INDIVIDUAL RESPONSIBILITIES

Businessmen have responsibilities. To maximize profit, businessmen conceptualize facts and integrate these facts to form values. This capacity to conceptualize facts and values makes businessmen responsible for the goods and services that they produce. These are not *social* responsibilities but *individual* responsibilities, because the basis of a businessman's responsibilities is the functioning of his or her individual mind.

In chapter 1, we saw that business ethicists believe that a corporation's status as an artificial entity poses a problem for explaining corporate responsibility. Mr. Godsey, our neighborhood grocer, has responsibilities because he is a flesh-and-blood person capable of deliberation. Corporations do not possess a rational faculty. Business ethicists assume that corporations must be able to deliberate to have responsibilities, so they have attempted to assign intentions to corporations *qua* corporations.[66] Peter French, for instance, argues that corporations have an internal decision structure that enables us to ascribe to them intentions, not reducible to the individuals who compose the corporation.[67]

There is no need to invent corporate intentionality. Corporations are people. Corporations are an association of flesh-and-blood human beings, who possess the capacity to deliberate. Corporations are no more artificial than families or sports clubs. The law treats a corporation as though it were a separate entity when a corporation is, in reality, an association of individuals. When lawyers state that a corporation is a legal person, they mean that a corporation has standing before the law, not that corporations exist as separate entities.

A juristic person and a natural person are not necessarily the same things. A deceased man no longer exists. Still, this man has standing before the law while his estate goes through probate. The deceased continues to exist as a juristic person with legal rights.[68] Historically, women did not have a juristic existence. A woman's legal identity was subsumed by her father's legal identity until she married, when the father transferred her legal identity to the husband.

Corporations have responsibilities because the individuals who compose the corporation have responsibilities. The CEO and board of directors have responsibilities because they make decisions that determine the corporation's direction. Employees have responsibilities because they make decisions within their specific roles. As evidence that corporations are not separate from the individuals who compose them, observe that Apple under Steve Jobs was a different Apple than under his predecessors.

Recall the Ford Pinto case from chapter 5. CSR's proponents allege that Ford's actions resulted from the absence of social responsibility. Not so. Individuals at Ford decided to proceed with the Pinto's production, knowing its design flaws. Ford is responsible for the ensuing deaths because these individuals are responsible. Had these individuals taken responsibility, the Pinto would likely have been redesigned.

Imagine if one of these individuals had said, "If someone dies, *I* will be the one responsible for his death. *I* will be responsible for the death of someone's son, father, brother, uncle, colleague, and friend. Their death will be on *me*." The Pinto went ahead because no individual at Ford regarded themselves as responsible for the consequences of Pinto's design flaws even though they signed off on the car's production.

An imagined social responsibility would not have prevented the Pinto. Society did not notice the design flaws. Society did not sign off on the Pinto's production. Society did not purchase a Pinto. Society was not driving a Pinto when another driver rear-ended it, igniting an explosion of the fuel tank. Society did not have burns over 90 percent of its body. Society did not lay in bed in agony.

Individuals caused the design flaws. Individuals were affected by the design flaws. Some individuals are, therefore, responsible to other individuals for these flaws and the consequences thereof.

UNDERMINING RESPONSIBILITY

Since individual responsibilities are the only genuine responsibilities, *social* responsibility means *no* responsibility. We can observe the absence of responsibility that social responsibility inculcates in the bystander effect. The bystander effect is social responsibility in practice.

When Kitty Genovese was stabbed behind her apartment building, she called out for help. Thirty-eight of Genovese's neighbors allegedly heard her screams and did nothing.[69] Society could not have taken responsibility for calling the police because society did not hear Genovese's screams. Assigning responsibility to society means that none of Genovese's neighbors are individually responsible for failing to call the police. Nevertheless, it was Genovese's neighbors who heard her screams and who chose not to respond.

The Nestlé case also does not demonstrate an absence of *social* responsibility but of *individual* responsibility. Particular individuals at Nestlé failed to take into consideration the fact that mothers in third-world countries lack access to clean drinking water. Imagine if one of these individuals had said, "The lives of babies are at stake, and if anything goes wrong, then *I* will be responsible. *I* will be responsible for the death of a baby who is someone's son or daughter, brother or sister, nephew or niece, a baby with so much potential ahead of it. *I* had better make sure that *I* have not overlooked anything."

Inventing a social responsibility would not have prevented these babies' deaths. An imagined social responsibility would not mean that the individuals at Nestlé who made negligent decisions are held responsible. On the contrary, social responsibility means that no one, in particular, is responsible to no one in particular. After all, society did not fail to take into account the conditions in third-world countries. Society was not fed baby formula mixed with contaminated water. Society did not lose its son or daughter.

BUSINESSMEN'S RESPONSIBILITIES

Businessmen have responsibilities as a regular part of being in business. Businessmen have responsibilities to their investors—to provide them with accurate information on the state of the company and to optimize the return on their investment. Businessmen have responsibilities to their customers—to stand behind the quality of their goods and services. Businessmen have responsibilities to their employees—to pay them on time, to treat them justly, and to respect their personal time.[70]

The factual basis of a businessman's responsibilities is a human being's capacity for deliberation. This capacity provides the factual basis of all of our responsibilities, including our responsibilities as a parent, a friend, a colleague, an employee, a sports coach, and a neighbor.

One argument asserts that businessmen have further responsibilities because businessmen must pay society back for the benefits society has provided them. Without society's grace, the argument goes, businessmen would not be able to maximize profit. Businessmen who do not pay back society are freeloaders, no different from welfare beneficiaries.[71]

President Barack Obama famously quipped, "If you've got a business, you didn't build that. Somebody else made that happen."[72] Elizabeth Warren similarly asserts that

> There is nobody in this country who got rich on his own. Nobody. You built a factory out there? Good for you. But I want to be clear: you moved your goods to market on the roads the rest of us paid for; you hired workers the rest of us paid to educate; you were safe in your factory because of police forces and fire forces that the rest of us paid for. You didn't have to worry that marauding

bands would come and seize everything at your factory, and hire someone to protect against this, because of the work the rest of us did.[73]

Some businessmen agree. Bill Courtney argues that his fellow businessmen "should feel grateful instead of entitled" to the use of government services, such as the fire and police departments, roads, bridges, and ports. He argues that "every business has a moral obligation to give back to the communities that make it possible for them to succeed."[74]

There are no unchosen obligations. Imagine a child growing up in a welfare state. The child is educated in a state kindergarten and state schools; he receives compulsory vaccinations, paid for by the state; he plays in state-furnished playgrounds; he walks to after-school activities on state-funded paths. When this child grows up, the state cannot turn around and say, "You owe us. We provided you with schools, vaccinations, playgrounds, and paths. Now is time to pay us back to show that our investment in you was worthwhile."[75] The right to impose unchosen obligations on individuals is the right to enslave.[76] Nevertheless, CSR's proponents imagine businessmen to be under precisely this type of obligation.

The government cannot monopolize services and offer them without charge and then demand that businessmen pay them back for the benefits. The government did not ask businessmen whether they wanted the government to provide these services.

Furthermore, most of these services could be provided by private enterprise, if the government let go of its monopoly. None other than Frederick Engels recognizes that in the 1800s, England had better roads than Germany and France because businessmen built them. He writes: "The whole British Empire, and especially England, which, sixty years ago, had as bad roads as Germany or France then had, is now covered by a network of the finest roadways; and these, too, like almost everything else in England, are the work of private enterprise, the State having done very little in this direction."[77]

A businessman has a responsibility to pay for the services for which he has contracted. He does not have a "social responsibility" to pay for services unilaterally provided to him without his consent.

SOCIAL RESPONSIBILITIES ARE ARBITRARY

Social responsibility has no factual basis. CSR's proponents can, therefore, assert anything as a social responsibility without feeling the need to justify their assertion. CSR's proponents advocate some causes that are worthwhile, such as the Back to Sleep campaign. They often use the cover of social responsibility to advocate causes that reflect their political biases, however. The "ethical investing" and "divestiture" movements, for example, advocate defunding causes that the proponents of CSR personally oppose, such as the use of fossil fuels.

If a social activist goes to a businessman and says, "I think you should be promoting this cause because it is important to *me*," then he would be laughed out of the office. If a social activist says that "You have a social responsibility to promote this cause," then the businessman is ideologically cornered into promoting the cause or being labeled irresponsible.[78]

Individual responsibilities can be challenged. Defense lawyers do so all of the time. The prosecution alleges that John Doe is responsible for the death of his wife. The defense attorney responds by pointing out that John Doe's wife was killed by a gun that had someone else's fingerprints on it and that John Doe did not have gunpowder residue on his hands.

Social responsibilities cannot be similarly challenged. Since there are no social responsibilities, no evidence can be offered to show that a businessman has a particular social responsibility or to refute the allegation.

People are sometimes led to support CSR because they want businessmen to be held responsible for their actions. These people want businessmen to be held *individually responsible*. They do not conceive of the issue in terms of individual responsibilities because they have been indoctrinated with the philosophy of collectivism since kindergarten, and so cannot conceive of a responsibility that is not social.

The rejection of businessmen's *social* responsibilities does not mean the rejection of businessmen's *responsibilities*. It means acknowledging that businessmen have the only type of responsibilities that are, in fact, possible—responsibilities as *individuals*.

INVALID CONCEPTS

Binswanger notes that there are two types of invalid concepts. Some concepts are invalid because they conceptualize non-existing units; for example, "parapsychology," "telepathy," and "telekinesis."[79] Other concepts are invalid because they misclassify units.[80]

Let us focus on the second mistake. As an example of this type of error, Binswanger describes a biologist who decides to abandon the old classification system for living organisms. Instead of dividing living organisms into *plants* and *animals*, this biologist proposes that living organisms be divided into *stripes* and *solids*. The *striped kingdom* includes zebras, tigers, and certain snakes, bees, and plants. The *solid kingdom* includes horses, lions, and other snakes, bees, and plants, and all single-celled organisms.

This biologist decides to further divide the *striped* and *solid* kingdoms according to whether a living organism is *monochromatic* or *colored* and *elongated* or *not*. Thus, whales and oaks are *elongated, monochromatic sol-*

ids; tigers and honey bees are *polychromatic stripes*; and lions and other bees are *monochromatic non-long solids*.[81]

The result is conceptual chaos.

The living organisms that this biologist misclassifies exist. This biologist did not invent whales, oaks, tigers, lions, or honey bees. The characteristics on which this biologist misclassified them also exist. Whales and oaks *are* elongated, monochromatic solids. Tigers and honey bees *are* polychromatic stripes. Rejecting this biologist's method of classification does not imply that we have to deny the existence of whales or that whales are elongated monochromatic solids.

The standard by which to judge a concept's validity is whether the concept serves a cognitive need. Advancing a moral-political agenda is not a justification for inventing a concept. As Binswanger explains, "there is an *objective* right and wrong in how we classify. The basis of that right and wrong lies in the need to obey the identity of man's conceptual equipment" (emphasis in original).[82]

CSR is a hodgepodge because social responsibility cannot be a standard of classification. The CSR folder must end up being filled with items that do not belong together because there is no basis in reality for the grouping.

BUSINESS ETHICS

Conceptual errors are not innocuous. CSR's practical effect is to displace the field of business ethics. Dirk Matten and Jeremy Moon, for instance, assert that "business ethics" is the "second most common CSR programme label" in European business education, as though CSR is another name for business ethics.[83]

When philanthropy is discussed under the heading of "business ethics," it is an open question as to whether businesses should be philanthropic. When the issue is discussed under the heading of "CSR," however, the legitimacy of business philanthropy is closed to discussion. The ideological framework assumes that businessmen operate their businesses by permission of society, and the only question left is the amount of philanthropy needed to meet society's expectations.

When non-experts utter the acronym "CSR," they typically mean *ethics*, and would not necessarily endorse the ideological baggage that comes with CSR. They use "CSR" because the language of social responsibility is the only framework they know for discussing ethics in business.

REASONS MATTER

CSR's proponents advocate for philanthropy and cause marketing, which is consonant with profit maximization. CSR's proponents cite Avon and Pampers as examples of CSR, and these practices are consonant with profit maximization. It might seem, therefore, that this chapter overstates the differences between CSR and profit maximization. There might be significant *ideological* differences; there are, however, no differences in the *practical* outcome. Both sides agree that businessmen should be philanthropic, support particular causes, and have certain responsibilities.

Reasons matter. CSR's problem is not what it expects of businessmen but that it expects businessmen to do these things on the premise that they operate by permission of society. When businessmen are philanthropic or promote a particular cause *in CSR's name*, they concede the principle that they are merely society's servants and must operate their businesses to society's satisfaction.

I once heard a story that illustrates the importance of reasons. Even if the story is not historically accurate, it nevertheless illustrates a profound point.[84] Private companies constructed British railroads. These companies petitioned the British government to confiscate private land on which to build their railroads. The companies justified the confiscation of private property on the grounds that their railroads would serve the public interest. A few years later, the British government decided to nationalize the railroads in the name of the public interest. When the railroad companies objected in the name of the right to property, their protests fell on deaf ears. The politicians pointed out that the railroad companies had already conceded that private property could be confiscated for the public interest.

When companies such as Avon and Pampers act in CSR's name, they are harming themselves, whatever the superficial benefit from an improvement to their reputation, and the boosting of employee morale. This self-harm consists of reducing themselves to the role of servants and elevating society to the status of their master.

ARTICULATING THE VALUE OF A COMPANY'S PRODUCTS

CSR is not good public relations. A public relations campaign grounded in CSR must result in a company convincing the public that the company is its servant. The proper approach to public relations is the model introduced by philosopher Alex Epstein through his company Center for Industrial Progress. Epstein is the author of *The Moral Case for Fossil Fuels*, so he appreciates oil's value. Epstein works with oil companies to train their management teams and employees in the value of the product that they produce and how to articulate this value to others.

Avon does not improve its reputation and boost employee morale by supporting the pink ribbon campaign. Avon does so by educating its employees and the public in the value of its cosmetics.

Pampers does not improve its reputation and boost employee morale by supporting the Back to Sleep campaign. Pampers does so by educating its employees and the public in the value of its disposable diapers.

If businessmen believe that their company's CSR program is what is important about their company and that there is no value in its goods or services, then they should quit the business and become social workers. Most businessmen recognize, at least implicitly, that the goods or services that they produce are of value. They do not know how to articulate this value to themselves or others, however. Epstein is addressing this problem in the oil industry. A rational course in business ethics would address this problem for future business leaders.

Such a course needs to address three issues. First, a rational course in business ethics needs to teach business students that profit maximization is moral by explaining to them how the technical skills that they learn in their other subjects aim at the creation of value. Instructors of business ethics need to cultivate an idealism in their students for their chosen profession. CSR undermines students' self-esteem by teaching them that profit-maximizing businessmen do well but do not do good. Business students should be no less proud of their major than science or medical students.

Second, a rational course in business ethics needs to teach business students about the virtues needed to conceptualize value—the virtues of rationality, independence, honesty, integrity, justice, productiveness, and pride. Business students need to learn that pragmatism does not work.[85] To maximize profit, businessmen need to become principled leaders who prioritize integrity over short-term gains.[86] Too often, students see virtue as a threat to profit maximization, believing that the pursuit of profit requires them to compromise their character, a compromise that some are happy to make.[87] These students are wrong. As we saw in chapter 4, students need to cultivate a moral character to be successful businessmen.

Third, a rational course in business ethics needs to teach students how to apply the virtues to specific cases. Jaana Woiceshyn's *How to Be Profitable and Moral* gives students lessons on the application of the virtues to real-life cases. For example, Woiceshyn recounts a dilemma faced by one of her executive students. The student was a field engineer who uses explosives to perforate oil wells for the company's clients. On one job, the student used two perforating guns—one fired; the other did not. The client's employee believed that both guns had fired and informed his manager that the job was successful. Though the well would produce less oil, it is unlikely anyone would discover that only one gun had fired.[88] Should Woiceshyn's student have told the truth? Read the book to find the answer. For our purposes, what is important is that a course on business ethics needs to teach students how to apply principles such as rationality, honesty, and integrity to such cases.

A rational course in business ethics would not imply that business ethics is an oxymoron. Students should come away with an appreciation of the integration of ethics and profit.

ARGUMENTS FOR CSR

We have not engaged with the specific arguments in support of CSR, for two reasons. First, the debate must focus on the morality of self-interest versus the morality of altruism, not on profit maximization versus CSR. Resolve this debate, and we resolve a range of other debates, including the debate between profit maximization and CSR. Until this debate is resolved, the opposing sides will speak past each other.

Second, one cannot challenge arguments in support of an invalid concept. The facts of reality do not bind the defenders of such a concept. Consequently, they can continuously shift the terms of the debate to maintain their conclusion. If the proponents of profit maximization demonstrate the flaws with *an* argument for CSR, its proponents can shift to a different argument or tweak CSR's meaning.

CSR UNDERMINES BUSINESS ETHICS

Despite being treated as the equivalent of business ethics, CSR does not address ethics in business. CSR guides businessmen on how they can serve society alongside their business activities; it does not guide businessmen on how to conduct those activities ethically. Since CSR is about extending altruism into business, this finding should not be of surprise. Altruism is about *sacrificing* wealth and has nothing to say about *creating* the wealth that is to be sacrificed.

Sternberg points out that for a business's activities to be ethical, they must first be *business* activities. An activity that is not a business activity may be ethical, but it cannot be an example of ethics in *business*.[89] Avon's support for the pink ribbon campaign may be ethical. This activity is not a business activity, however, and, therefore, it cannot be cited to establish whether or not Avon is an ethical business. Telling Avon to support breast cancer research does not tell Avon how to conduct its *business* ethically.

A business can be ethical by CSR's standards and still be unethical in its business practices. This conclusion is not armchair speculation; it is evidenced by the history of business ethics. Enron, for example, was held up by

CSR's proponents as an example of an ethical business. Robert L. Bradley Jr. notes that academics widely respected Enron for its emphasis on CSR.[90] David Vogel notes that Enron "established a social responsibility task force . . . and was known for its generous philanthropic contributions."[91]

Similarly, CSR's proponents respected Fannie Mae for facilitating subprime mortgages to low-income earners. Marianne M. Jennings notes that the year before Fannie Mae was found to be manipulating earnings, *Business Ethics* ranked it "as the most ethical company in America."[92]

CSR's proponents misevaluated these companies because they evaluated their *side* activities, not their *business* activities. They were looking for evidence of ethics in the wrong place. This oversight is not accidental. CSR requires it. The proper approach is to advise businessmen on how to conduct their *business* activities ethically.

EVALUATING BUSINESSMEN OBJECTIVELY

CSR undermines our ability to evaluate businessmen objectively by introducing a goal that competes with profit maximization. Businessmen are evaluated by their ability to *maximize* profit *and* to *sacrifice* it. Depending on their success at either goal, a businessman can avoid accountability by switching the terms of evaluation. A businessman maximizing profit is happy to be evaluated by the standard of profit maximization. A businessman who is underperforming can excuse his poor performance by appealing to CSR. As Woiceshyn explains, "Lagging profits can always be excused by the promotion of a 'social good.'"[93]

This problem is inherent in attempting to evaluate a person by the standard of two *final* ends. This problem is compounded in CSR's case because it is an invalid concept. Recall Dow Votaw's observation: "The term [CSR] . . . means something, but not always the same thing, to everybody."[94] A businessman who is performing well by the standards of CSR-as-interpreted-by-his-investors may not be performing well by the standards of CSR-as-interpreted-by-Ralph-Nader.

The objective evaluation of businessmen requires an objective standard. Profit maximization provides this standard. CSR does not. Though CSR's proponents purport to bring accountability into business, an invalid concept is incapable of holding businessmen to account.

THE MORAL HIGH GROUND

Jim Steele was president of worldwide sales at Salesforce.com. He states that Salesforce's volunteer program "brought the notion of serving the community 'to real life'" for him.[95] He was happy working for a company that embraced community service from "day one" because he can go home to his family and say, "Look what I'm doing," and "be proud of it."[96] Consider the implications. Steele can stand before his family proud of doing community service. He cannot stand before his wife and children proud of the value created by Salesforce.

CSR's mantra is that businessmen should do good while doing well. Businessmen should not feel the need to make amends for maximizing profit. Profit signifies the creation of objective value. Businessmen, therefore, do good by doing well.

CSR does not recognize the good that businessmen do because CSR is an invalid concept created to advance the moral-political agenda of altruism and collectivism. By the standards of these moral and political philosophies, there is nothing morally good about creating value.

We can oppose CSR without opposing many of the activities advocated in CSR's name, such as philanthropy and cause marketing. To oppose CSR means to oppose uniting valid business activities with the philosophies of altruism and collectivism.

CSR implies that businessmen who want to take the moral high ground must reject profit maximization in favor of social responsibility. CSR's proponents are wrong. The moral high ground belongs to the maximizers of profit.

NOTES

1. Aristotle, "Physics," in *The Complete Works of Aristotle: The Revised Oxford Translation*, ed. Jonathan Barnes (Princeton, NJ: Princeton University Press, 1984), 332–33. Cf. Henry B. Veatch and Francis H. Parker, *Logic as a Human Instrument* (New York: Harper & Row, 1959), 226–27.
2. Rand gives a similar example in Ayn Rand, *The Art of Nonfiction: A Guide for Writers and Readers*, ed. Robert Mayhew (New York: Plume, 2001), 55–56.
3. Philip Kotler and Nancy Lee, *Corporate Social Responsibility: Doing the Most Good for Your Company and Your Cause* (Hoboken, NJ: John Wiley & Sons, 2005), 89–91; Michael E. Porter and Mark R. Kramer, "The Competitive Advantage of Corporate Philanthropy," in *Harvard Business Review on Corporate Responsibility* (Boston, MA: Harvard Business School Press, 2003), 53.
4. Kotler and Lee, *Corporate Social Responsibility*, 265.
5. Andrew Bernstein, *Capitalism Unbound: The Incontestable Moral Case for Individual Rights* (Lanham, MD: University Press of America, 2010), 52.
6. Kotler and Lee, *Corporate Social Responsibility*, 121–22.
7. Walter Isaacson, *Steve Jobs* (London: Little, Brown, 2011), 423–24.
8. Kotler and Lee, *Corporate Social Responsibility*, 55–56.
9. For reasons why we should be cautious about climate change alarmism, see Alex Epstein, *The Moral Case for Fossil Fuels* (New York: Penguin, 2014).
10. Ben and Jerry make a tenuous link by suggesting that climate change is a threat to their swirled ice cream. Their message is, in effect, save the planet, save your favorite ice cream.
11. Ben Cohen and Jerry Greenfield, *Ben & Jerry's Double-Dip: How to Run a Values-Led Business and Make Money, Too* (New York: Simon & Schuster, 1998). Note that the title of Ben and Jerry's book posits the pursuit of values as something different from making money.

12. Marc Benioff and Karen Southwick, *Compassionate Capitalism: How Corporations Can Make Doing Good an Integral Part of Doing Well* (Franklin Lakes, NJ: Career Press, 2004), 26.

13. See, for example, the BB&T Foundation's gift to establish the Wheeling Jesuit University's Institute for the Study of Capitalism. Edward W. Younkins, "Preface," in *Capitalism and Commerce in Imaginative Literature: Perspectives on Business from Novels and Plays*, ed. Edward W. Younkins (Lanham, MD: Lexington Books, 2016), xii.

14. For a discussion of BB&T's success under Allison's principled leadership, see Shelley A. Kirkpatrick, "Lead through Vision and Values," in *Handbook of Principles of Organizational Behavior*, ed. Edwin A. Locke (West Sussex: John Wiley & Sons, 2009).

15. Archie B. Carroll, "A History of Corporate Social Responsibility: Concepts and Practices," in *The Oxford Handbook of Corporate Social Responsibility*, ed. Andrew Crane et al. (Oxford: Oxford University Press, 2009), 25.

16. Howard R. Bowen, *Social Responsibilities of the Businessman* (New York: Harper & Brothers, 1953), 39. The Federal Council of the Churches of Christ in America holds the book's copyright, indicating the religious influence on Bowen's thinking.

17. Benioff and Southwick, *Compassionate Capitalism*, 19.

18. Ibid., 60.

19. Ibid., 213.

20. Quoted in Alex Epstein and Yaron Brook, "Why Conservatives Can't Stop the Growth of the State," in *Why Businessmen Need Philosophy: The Capitalist's Guide to the Ideas Behind Ayn Rand's* Atlas Shrugged, ed. Debi Ghate and Richard E. Ralston (New York: New American Library, 2011), 163.

21. Casey A. Klofstad, *Civic Talk: Peers, Politics, and the Future of Democracy* (Philadelphia: Temple University Press, 2011), 41.

22. Bruce Juell, *The Retirement Activities Guide: 165 Ideas for Finding Fulfillment and Meaning* (Rolling Hills Estate, CA: 3rd Age Press, 2006), 262.

23. Douglas Jacobsen and Rhonda Hustedt Jacobsen, *No Longer Invisible: Religion in University Education* (Oxford: Oxford University Press, 2012), 116.

24. Lucien Lévy-Bruhl, *The Philosophy of Auguste Comte* (London: Sonnenschein & Co., 1903), 310. John Stuart Mill notes that Comte did not support the Christian doctrine of love your neighbor as yourself because he believed that we should not love ourselves at all. John Stuart Mill, *Auguste Comte and Positivism* (London: Routledge, 1908), 138–39. For a discussion of Comte and altruism, see Leonard Peikoff, *The Ominous Parallels: The End of Freedom in America* (New York: Meridian, 1993), 85; Gregory Salmieri, "Egoism and Altruism: Selfishness and Sacrifice," in *A Companion to Ayn Rand*, ed. Allan Gotthelf and Gregory Salmieri (Malden, MA: John Wiley & Sons, 2016), 139–41.

25. John 13:1–17 NIV.

26. Bowen, *Social Responsibilities of the Businessman*, 33. Bowen defines "profit" as a businessman's share of the "national income," implying that the wealth created by businessmen originally belongs to society, and the question is how much of this income society should distribute to businessmen. P. 147.

27. F. Ernest Johnson, "Commentary on the Ethical Implications of the Study," in *Social Responsibilities of the Businessman*, by Howard R. Bowen (New York: Harper & Brothers, 1953), 242. Johnson based his conclusions on his reading of Bowen.

28. Domènec Melé, "Corporate Social Responsibility Theories," in *The Oxford Handbook of Corporate Social Responsibility*, ed. Andrew Crane et al. (Oxford: Oxford University Press, 2009), 49.

29. Quoted in Carroll, "A History of Corporate Social Responsibility," 29.

30. Norman E. Bowie, "Changing the Rules," in *Ethical Theory and Business*, ed. Tom L. Beauchamp and Norman E. Bowie (Englewood Cliffs, NJ: Prentice-Hall, 1983), 103.

31. Keith Davis and Robert L. Blomstrom, *Business, Society, and Environment: Social Power and Social Response* (New York: McGraw-Hill, 1971), 95.

32. For a discussion of the antitrust case against Microsoft, see Dominick T. Armentano, *Antitrust: The Case for Repeal*, revised 2nd ed. (Auburn: Ludwig von Mises Institute, 2007), 1–12; Robert White, "Ayn Rand Versus Adam Smith," *The Journal of Ayn Rand Studies* 7, no.

1 (Fall 2005): 167–74; Harry Binswanger, "Antitrust: 'Free Competition' at Gunpoint," in *The Abolition of Antitrust*, ed. Gary Hull (New Brunswick, NJ: Transaction Publishers, 2006), 133–38.

33. Quoted in Benioff and Southwick, *Compassionate Capitalism*, 138. Crompton is now in charge of employee giving at Apple.

34. Milton Friedman, "The Social Responsibility of Business Is to Increase Its Profits," in *Economic Morality: Ancient to Modern Readings*, ed. Henry C. Clark and Eric Allison (Lanham, MD: Lexington Books, 2015), 325.

35. Archie B. Carroll et al., *Corporate Responsibility: The American Experience* (Cambridge: Cambridge University Press, 2012), 344.

36. https://z.co.nz

37. *The Z Why* (Wellington: Z Energy, 2017), 51.

38. CSR's proponents seem to be advocating for what is commonly called "crony capitalism" (or, more appropriately, "crony *statism*").

39. Yaron Brook and Don Watkins, *Free Market Revolution: How Ayn Rand's Ideas Can End Big Government* (New York: Palgrave Macmillan, 2012), 115.

40. For a discussion of the argument from intimidation, which is widespread in the CSR literature, see Ayn Rand, "The Argument from Intimidation," in *The Virtue of Selfishness: A New Concept of Egoism* (New York: Signet, 1964).

41. Bowie, "Changing the Rules," 103.

42. For a discussion of the entity status of corporations, see Robert Hessen, *In Defense of the Corporation* (Stanford: Hoover Institution Press, 1979); Robert White, "Corporations Are People Too: An Argument for Corporate Moral Personhood," *The Journal of Ayn Rand Studies* 14, no. 2 (December 2014).

43. Hessen, *In Defense of the Corporation*, 15–22.

44. Leonard Peikoff, *Objectivism: The Philosophy of Ayn Rand* (New York: Meridian, 1993), 130.

45. Mark 12:43–44 NIV.

46. Epstein and Brook, "Why Conservatives Can't Stop the Growth of the State," 163.

47. Carroll et al., *Corporate Responsibility*, 6.

48. Quoted in ibid., 7.

49. Geoffrey P. Lantos, "The Boundaries of Strategic Corporate Social Responsibility," *Journal of Consumer Marketing* 18, no. 7 (2001): 595.

50. Jeremy Moon, "Corporate Social Responsibility: An Overview," in *International Directory of Corporate Philanthropy* (London: Europa Publications, 2002), 4.

51. Duane Windsor, "Corporate Social Responsibility: Three Key Approaches," *Journal of Management Studies* 43, no. 1 (January 2006): 94.

52. Andrew Crane et al., "The Corporate Social Responsibility Agenda," in *The Oxford Handbook of Corporate Social Responsibility*, ed. Andrew Crane et al. (Oxford: Oxford University Press, 2009), 6.

53. Harry Binswanger, *How We Know: Epistemology on an Objectivist Foundation* (New York: TOF Publications, 2014), 231.

54. Aristotle, "Nicomachean Ethics," in *The Complete Works of Aristotle: The Revised Oxford Translation*, ed. Jonathan Barnes (Princeton, NJ: Princeton University Press, 1984), 1754.

55. Ibid., 1758.

56. Ibid., 1752.

57. Ibid., 1754.

58. Ibid., 1755.

59. T. H. Irwin, "Reason and Responsibility in Aristotle," in *Essays on Aristotle's Ethics*, ed. Amélie Oksenberg Rorty (Berkeley: University of California Press, 1980), 131.

60. For an interesting survey of the competing theories of responsibility, see Diana Hsieh, *Responsibility & Luck: A Defense of Praise and Blame* (Sedalia, CO: Philosophy in Action, 2013).

61. Ayn Rand, *The Fountainhead* (London: HarperCollins, 1994), 665. Cf. C. Bradley Thompson, "Americanism and the Spirit of Liberty," in *A New Textbook of Americanism: The Politics of Ayn Rand*, ed. Jonathan Hoenig (Chicago: Capitalistpig Publications, 2018), 145–48.

62. For a discussion of the meaning and legitimacy of "society," see White, "Corporations Are People Too," 106–107.

63. Michael Muthukrishna and Joseph Henrich, "Innovation in the Collective Brain," *Philosophical Transactions* 371, no. 1690 (2016).

64. Ibid., 2 and 4.

65. Ibid., 1 and 4.

66. Thomas Donaldson, *Corporations and Morality* (Englewood Cliffs, NJ: Prentice-Hall, 1982), 20–21.

67. White, "Corporations Are People Too," 101.

68. Donaldson, *Corporations and Morality*, 21.

69. Catherine Pelonero, *Kitty Genovese: A True Account of a Public Murder and Its Private Consequences* (New York: Skyhorse Publishing, 2014). The traditional account of the Genovese case illustrates the problems with social responsibility, even though this account is now regarded as unreliable.

70. For a discussion of the relationship between independence and responsibility, see John A. Allison, *The Leadership Crisis and the Free Market Cure: Why the Future of Business Depends on the Return to Life, Liberty, and the Pursuit of Happiness* (New York: McGraw Hill, 2015), 41–42.

71. Bill Courtney, *Against the Grain: A Coach's Wisdom on Character, Faith, Family, and Love* (New York: Hachette Books, 2014), 148.

72. Quoted in ibid., 147.

73. Quoted in Joan Walsh, *What's the Matter with White People? Finding Our Way in the Next America* (New York: Touchstone, 2012), 300. Warren articulates an assumption common in the business ethics literature. Thomas Donaldson, for instance, claims that the needs of corporations are met by a "network of support systems," which include "roads, utilities, and . . . a labor pool which must itself be housed and provided with schools, parks, and commercial facilities." Donaldson, *Corporations and Morality*, 8.

74. Courtney, *Against the Grain*, 147.

75. Cf. Zane Ma Rhea, *Leading and Managing Indigenous Education in the Postcolonial World* (London: Routledge, 2015), 44.

76. Ayn Rand, "Man's Rights," in *The Virtue of Selfishness: A New Concept of Egoism* (New York: Signet, 1964), 113.

77. Frederick Engels, *The Condition of the Working-Class in England in 1844*, trans. Florence Kelley Wischnewetzky (Frankfurt: Outlook Verlag, 2019), 23.

78. An environmental control director observes that if a business proposal cannot be justified in terms of profit, the proposal's proponents assert that the proposal is justified on environmental grounds because then no one can object. The same observation applies to proposals justified based on CSR. Robert W. Ackerman, *The Social Challenge to Business* (Cambridge, MA: Harvard University Press, 1975), 292.

79. Binswanger, *How We Know*, 228–29.

80. Ibid., 229–32.

81. Ibid., 230.

82. Ibid., 230–31.

83. Dirk Matten and Jeremy Moon, "Corporate Social Responsibility Education in Europe," *Journal of Business Ethics* 54, no. 4 (2004): 326.

84. For a discussion of the importance of principles, see Leonard Peikoff, "Why Should One Act On Principle?" in *Why Businessmen Need Philosophy: The Capitalist's Guide to the Ideas Behind Ayn Rand's* Atlas Shrugged, ed. Debi Ghate and Richard E. Ralston (New York: New American Library, 2011).

85. For an explanation of why pragmatism is impractical, see Tara Smith, "The Menace of Pragmatism," *The Objective Standard* 3, no. 3 (Fall 2008).

86. For a discussion of the application of the virtues to leadership, see Allison, *The Leadership Crisis and the Free Market Cure*.

87. Their views are shared by Richard Sennett, *The Corrosion of Character: The Personal Consequences of Work in the New Capitalism* (New York: W. W. Norton, 1998).
88. Jaana Woiceshyn, *How to Be Profitable and Moral: A Rational Egoist Approach to Business* (Lanham, MD: Hamilton Books, 2012), 65.
89. Elaine Sternberg, "The Need for Realism in Business Ethics," *Reason Papers* 31 (Fall 2009): 34; Elaine Sternberg, *Just Business: Business Ethics in Action*, 2nd ed. (Oxford: Oxford University Press, 2000), 67.
90. Robert L. Bradley Jr., *Capitalism at Work: Business, Government, and Energy* (Salem, MA: M & M Scrivener Press, 2009), 8.
91. David Vogel, *The Market for Virtue: The Potential and Limits of Corporate Social Responsibility* (Washington, DC: The Brookings Institution, 2006), 38–39.
92. Marianne M. Jennings, "The Sloppiness of Business Ethics," *Reason Papers* 31 (Fall 2009): 109.
93. Woiceshyn, *How to Be Profitable and Moral*, 130.
94. Carroll et al., *Corporate Responsibility*, 7.
95. Benioff and Southwick, *Compassionate Capitalism*, 13.
96. Ibid., 15.

Conclusion

Profit maximization is moral because businessmen maximize profit by conceiving of the ends that goods and services can serve.

Profit maximization must meet two conditions to be moral. A businessman must produce goods or services that are of legitimate value (the "*what* condition") and must do so virtuously (the "*how* condition"). Profit maximization meets the first condition because businessmen maximize profit by conceptualizing values and conceiving of goods or services that can serve these values. Profit maximization meets the second condition because businessmen need to cultivate the virtues to conceptualize value.

In a free market, profit signifies a businessman's success at conceptualizing objective values. Profit is the market mechanism through which businessmen learn whether their value judgments are correct. In a regulated market, businessmen can maximize profit without creating goods or services that are of objective value. Still, profit maximization is only moral when businessmen seek to make profit from the creation of objective values.

Businessmen should *maximize* profit because profit maximization is foremost an intellectual enterprise. To maximize profit, businessmen must have active minds. A self-imposed limit on profit would be a self-imposed limit on thought.

The creation of the wheel, the refrigerator, and the shipping container evidence the claim that businessmen maximize profit through conceptualizing value. The lives of Morgan, Rockefeller, and Edison evidence the claim that businessmen need the virtues to conceptualize value.

The moral case for profit maximization does not require businessmen to set aside non-profit considerations, to prioritize profit above other values, or to extend a "market mentality" to every area of human life. The moral case for profit maximization also does not imply that businessmen are necessarily moral or that everyone is under a duty to maximize profit.

The traditional defenses of profit maximization are incomplete because they do not make a moral case. The case for profit maximization is traditionally framed in economic terms. The economic case cannot defend profit maximization on its own because morality trumps economics. Economic principles can form part of the evidence that a person takes into account when deciding a course of action. Morality, however, is the final determiner because morality establishes the ends that a person must strive to achieve.

Businessmen who choose profit maximization over corporate social responsibility take the moral high road. CSR is an invalid concept created to advance an altruist-collectivist agenda. Though CSR's proponents equate it with business ethics, CSR does not provide businessmen with guidance on how to conduct their businesses ethically. True business ethics is to be found in understanding businessmen's role in creating objective value and the virtues needed for them to do so.

Profit maximization is moral because the goods and services that we see all around us make our lives better off. Today's standard of living is made possible by the businessmen who conceived of dishwashers, video conference platforms, smartwatches, and countless other products, large and small, and the ends that these products serve.

INDUCTION'S ROLE

The moral case for profit maximization is *inductive*, not *deductive*.[1] We find the evidence for the morality of profit maximization in the world that we see around us, not in the deduction of conclusions from premises.

The moral case for profit maximization identifies the *one in the many*. The moral case for profit maximization is an abstract statement of the moral case for producing the supermarkets from which people purchase their weekly groceries, the cane our grandmother uses to walk, the smartphone that our daughter uses to navigate a new city, and the website that our wife uses to book family holidays.

Chapters 1 and 2 ground the concepts of "profit" and "value" in the facts of reality by identifying the facts that give rise to these concepts. Chapters 3 and 4 point the reader to the facts of reality that support the moral case for profit maximization.

Inductive arguments require intellectual work on the reader's part. This book indicates the evidence for the morality of profit maximization. To be convinced, you need to see the evidence first-hand by looking out at the world. Examining the words on this book's pages is insufficient.

Peikoff tells an instructive story of how the concept of "causality" became solidified in his mind. When Peikoff was young, his understanding of causality was abstract and not grounded in the facts that give rise to the concept. Rand suggested that Peikoff goes for a walk around New York City to look for examples of cause and effect. To Peikoff's surprise, he saw causality everywhere, in trucks turning, people moving, feathers floating, and planes flying.[2]

If you judge the ideas in this book worth exploring further, then you may find it useful to do a "causality walk" for profit maximization. For a day or even a week, give your mind a standing order to pay attention to the following issues:

How do the goods and services that you purchase serve your ends? You purchase running shoes. Why did you purchase *these* shoes from all of the other shoes that you could have bought?

Where do your purchases fit within your hierarchy of values? You purchased running shoes instead of purchasing a new book, taking your family out to dinner, or putting the money toward an overseas vacation. Why were these running shoes more important to you than the other things on which you could have spent this money?

How are your values expressed through the goods and services that you purchase? Did you purchase running shoes because you love running, or for some other reason?

Consider the thought that went into producing the goods and services that you purchase. Pay attention to the small items whose value you may overlook. Perhaps there is a ballpoint pen lying on your desk. Think about the chemistry and engineering problems that had to be solved to invent the ballpoint pen. The Biro brothers had to identify ink that dried quickly. They had to develop a ball-socket mechanism that would prevent the ink from drying while in the reservoir, and that would effectively transfer the ink from the reservoir to the paper.[3] In a world of smartphones and electronic paper, we take the ballpoint pen for granted. We must remind ourselves that, historically, such seemingly insignificant inventions are remarkable intellectual achievements deserving of our admiration.

Consider the virtues that a person had to cultivate to create these goods and services. In the case of the ballpoint pen, the Biro brothers brought into existence a device that surpassed all other writing instruments of the time and is still in use over eighty years later. What virtues did the Biro brothers need to achieve this feat? Do the people around you share these virtues?

Observe the double thank-you moments in your life. At the end of a taxi ride, you thank the driver, and the driver thanks you. These double thank-you moments reflect the fact that you both benefit from the trade. There have likely been numerous double thank-you moments in your life. You may not have noticed them before, let alone reflected on their philosophical significance.

BUSINESSMEN DO NOT NECESSARILY SUPPORT PROFIT MAXIMIZATION

The moral case for profit maximization does not depend on businessmen living up to the exalted view of profit defended in this book. Businessmen are experts on the particular goods and services that they produce, and they usually understand the value of these particular goods and services to their customers. Businessmen, however, are not philosophers, and there is no reason to expect businessmen to have a better grasp of profit maximization in the abstract than anyone else.

Some businessmen do not recognize that they are maximizing profit. These businessmen typically claim that they are concerned with creating value for their customers, not with profit maximization.[4] These businessmen do not recognize that the latter signifies their success at achieving the former, at least in a free market.

Some businessmen think that they are profit maximizers when they do not care about *what* they produce or *how* they produce it, so long as they get the cash.

The movie *Executive Suite* dramatizes this fallacy in the concluding boardroom scene. Loren Shaw argues that corporations must be financial institutions "yielding the highest and safest return on investment." His opponent, Don Walling, cites the quality of the K-F line as an example of the problem with Shaw's thinking. The K-F line's finish cracks, the veneer splits off, and the legs come loose. Shaw defends the K-F line's poor quality on the grounds that it is "price merchandise," which "serves a definite purpose in the profit structure of this company." Walling insists that if the Board appoints him CEO, the company will produce low-cost goods. These goods will not be low-cost because they are of poor quality, however. They will be low-cost because they are "new and different . . . as different from anything we're making today, as a modern automobile is different from a covered wagon." Customers, Walling argues, will want to purchase these low-cost goods because they have "beauty and function and *value*" (emphasis mine).[5]

Shaw thinks that he is the one aiming at profit maximization. He is wrong. Walling is the one concerned with profit maximization because he wants to produce a low-cost product that will be of value to his customers.

Critics might think that businessmen will love this book. Businessmen, however, have been raised in a culture of altruism like everyone else. Businessmen, therefore, do not necessarily want to think of themselves as profit maximizers and do not want other people to see them as such. Many businessmen are happy to accept the role of servants, and these businessmen would be the first to condemn a book defending their pursuit of profit.[6] For evidence, observe CSR's widespread appeal among businessmen.

PROFIT MAXIMIZATION'S NEGATIVE CONSEQUENCES

This book may be accused of downplaying the negative consequences of profit maximization. Businessmen's ethical breaches are acknowledged. The negative consequences of profit maximization are not. Much has been written about the supposed negatives of profit maximization. This book's purpose is to remind readers of the positives. The real negatives need to be judged in light of these benefits.

The *benefits* of profit maximization are the benefits of the goods and services that businessmen produce. The *negatives* are the negatives of these goods and services. The negatives are the negatives of supermarkets, hair salons, briefcases, spectacles, and smartwatches.

The negatives of goods and services are accounted for in the claim that goods and services are *values*. We do not weigh the value of a good or service against the negatives. Value judgments must take into account the negatives. To say, "This good (or service) is a *value*" is to say, in effect, that given the negatives of this good (or service), the benefits make the good (or service) worth pursuing.

Consider three negatives that arise from the production of certain goods and services—waste, digital addiction, and obesity.

Waste is a byproduct of the production of goods and services. Consider fumes from smokestacks, which is the classic symbol of the Industrial Revolution's many alleged evils. Inhaling these fumes is not good for one's health. When we assess the value status of these factories, we need to place the health hazards in context. If these factories more than double the human lifespan, then these factories—*with their toxic fumes*—are a value, because, all things considered, they make our lives better off.[7]

Of course, the fumes *are* a health hazard, and it is even better if we can negate their toxicity. The appropriate approach, however, is not to point to toxic fumes, out of context, as evidence of profit maximization's evil. The appropriate approach is to look at toxic fumes as a scientific problem to be solved. The same approach applies to all forms of waste.

Digital addiction and obesity are problems that would not exist without smartphones and fast food outlets. Similarly, car accidents would not exist without cars, and jet lag would not exist without jets. Cars and jets are not condemned, because these technologies are so thoroughly integrated into our lives that we cannot imagine our world without them.

Smartphones and fast food outlets make genuine contributions to our lives. The contributions of smartphones are too numerous to enumerate. Let me mention one. A smartphone, coupled with a smartwatch, saves lives. Kate Donald is a forty-year-old mother of three, who has epilepsy. While home alone, she suffered a seizure. She was wearing an Apple Watch Series 4. The watch detected the fall, and started tapping her on the wrist and sounded an alarm. When there was no response, the watch called emergency services and sent a text message to her husband. Kate's husband called a neighbor who let himself into the house. Seeing Kate on the floor, the neighbor called an ambulance, only to find that it was already on its way. The watch sent Kate's husband updates on her location as the ambulance drove her to the hospital.[8]

The contributions of fast food outlets may not be so obvious. Let us mention one benefit. The standardization of food across countries is a genuine value. There is value in having a diversity of foods and trying local cuisines. There are also times when there is value in eating something familiar. McDonald's can be a savior for the parents of a young child visiting a new country with exotic foods that the child finds uneatable.

Digital addiction, obesity, and similar problems are not the responsibility of businessmen. These problems arise from individuals not taking responsibility for their own lives. A smartphone's owner is responsible for ensuring that he uses the phone in a way that does not disrupt his sleep. McDonald's customers are responsible for how many meals they eat and whether they agree for their orders to be supersize.[9]

Profit maximization promotes solutions to the problems that arise from profit maximization. The negatives of production are opportunities for businessmen to create value.

Digital addiction is a genuine problem. Profit-maximizing businessmen offer digital detox holidays, spectacles that filter blue light, and operating systems and applications with "dark mode," all of which are designed to negate some of the problems associated with digital devices.

Obesity is also a genuine problem. Profit-maximizing businessmen create diet programs, self-help books, and gyms with personal trainers.

Assigning significance to the negatives of profit maximization is disingenuous when we live in a world where a robot can vacuum our house, we can ask a cylindric device in our living room to play from a catalog of over forty million songs, and in which we can explore the streets of every major city from a laptop or phone.

BUSINESSMEN ARE THE REAL DO-GOODERS

This book has not made a case for self-interest. Nevertheless, the moral case for profit maximization provides evidence of self-interest's morality. By the standards of self-interest, the life of a Morgan, a Rockefeller, and an Edison has moral merit. Consider the life that has moral merit by altruism's standards.

Larissa MacFarquhar tells the true story of "do-gooders" Charles and Dorothy in her book *Strangers Drowning*. Charles earns a minuscule wage as a carpenter, while Dorothy works part time in a nursing home. Charles and Dorothy live in a shared house. Charles suggests to Dorothy that they should live on the street so that they can give their rent money to people who need it more.[10]

By altruism's standards, Charles is a do-gooder because he wants to sacrifice his wages for the sake of those more in need. Morgan, Rockefeller, and Edison were not do-gooders, by this standard, because they did not sacrifice.

The moral case for profit maximization challenges us to question our moral assumptions. By a properly self-interested standard of morality, Morgan, Rockefeller, and Edison are the real do-gooders. The life of a Charles must be expunged from the smorgasbord of lives from which we may legitimately choose.

ACKNOWLEDGMENTS

In the spirit of the moral case for profit maximization, I would like to acknowledge the businessmen who have contributed to this book. Of course, these businessmen have not read this book, and may not agree with my thesis, so acknowledging their contribution does not imply their endorsement.

I want to acknowledge

—Adam Leeb and Patrick Paul for creating the Freewrite, on which I wrote the first draft. For years I struggled with premature editing. The Freewrite is designed to solve this problem.

—Steve Jobs and Bill Gates for creating the MacBook Pro and Microsoft Word, on which I completed this book.

—The software engineers at Thomson Reuters for creating Endnote, which I used to manage the book's citations and compile the bibliography. Anyone who has struggled to conform citations to a single style will appreciate Endnote's value.

—Jeff Bezos for creating Amazon. I can order a physical book online, and it will arrive within a week. I can also order a digital book online, and it will appear on my Kindle within seconds. As someone who used to wait over six months for books to ship from the United States to New Zealand, in the pre-Amazon era, I cannot overstate the value that Amazon creates in my life.

THE SPIRITUAL FUEL THAT BUSINESSMEN PROVIDE US

I am an optimist. There are good reasons for being worried about the state of the culture and the political direction of the world. If I focused exclusively on culture and politics, I would have to be a pessimist. My optimism is maintained because I live in a world in which smartphones, smartwatches, robotic vacuum cleaners, and driverless cars are possible. Rarely mentioned in discussions of profit maximization is the spiritual fuel that businessmen provide to the rest of us in demonstrating the greatness of which human beings are still capable.[11]

In his epic documentary series *The Ascent of Man*, Jacob Bronowski observes that the "most powerful drive in the ascent of man is his pleasure in his own skill. He loves to do what he does well and, having done it well, he loves to do it better."[12] Bronowski notes that we can see this pleasure in science and art. I would add that we can also observe this pleasure in business. And what a marvelous sight it is.

There are days of the year on which we honor children, women, manual laborers, and soldiers who died in battle. Perhaps there should also be a day on which we raise a glass to the businessmen who carry the world on their shoulders and say, "Well done."

NOTES

1. For a defense of induction, see David Harriman, *The Logical Leap: Induction in Physics* (New York: New American Library, 2010).
2. Leonard Peikoff, *Objective Communication: Writing, Speaking, and Arguing*, ed. Barry Wood (New York: New American Library, 2013), 30.
3. For a history of the ballpoint pen, see György Moldova, *Ballpoint: A Tale of Genius and Grit, Perilous Times, and the Invention That Changed the Way We Write*, trans. David Robert Evans (North Adams, MA: New Europe Books, 2012).
4. Max Anderson and Peter Escher, *The MBA Oath: Setting a Higher Standard for Business Leaders* (New York: Portfolio, 2010), 86–87. Anderson and Escher give the example of Big Profit Paste, an imaginary toothpaste company that substitutes an ingredient with a cheaper, less effective one, in order to lower the costs of production and thereby maximize its profit. Anderson and Escher claim that a company would fail to maximize profit if it were to reject the substitute in the name of creating value for its customers.
5. Ernest Lehman, *Executive Suite* (Metro-Goldwyn-Mayer, 1954), 1 hour, 32 min. For a discussion of the movie *Executive Suite*, see Edward W. Younkins, *Exploring Capitalist Fiction: Business through Literature and Film* (Lanham, MD: Lexington Books, 2014), 137–45.
6. Robert K. Greenleaf attempts to reconcile the religious belief in service to others with business leadership through the idea of "servant-leadership." Greenleaf was influential among business leaders because he provided a rationalization for businessmen to pretend to themselves that their business success is altruistic. Robert K. Greenleaf, *Servant Leadership: A Journey into the Nature of Legitimate Power and Greatness*, 25th anniversary ed. (Mahway, NJ: Paulist Press, 2002). For an example of a CEO who followed Greenleaf's philosophy, see Cheryl Bachelder, *Dare to Serve: How to Drive Superior Results by Serving Others* (Oakland, CA: Berrett-Koehler Publishers, 2015).

7. For an explanation of the philosophical flaws with this type of argument, see Ayn Rand, "The Anti-Industrial Revolution," in *Return of the Primitive: The Anti-Industrial Revolution*, ed. Peter Schwartz, new expanded edition of *The New Left: The Anti-Industrial Revolution* (New York: Meridian, 1999).

8. Stephanie Bedo, "Emergency Texts from Apple Watch Set Off Chain Reaction to Save Mum-of-Three's Life," *news.com.au* (31 July 2019).

9. The movie *Super Size Me* claims that McDonald's promotes poor nutrition for its own profit. Morgan Spurlock, *Super Size Me* (The Con, 2004). The rules governing the self-described "experiment" require Spurlock to grant control over his diet to McDonald's. Spurlock does not take responsibility for his meals.

10. Larissa MacFarquhar, *Strangers Drowning: Voyages to the Brink of Moral Extremity* (New York: Penguin Press, 2015), 31–32.

11. For a description of a culture that celebrated human achievement in a way unimaginable to current generations, see Leonard Peikoff, *Why Ancient Greece Is My Favorite Civilization* (Irvine, CA: Ayn Rand Institute, 1997).

12. Jacob Bronowski, *The Ascent of Man* (London: BBC Books, 2011), 93.

Bibliography

Ackerman, Robert W. *The Social Challenge to Business*. Cambridge, MA: Harvard University Press, 1975.

Allison, John A. "Foreword." In *Perspectives on Ayn Rand's Contributions to Economic and Business Thought*, edited by Edward W. Younkins, xiii–xiv. Lanham, MD: Lexington Books, 2018.

———. *The Leadership Crisis and the Free Market Cure: Why the Future of Business Depends on the Return to Life, Liberty, and the Pursuit of Happiness*. New York: McGraw Hill, 2015.

Anderson, Max, and Peter Escher. *The MBA Oath: Setting a Higher Standard for Business Leaders*. New York: Portfolio, 2010.

Anthony, Robert N. "The Trouble with Profit Maximization." *Harvard Business Review* 38, no. 6 (1960): 127–34.

Aristotle. "Nicomachean Ethics." Translated by W. D. Ross and J. O. Urmson. In *The Complete Works of Aristotle: The Revised Oxford Translation*, edited by Jonathan Barnes, 1729–867. Vol. 2. Princeton, NJ: Princeton University Press, 1984.

———. "Physics." Translated by R. P. Hardie and R. K. Gaye. In *The Complete Works of Aristotle: The Revised Oxford Translation*, edited by Jonathan Barnes, 315–446. Vol. 1. Princeton, NJ: Princeton University Press, 1984.

Armentano, Dominick T. *Antitrust and Monopoly: Anatomy of a Policy Failure*. Second ed. Oakland, CA: The Independent Institute, 1990.

———. *Antitrust: The Case for Repeal*. Revised 2nd ed. Auburn: Ludwig von Mises Institute, 2007.

Asongu, J. J. *Strategic Corporate Social Responsibility in Practice*. Lawrenceville, GA: Greenview Publishing Company, 2007.

Bachelder, Cheryl. *Dare to Serve: How to Drive Superior Results by Serving Others*. Oakland, CA: Berrett-Koehler Publishers, 2015.

Baier, Kurt. "Egoism." In *A Companion to Ethics*, edited by Peter Singer, 197–204. Oxford: Blackwell Reference, 1991.

Bakan, Joel. *The Corporation: The Pathological Pursuit of Profit and Power*. New York: Free Press, 2004.

Baynes, Chris. "New Zealand's New Prime Minister Calls Capitalism a 'Blatant Failure.'" *Independent* (21 October 2017).

Bedo, Stephanie. "Emergency Texts from Apple Watch Set Off Chain Reaction to Save Mum-of-Three's Life." *news.com.au* (31 July 2019).

Benioff, Marc, and Karen Southwick. *Compassionate Capitalism: How Corporations Can Make Doing Good an Integral Part of Doing Well*. Franklin Lakes, NJ: Career Press, 2004.

Berliner, Michael S., ed. *Letters of Ayn Rand*. New York: Dutton, 1995.

Bernstein, Andrew. *Capitalism Unbound: The Incontestable Moral Case for Individual Rights*. Lanham, MD: University Press of America, 2010.

———. "Heroes and Villains in American Education." *The Objective Standard* 13, no. 3 (Fall 2018): 14–40.

Binswanger, Harry. "Antitrust: 'Free Competition' at Gunpoint." In *The Abolition of Antitrust*, edited by Gary Hull, 121–42. New Brunswick, NJ: Transaction Publishers, 2006.

———. *How We Know: Epistemology on an Objectivist Foundation*. New York: TOF Publications, 2014.

Biondi, Carrie-Ann. "Counter-Culture Capitalist." In *Steve Jobs and Philosophy: For Those Who Think Different*, edited by Shawn E. Klein, 15–25. Chicago: Open Court, 2015.

Bolton, Bill, and John Thompson. *Entrepreneurs: Talent, Temperament and Opportunity*. 3rd ed. Oxon: Routledge, 2013.

Bowden, Thomas A. "Antitrust: The War against Contract." In *The Abolition of Antitrust*, edited by Gary Hull, 95–118. New Brunswick, NJ: Transaction Publishers, 2006.

Bowen, Howard R. *Social Responsibilities of the Businessman*. New York: Harper & Brothers, 1953.

Bowie, Norman E. "Business Ethics." In *New Directions in Ethics: The Challenge of Applied Ethics*, edited by Joseph P. DeMarco and Richard M. Fox, 158–72. New York: Routledge & Kegan Paul, 1986.

———. "Changing the Rules." In *Ethical Theory and Business*, edited by Tom L. Beauchamp and Norman E. Bowie, 103–106. Englewood Cliffs, NJ: Prentice-Hall, 1983.

Bradley Jr., Robert L. *Capitalism at Work: Business, Government, and Energy*. Salem, MA: M & M Scrivener Press, 2009.

Branden, Nathaniel. "Alienation." In *Capitalism: The Unknown Ideal*, edited by Ayn Rand, 270–96. New York: Signet, 1967.

———. *The Psychology of Self-Esteem: A Revolutionary Approach to Self-Understanding That Launched a New Era in Modern Psychology*. 32nd anniversary ed. San Francisco: Jossey-Bass, 2001.

Brennan, Jason. "Do Markets Corrupt?" In *Economics and the Virtues: Building a New Moral Foundation*, edited by Jennifer Baker and Mark D. White, 236–55. Oxford: Oxford University Press, 2016.

Bronowski, Jacob. *The Ascent of Man*. London: BBC Books, 2011.

Brook, Yaron, and Don Watkins. *Equal Is Unfair: America's Misguided Fight Against Income Inequality*. New York: St. Martin's Press, 2016.

———. *Free Market Revolution: How Ayn Rand's Ideas Can End Big Government*. New York: Palgrave Macmillan, 2012.

———, eds. *In Pursuit of Wealth: The Moral Case for Finance*. Irvine, CA: Ayn Rand Institute Press, 2017.

Brooks, Leonard J., and Paul Dunn. *Business and Professional Ethics for Directors, Executives & Accountants*. 8th ed. Boston, MA: Cengage Learning, 2017.

Buch, Esteban. *Beethoven's Ninth: A Political History*. Translated by Richard Miller. Chicago: University of Chicago Press, 2004.

Buechner, M. Northrup. *Objective Economics: How Ayn Rand's Philosophy Changes Everything about Economics*. Lanham, MD: University Press of America, 2011.

Bulliet, Richard W. *The Wheel: Inventions & Reinventions*. New York: Columbia University Press, 2016.

Burnett, Gene M. *Florida's Past: People and Events that Shaped the State*. Vol. 2. Sarasota, FL: Pineapple Press, 1988.

Carroll, Archie B. "A History of Corporate Social Responsibility: Concepts and Practices." In *The Oxford Handbook of Corporate Social Responsibility*, edited by Andrew Crane, Abagail McWilliams, Dirk Matten, Jeremy Moon, and Donald S. Siegel, 19–46. Oxford: Oxford University Press, 2009.

Carroll, Archie B., Kenneth J. Lipartito, James E. Post, Patricia H. Werhane, and Kenneth E. Goodpaster. *Corporate Responsibility: The American Experience*. Cambridge: Cambridge University Press, 2012.

Carson, Rachel. *Silent Spring*. 40th anniversary ed. New York: Mariner Books, 2002.
Carson, Thomas L. "Friedman's Theory of Corporate Social Responsibility." *Business and Professional Ethics Journal* 12, no. 1 (1993): 3–32.
———. "My Correspondence with Milton Friedman about the Social Responsibilities of Business." *Business and Society Review* 123, no. 2 (2018): 217–42.
Chernow, Ron. *Titan: The Life of John D. Rockefeller, Sr.* New York: Vintage Books, 1998.
Chonko, Larry B., and Eli Jones. "Sales Force Agility, Strategic Thinking, and Value Propositions." In *The Oxford Handbook of Strategic Sales and Sales Management*, edited by David W. Cravens, Kenneth Le Meunier-FitzHugh, and Nigel F. Piercy, 518–38. Oxford: Oxford University Press, 2012.
Cipolla, Carlo M. *Before the Industrial Revolution: European Society and Economy, 1000–1700*. 3rd ed. New York: W. W. Norton, 1984.
Clark, Henry C., and Eric Allison, eds. *Economic Morality: Ancient to Modern Readings*. Lanham, MD: Lexington Books, 2015.
Clarkson, Kenneth W., Roger LeRoy Miller, and Frank B. Cross. *Business Law: Text and Cases*. 13th ed. Stamford, CT: Cengage Learning, 2014.
Coffee, John C. "'No Soul to Damn: No Body to Kick': An Unscandalized Inquiry into the Problem of Corporate Punishment." *Michigan Law Review* 79, no. 3 (1981): 386–459.
Cohen, Ben, and Jerry Greenfield. *Ben & Jerry's Double-Dip: How to Run a Values-Led Business and Make Money, Too*. New York: Simon & Schuster, 1998.
Cohen, William. "Occupy Wall St Movement an Exercise in Contradictions." *New Zealand Herald* (18 October 2011).
Coppola, Francis Ford, and Mario Puzo. *The Godfather*. Directed by Francis Ford Coppola. Movie. Paramount Pictures, 1972.
———. *The Godfather Part II.* Directed by Francis Ford Coppola. Movie. Paramount Pictures, 1974.
Cornut-Gentille d'Arcy, Chantal. "*Absolutely Fabulous*: 'Money Makes the World Go Round' or a Politicised Notion of Fulfilment." In *Culture and Power: Challenging Discourses*, edited by María José Coperías Aguilar, 59–70. València: Universitat de València, 2000.
Courtney, Bill. *Against the Grain: A Coach's Wisdom on Character, Faith, Family, and Love*. New York: Hachette Books, 2014.
Courtois, Stéphane, Nicolas Werth, Jean-Louis Panné, Andrezej Paczkowski, Karel Bartošek, and Jean-Louis Margolin. *The Black Book of Communism: Crimes, Terror, Repression*. Translated by Jonathan Murphy and Mark Kramer. Cambridge, MA: Harvard University Press, 1999.
Cowan, Robin, and Mario J. Rizzo. "Fundamental Issues in the Justification of Profits." In *Profits and Morality*, edited by Robin Cowan and Mario J. Rizzo, 1–21. Chicago: The University of Chicago Press, 1995.
Crane, Andrew, Abagail McWilliams, Dirk Matten, Jeremy Moon, and Donald S. Siegel. "Conclusion." In *The Oxford Handbook of Corporate Social Responsibility*, edited by Andrew Crane, Abagail McWilliams, Dirk Matten, Jeremy Moon, and Donald S. Siegel, 568–75. Oxford: Oxford University Press, 2009.
———. "The Corporate Social Responsibility Agenda." In *The Oxford Handbook of Corporate Social Responsibility*, edited by Andrew Crane, Abagail McWilliams, Dirk Matten, Jeremy Moon, and Donald S. Siegel, 3–15. Oxford: Oxford University Press, 2009.
Cusumano, Michael A. *The Business of Software: What Every Manager, Programmer, and Entrepreneur Must Know to Thrive and Survive in Good Times and Bad*. New York: Free Press, 2004.
Daniels, Eric. "Reversing Course: American Attitudes about Monopolies, 1607-1890." In *The Abolition of Antitrust*, edited by Gary Hull, 63–94. New Brunswick, NJ: Transaction Publishers, 2006.
Davies, Russell T., and Benjamin Cook. *The Writer's Tale: The Final Chapter*. London: BBC Books, 2010.
Davis, Keith. "The Case for and Against Business Assumption of Social Responsibilities." *The Academy of Management Journal* 16, no. 2 (June 1973): 312–22.

Davis, Keith, and Robert L. Blomstrom. *Business, Society, and Environment: Social Power and Social Response*. New York: McGraw-Hill, 1971.
Debré, Patrice. *Louis Pasteur*. Translated by Elborg Forster. Baltimore: The Johns Hopkins University Press, 1998.
Den Uyl, Douglas J., and Douglas B. Rasmussen. *Liberty and Nature: An Aristotelian Defense of Liberal Order*. La Salle, IL: Open Court, 1991.
Diamandis, Peter H., and Steven Kotler. *Abundance: The Future Is Better Than You Think*. New York: Free Press, 2012.
Dobson, Geoffrey P. *A Chaos of Delight: Science, Religion and Myth and the Shaping of Western Thought*. Oxon: Routledge, 2014.
Donaldson, Thomas. *Corporations and Morality*. Englewood Cliffs, NJ: Prentice-Hall, 1982.
Drewitt, F. Dawtry. *The Life of Edward Jenner: Naturalist, and Discoverer of Vaccination*. Cambridge: Cambridge University Press, 2013.
Dube, Allison. "In Defence of a Utilitarian University Education." In *Liberal Education and the Idea of the University: Arguments and Reflections on Theory and Practice*, edited by Karim Dharamsi and James Zimmer, 61–84. Wilmington, DE: Vernon Press, 2019.
Engels, Frederick. *The Condition of the Working-Class in England in 1844*. Translated by Florence Kelley Wischnewetzky. Frankfurt: Outlook Verlag, 2019.
Epstein, Alex. *The Moral Case for Fossil Fuels*. New York: Penguin, 2014.
Epstein, Alex, and Yaron Brook. "Why Conservatives Can't Stop the Growth of the State." In *Why Businessmen Need Philosophy: The Capitalist's Guide to the Ideas Behind Ayn Rand's* Atlas Shrugged, edited by Debi Ghate and Richard E. Ralston, 147–68. New York: New American Library, 2011.
Etzioni, Amitai. "Introduction: Voluntary Simplicity—Psychological Implications, Societal Consequences." In *Voluntary Simplicity: Responding to Consumer Culture*, edited by Daniel Doherty and Amitai Etzioni, 1–25. Lanham, MD: Rowman & Littlefield, 2003.
Folsom, Burton W. *The Myth of the Robber Barons: A New Look at the Rise of Big Business in America*. 5th ed. Herndon, VA: Young America's Foundation, 2007.
Francis. *Apostolic Exhortation: Evangelii Gaudium of the Holy Father Francis to the Bishops, Clergy, Consecrated Persons and the Lay Faithful on the Proclamation of the Gospel in Today's World*. Vatican City: Vatican Press, 2013.
Franklin, Paul M., and Nancy Mikula. *Backroads of Florida: Your Guide to Great Day Trips and Weekend Getaways*. Minneapolis: Voyageur Press, 2009.
Friedman, Milton. *Capitalism and Freedom*. Fortieth anniversary ed. Chicago: The University of Chicago Press, 2002.
———. "The Social Responsibility of Business Is to Increase Its Profits." In *Economic Morality: Ancient to Modern Readings*, edited by Henry C. Clark and Eric Allison, 320–27. Lanham, MD: Lexington Books, 2015.
Galbraith, John Kenneth. *The Affluent Society*. Cambridge, MA: Riverside Press, 1958.
Gantz, Carroll. *Refrigeration: A History*. Jefferson, NC: McFarland & Company, 2015.
Ghate, Debi. "The Businessmen's Crucial Role: Material Men of the Mind." In *Why Businessmen Need Philosophy: The Capitalist's Guide to the Ideas Behind Ayn Rand's* Atlas Shrugged, edited by Debi Ghate and Richard E. Ralston, 45–64. New York: New American, 2011.
Goldsmith, M. M. *Private Vices, Public Benefits: Bernard Mandeville's Social and Political Thought*. Cambridge: Cambridge University Press, 1985.
Gotthelf, Allan. "Ayn Rand's Theory of Concepts: Rethinking Abstraction and Essence." In *Concepts and Their Role in Knowledge: Reflections on Objectivist Epistemology*, edited by Allan Gotthelf and James G. Lennox, 3–40. Pittsburgh: University of Pittsburgh Press, 2013.
———. *Teleology, First Principles, and Scientific Method in Aristotle's Biology*. Oxford: Oxford University Press, 2012.
Gray, Jamie. "Insurance Company Boards Must Act Now to Fix Culture and Conduct, FMA Boss Says." *New Zealand Herald* (29 January 2019).
Gray, John. *Men Are from Mars, Women Are from Venus: The Classic Guide to Understanding the Opposite Sex*. 20th anniversary ed. New York: Harper, 2012.

Greenleaf, Robert K. *Servant Leadership: A Journey into the Nature of Legitimate Power and Greatness*. 25th anniversary ed. Mahwah, NJ: Paulist Press, 2002.

Greenspan, Alan. "Antitrust." In *Capitalism: The Unknown Ideal*, edited by Ayn Rand, 63–71. New York: Signet, 1967.

Greiner, Donna, and Theodore B. Kinni. *Ayn Rand and Business*. New York: Texere, 2001.

Haig, Matt. *Brand Failures: The Truth about the 100 Biggest Branding Mistakes of All Time*. London: Kogan Page, 2005.

Hammer, Michael. "Violent Music: Sony, Slayer, and Self-Regulation." In *Case Studies in Business, Society, and Ethics*, edited by Tom L. Beauchamp, 87–92. 5th ed. Upper Saddle River, NJ: Pearson Education, 2004.

Harriman, David. *The Logical Leap: Induction in Physics*. New York: New American Library, 2010.

Hawkesby, Kate. "Roseanne, Racism and Choosing Values over Profit." *New Zealand Herald* (31 May 2018).

Hayek, F. A. "The Pretence of Knowledge." *The American Economic Review* 79, no. 6 (December 1989): 3–7.

Hazlitt, Henry. *Economics in One Lesson*. 50th anniversary ed. San Francisco: Laissez Faire Books, 1996.

Heal, Geoffrey. *When Principles Pay: Corporate Social Responsibility and the Bottom Line*. New York: Columbia University Press, 2008.

Hessen, Robert. *In Defense of the Corporation*. Stanford: Hoover Institution Press, 1979.

Hilse, Audra. "Norman Borlaug: The Man Who Taught People to Feed Themselves." *The Objective Standard* 5, no. 1 (Spring 2010): 69–74.

Hitchens, Christopher. *The Missionary Position: Mother Teresa in Theory and Practice*. London: Verso, 1995.

Hospers, John. "Ayn Rand's Philosophical Significance." *Reason Papers*, no. 23 (Fall 1998): 92–95.

Hsieh, Diana. *Responsibility & Luck: A Defense of Praise and Blame*. Sedalia, CO: Philosophy in Action, 2013.

Huemer, Michael. "Is Benevolent Egoism Coherent?" *The Journal of Ayn Rand Studies* 3, no. 2 (Spring 2002): 259–88.

Hull, Gary, ed. *The Abolition of Antitrust*. New Brunswick, NJ: Transaction Publishers, 2006.

Hume, David. *A Treatise of Human Nature*. Edited by L. A. Selby-Bigge. Oxford: Clarendon Press, 1958.

Irwin, T. H. "Reason and Responsibility in Aristotle." In *Essays on Aristotle's Ethics*, edited by Amélie Oksenberg Rorty, 117–55. Berkeley: University of California Press, 1980.

Isaacson, Walter. *Steve Jobs*. London: Little, Brown, 2011.

Izzo, John, and Jeff Vanderwielen. *The Purpose Revolution: How Leaders Create Engagement and Competitive Advantage in an Age of Social Good*. Oakland, CA: Berrett-Koehler Publishers, 2018.

Jackson, Peter, director. *They Shall Not Grow Old*. Movie. WingNut Films, 2018.

Jacobsen, Douglas, and Rhonda Hustedt Jacobsen. *No Longer Invisible: Religion in University Education*. Oxford: Oxford University Press, 2012.

Jennings, Marianne M. *Business Ethics: Case Studies and Selected Readings*. 8th ed. Stamford, CT: Cengage Learning, 2015.

———. "The Sloppiness of Business Ethics." *Reason Papers* 31 (Fall 2009): 109–24.

Johnson, Ericka. *Dreaming of a Mail-Order Husband: Russian-American Internet Romance*. Durham, NC: Duke University Press, 2007.

Johnson, F. Ernest. "Commentary on the Ethical Implications of the Study." In *Social Responsibilities of the Businessman*, by Howard R. Bowen, 233–59. New York: Harper & Brothers, 1953.

Josephson, Matthew. *Edison: A Biography*. New York: History Book Club, 1959.

Journo, Elan. "What Motivates the Jihad on America." In *Winning the Unwinnable War: America's Self-Crippled Response to Islamic Totalitarianism*, edited by Elan Journo, 23–50. Lanham, MD: Lexington Books, 2009.

Juell, Bruce. *The Retirement Activities Guide: 165 Ideas for Finding Fulfillment and Meaning*. Rolling Hills Estate, CA: 3rd Age Press, 2006.

Kahan, Alan S. *Mind vs. Money: The War between Intellectuals and Capitalism*. New Brunswick, NJ: Transaction Publishers, 2010.

Kant, Immanuel. *Critique of Pure Reason*. Translated by Norman Kemp Smith. London: MacMillan, 1929.

Kelley, David. *A Life of One's Own: Individual Rights and the Welfare State*. Washington, DC: Cato Institute, 1998.

Kirkpatrick, Jerry. *In Defense of Advertising: Arguments from Reason, Ethical Egoism, and Laissez-Faire Capitalism*. Claremont, CA: TLJ Books, 2007.

Kirkpatrick, Shelley A. "Lead through Vision and Values." In *Handbook of Principles of Organizational Behavior*, edited by Edwin A. Locke, 367–87. West Sussex: John Wiley & Sons, 2009.

Klein, Naomi. *No Logo: No Space, No Choice, No Jobs*. 10th anniversary ed. New York: Picador, 2010.

Klofstad, Casey A. *Civic Talk: Peers, Politics, and the Future of Democracy*. Philadelphia: Temple University Press, 2011.

Kotler, Philip, and Nancy Lee. *Corporate Social Responsibility: Doing the Most Good for Your Company and Your Cause*. Hoboken, NJ: John Wiley & Sons, 2005.

Kottler, Jeffrey A. *Doing Good: Passion and Commitment for Helping Others*. Philadelphia: Brunner-Routledge, 2000.

Lantos, Geoffrey P. "The Boundaries of Strategic Corporate Social Responsibility." *Journal of Consumer Marketing* 18, no. 7 (2001): 595–632.

Lasbury, Mark E. *The Realization of Star Trek Technologies: The Science, Not Fiction, Behind Brain Implants, Plasma Shields, Quantum Computing, and More*. Switzerland: Springer, 2017.

Leeper, Mary Ann. "Social Commitment and Entrepreneurship." In *Women in Business: The Changing Face of Leadership*, edited by Patricia Werhane, Margaret Posig, Lisa Gundry, Laurel Ofstein, and Elizabeth Powell, 99–108. Westport: Praeger Publishers, 2007.

Lehman, Ernest. *Executive Suite*. Directed by Robert Wise. Movie. Metro-Goldwyn-Mayer, 1954.

Leonard, Annie. *The Story of Stuff: How Our Obsession with Stuff Is Trashing the Planet, Our Communities, and Our Health—and a Vision for Change*. New York: Free Press, 2010.

Levinson, Marc. *The Box: How the Shipping Container Made the World Smaller and the World Economy Bigger*. Second ed. Princeton, NJ: Princeton University Press, 2016.

Lévy-Bruhl, Lucien. *The Philosophy of Auguste Comte*. London: Sonnenschein & Co., 1903.

Lewis, C. S. *Mere Christianity*. Revised and amplified ed. [London]: Collins, 1958.

Lewis, John David. *Nothing Less Than Victory: Decisive Wars and the Lessons of History*. Princeton, NJ: Princeton University Press, 2010.

Locke, Edwin A. *The Prime Movers: Traits of the Great Wealth Creators*. Second ed. Irvine, CA: The Ayn Rand Bookstore, 2008.

———. "The Traits of Business Heroes in *Atlas Shrugged*." In *Perspectives on Ayn Rand's Contributions to Economic and Business Thought*, edited by Edward W. Younkins, 203–21. Lanham, MD: Lexington Books, 2018.

Locke, Edwin A., and Ellen Kenner. *The Selfish Path to Romance: How to Love with Passion and Reason*. Doylestown, PA: Platform Press, 2011.

Locke, Edwin A., and Jaana Woiceshyn. "Why Businessmen Should Be Honest: The Argument from Rational Egoism." *Journal of Organizational Behavior* 16, no. 5 (September 1995): 405–14.

Lodewyckx, Esther. "Non-Profit Organizations." In *Financial Accounting: Fresh Perspectives*, edited by Roelien Theron, 425–54. Cape Town: Pearson Education South Africa, 2007.

Long, David. *Henry Ford: Industrialist*. New York: Cavendish Square Publishing, 2016.

Lucas Jr., Henry C. *The Search for Survival: Lessons from Disruptive Technologies*. Santa Barbara, CA: Praeger, 2012.

Lutz, David W. "Beyond Business Ethics." *Oikonomia: Journal of Ethics and Social Sciences* 2 (2003): 1–15.

MacFarquhar, Larissa. *Strangers Drowning: Voyages to the Brink of Moral Extremity*. New York: Penguin Press, 2015.

Machan, Tibor R. *Ayn Rand*. New York: Peter Lang, 1999.

———. "Business Ethics in a New Key." *Journal of Private Enterprise* 21, no. 2 (Spring 2006): 1–33.

———. *The Morality of Business: A Profession for Human Wealthcare*. New York: Springer, 2007.

———. *The Promise of Liberty: A Non-Utopian Vision*. Lanham, MD: Lexington Books, 2009.

Machiavelli, Niccolò. *The Prince*. Translated by Peter Bondanella and Mark Musa. Oxford: Oxford University Press, 1998.

Malthus, T. R. *An Essay on the Principle of Population*. Mineola, NY: Dover Publications, 2007.

Manchester, William. *A World Lit Only by Fire: The Medieval Mind and the Renaissance—Portrait of an Age*. New York: Hachette Book Group, 1992.

Mandeville, Bernard. "'The Grumbling Hive,' in *Fable of the Bees*." In *Economic Morality: Ancient to Modern Readings*, edited by Henry C. Clark and Eric Allison, 151–60. Lanham, MD: Lexington Books, 2015.

Martin, Roger L. "The Virtue Matrix: Calculating the Return on Corporate Responsibility." In *Harvard Business Review on Corporate Responsibility*, 83–103. Boston, MA: Harvard Business School Press, 2003.

Matten, Dirk, and Jeremy Moon. "Corporate Social Responsibility Education in Europe." *Journal of Business Ethics* 54, no. 4 (2004): 323–37.

Mattera, Jason. *Crapitalism: Liberals Who Make Millions Swiping Your Tax Dollars*. New York: Threshold Editions, 2014.

McCullough, David. *The Wright Brothers: The Dramatic Story Behind the Legend*. London: Simon & Schuster, 2015.

McKeown, Greg. *Essentialism: The Disciplined Pursuit of Less*. London: Virgin Books, 2014.

Melé, Domènec. "Corporate Social Responsibility Theories." In *The Oxford Handbook of Corporate Social Responsibility*, edited by Andrew Crane, Abagail McWilliams, Dirk Matten, Jeremy Moon, and Donald S. Siegel, 47–82. Oxford: Oxford University Press, 2009.

Mill, John Stuart. *Auguste Comte and Positivism*. London: Routledge, 1908.

Miller Jr., Fred D. *Out of the Mouths of Babes: The Infant Formula Controversy*. Bowling Green, OH: The Social Philosophy and Policy Center, 1983.

Moldova, György. *Ballpoint: A Tale of Genius and Grit, Perilous Times, and the Invention That Changed the Way We Write*. Translated by David Robert Evans. North Adams, MA: New Europe Books, 2012.

Moon, Jeremy. *Corporate Social Responsibility: A Very Short Introduction*. Oxford: Oxford University Press, 2014.

———. "Corporate Social Responsibility: An Overview." In *International Directory of Corporate Philanthropy*, 3–14. London: Europa Publications, 2002.

Muller, Mike. *The Baby Killer: A War on Want Investigation into the Promotion and Sale of Powdered Baby Milks in the Third World*. London: War on Want, 1974.

Munro, Roana. *Oranges and Sunshine*. Directed by Jim Loach. Movie. See-Saw Films, 2010.

Murguía, Salvador Jimenez. *Epic Fails: The Edsel, the Mullet, and Other Icons of Unpopular Culture*. Lanham, MD: Rowman & Littlefield Publishers, 2018.

Muthukrishna, Michael, and Joseph Henrich. "Innovation in the Collective Brain." *Philosophical Transactions* 371, no. 1690 (2016): 1–14.

Nader, Ralph. "The Case for Federal Chartering." In *Corporate Power in America*, edited by Ralph Nader and Mark J. Green, 67–93. New York: Grossman Publishers, 1973.

———. *Unsafe at Any Speed: The Designed-in Dangers of the American Automobile*. New York: Grossman, 1972.

Nathanson, Jeff. *Catch Me If You Can*. Directed by Steven Spielberg. Movie. DreamWorks, 2002.

Nicholson, Brian, Ron Babin, and Mary C. Lacity. "Introduction." In *Socially Responsible Outsourcing: Global Sourcing with Social Impact*, edited by Brian Nicholson, Ron Babin, and Mary C. Lacity, 1–15. London: Palgrave Macmillan UK, 2016.

Nielsen, Kai. *Why Be Moral?* Buffalo, NY: Prometheus Books, 1989.

Novak, Michael. *The Spirit of Democratic Capitalism*. Lanham, MD: Madison Books, 1991.

Oleson, Erik. "Fallout." Directed by Daniel Percival. In *The Man in the High Castle*. TV series. Amazon Studios, 2016.

Ollman, Bertell, ed. *Market Socialism: The Debate among Socialists*. New York: Routledge, 1998.

Österberg, Jan. *Self and Others: A Study of Ethical Egoism*. Dordrecht: Kluwer Academic Publishers, 1988.

Pape, Scott. *The Barefoot Investor: The Only Money Guide You'll Ever Need*. Milton, Queensland: John Wiley & Sons, 2017.

Pascal, Janet B. *Arthur Conan Doyle: Beyond Baker Street*. New York: Oxford University Press, 2000.

Pasles, Paul C. *Benjamin Franklin's Numbers: An Unsung Mathematical Odyssey*. Princeton: Princeton University Press, 2008.

Pasnau, Robert. *Thomas Aquinas on Human Nature: A Philosophical Study of* Summa Theologiae Ia 75–89. Cambridge: Cambridge University Press, 2002.

Peikoff, Leonard. *The DIM Hypothesis: Why the Lights of the West Are Going Out*. New York: New American Library, 2012.

———. *Objective Communication: Writing, Speaking, and Arguing*, edited by Barry Wood. New York: New American Library, 2013.

———. *Objectivism through Induction*. Audiotaped lecture. Irvine, CA: Ayn Rand Institute, 1997.

———. *Objectivism: The Philosophy of Ayn Rand*. New York: Meridian, 1993.

———. *The Ominous Parallels: The End of Freedom in America*. New York: Meridian, 1993.

———. *Understanding Objectivism: A Guide to Learning Ayn Rand's Philosophy*. New York: New American Library, 2012.

———. *Why Ancient Greece Is My Favorite Civilization*. Videotaped lecture. Irvine, CA: Ayn Rand Institute, 1997.

———. "Why Should One Act On Principle?" In *Why Businessmen Need Philosophy: The Capitalist's Guide to the Ideas Behind Ayn Rand's* Atlas Shrugged, edited by Debi Ghate and Richard E. Ralston, 233–48. New York: New American Library, 2011.

Pelonero, Catherine. *Kitty Genovese: A True Account of a Public Murder and Its Private Consequences*. New York: Skyhorse Publishing, 2014.

Pigden, Charles R. "Naturalism." In *A Companion to Ethics*, edited by Peter Singer, 421–31. Oxford: Blackwell Publishers, 1993.

Plato. "Republic." Translated by G. M. A. Grube. Translation revised by C. D. C. Reeve. In *Plato: Complete Works*, edited by John M. Cooper, 971–1223. Indianapolis: Hackett Publishing Company, 1997.

Podritske, Marlene, and Peter Schwartz. *Objectively Speaking: Ayn Rand Interviewed*. Lanham, MD: Lexington Books, 2009.

Poirot, Paul L. "He Gains Most Who Serves Best." *The Freeman* 25, no. 5 (May 1975): 313–16.

Pojman, Louis P., and James Fieser. *Ethics: Discovering Right and Wrong*. 7th ed. Boston, MA: Wadsworth, 2012.

Pope, Kamila. *Understanding Planned Obsolescence: Unsustainability through Production, Consumption and Waste Generation*. London: Kogan Page, 2017.

Porter, Michael E., and Mark R. Kramer. "The Competitive Advantage of Corporate Philanthropy." In *Harvard Business Review on Corporate Responsibility*, 27–64. Boston, MA: Harvard Business School Press, 2003.

Rachels, James, and Stuart Rachels. *The Elements of Moral Philosophy*. 5th ed. New York: McGraw-Hill, 2007.

Ramseyer, J. Mark. *Business Organizations*. Second ed. New York: Wolters Kluwer, 2017.

Rand, Ayn. "America's Persecuted Minority: Big Business." In *Capitalism: The Unknown Ideal*, 44–62. New York: Signet, 1967.
———. "The Anatomy of Compromise." In *Capitalism: The Unknown Ideal*, 144–49. New York: Signet, 1967.
———. "The Anti-Industrial Revolution." In *Return of the Primitive: The Anti-Industrial Revolution*, edited by Peter Schwartz, 270–90. New expanded edition of *The New Left: The Anti-Industrial Revolution*. New York: Meridian, 1999.
———. "Antitrust: The Rule of Unreason." In *The Voice of Reason: Essays in Objectivist Thought*, edited by Leonard Peikoff, 254–59. New York: Meridian, 1990.
———. "The Argument from Intimidation." In *The Virtue of Selfishness: A New Concept of Egoism*, 162–68. New York: Signet, 1964.
———. *The Art of Nonfiction: A Guide for Writers and Readers*. Edited by Robert Mayhew. New York: Plume, 2001.
———. *Atlas Shrugged*. New York: Signet, 1992.
———. "Bootleg Romanticism." In *The Romantic Manifesto: A Philosophy of Literature*, 129–41. Revised ed. New York: Signet, 1975.
———. "The Comprachicos." In *Return of the Primitive: The Anti-Industrial Revolution*, edited by Peter Schwartz, 51–95. New expanded edition of *The New Left: The Anti-Industrial Revolution*. New York: Meridian, 1999.
———. "The Ethics of Emergencies." In *The Virtue of Selfishness: A New Concept of Egoism*, 49–56. New York: Signet, 1964.
———. *For the New Intellectual: The Philosophy of Ayn Rand*. New York: Signet, 1961.
———. *The Fountainhead*. London: HarperCollins, 1994.
———. *Introduction to Objectivist Epistemology*. Edited by Harry Binswanger and Leonard Peikoff. Expanded second ed. New York: Meridian, 1990.
———. "Man's Rights." In *The Virtue of Selfishness: A New Concept of Egoism*, 108–17. New York: Signet, 1964.
———. "The Metaphysical Versus the Man-Made." In *Philosophy: Who Needs It*, 23–34. New York: Signet, 1984.
———. "The Objectivist Ethics." In *The Virtue of Selfishness: A New Concept of Egoism*, 13–39. New York: Signet, 1964.
———. "The Psycho-Epistemology of Art." In *The Romantic Manifesto: A Philosophy of Literature*, 15–24. Revised ed. New York: Signet, 1975.
———. "What Is Capitalism?" In *Capitalism: The Unknown Ideal*, 11–34. New York: Signet, 1967.
Ratigan, Dylan. *Greedy Bastards: How We Can Stop Corporate Communists, Banksters, and Other Vampires from Sucking America Dry*. New York: Simon & Schuster, 2012.
Reisman, George. *Capitalism: A Treatise on Economics*. Ottawa, IL: Jameson Books, 1998.
Rhea, Zane Ma. *Leading and Managing Indigenous Education in the Postcolonial World*. London: Routledge, 2015.
Ridley, Matt. *The Rational Optimist: How Prosperity Evolves*. London: Fourth Estate, 2011.
Robbins, Tim. *Dead Man Walking*. Directed by Tim Robbins. Movie. Gramercy Pictures, 1995.
Robertson, Thomas. *The Malthusian Moment: Global Population Growth and the Birth of American Environmentalism*. New Brunswick, NJ: Rutgers University Press, 2012.
Roemer, John E. *A Future for Socialism*. Cambridge, MA: Harvard University Press, 1994.
Salazar, José, and Bryan W. Husted. "Principals and Agents: Further Thoughts on the Friedmanite Critique of Corporate Social Responsibility." In *The Oxford Handbook of Corporate Social Responsibility*, edited by Andrew Crane, Abagail McWilliams, Dirk Matten, Jeremy Moon, and Donald S. Siegel, 137–55. Oxford: Oxford University Press, 2009.
Salmieri, Gregory. "Conceptualization and Justification." In *Concepts and Their Role in Knowledge: Reflections on Objectivist Epistemology*, edited by Allan Gotthelf and James G. Lennox, 41–84. Pittsburgh: University of Pittsburgh Press, 2013.
———. "Egoism and Altruism: Selfishness and Sacrifice." In *A Companion to Ayn Rand*, edited by Allan Gotthelf and Gregory Salmieri, 130–56. Malden, MA: John Wiley & Sons, 2016.

Sandel, Michael. *What Money Can't Buy: The Moral Limits of Markets*. London: Allen Lane, 2012.
Saunders, Jennifer. "Iso Tank." Directed by Bob Spiers. In *Absolutely Fabulous*. TV series. BBC, 1992.
Schlender, Brent, and Rick Tetzeli. *Becoming Steve Jobs: The Evolution of a Reckless Upstart into a Visionary Leader*. New York: Crown Business, 2015.
Schor, Juliet B., and Douglas B. Holt, eds. *The Consumer Society Reader*. New York: The New Press, 2000.
Schwartz, Gary T. "The Myth of the Ford Pinto Case." *Rutgers Law Review* 43 (1990): 1013–68.
Sennett, Richard. *The Corrosion of Character: The Personal Consequences of Work in the New Capitalism*. New York: W. W. Norton, 1998.
Shute, Nevil. *Trustee from the Toolroom*. London: Vintage, 2009.
Simon, Julian L. *The Ultimate Resource 2*. Revised ed. Princeton, NJ: Princeton University Press, 1996.
Simpson, Brian P. *Markets Don't Fail!* Lanham, MD: Lexington Books, 2005.
Simpson, Peter. *Goodness and Nature: A Defence of Ethical Naturalism*. Dordrecht: Martinus Nijhoff Publishers, 1987.
Smith, Adam. *The Wealth of Nations*. London: David Campbell Publishers, 1910.
Smith, Tara. *Ayn Rand's Normative Ethics: The Virtuous Egoist*. New York: Cambridge University Press, 2006.
———. "The Importance of the Subject in Objective Morality: Distinguishing Objective from Intrinsic Value." In *Objectivism, Subjectivism, and Relativism in Ethics*, edited by Ellen Frankel Paul, Fred D. Miller Jr., and Jeffery Paul, 126–48. Cambridge: Cambridge University Press, 2008.
———. "The Menace of Pragmatism." *The Objective Standard* 3, no. 3 (Fall 2008): 71–93.
———. "Money *Can* Buy Happiness." *Reason Papers* 26 (Summer 2003): 7–19.
———. "Unborrowed Vision: Independence and Egoism in *The Fountainhead*." In *Essays on Ayn Rand's* The Fountainhead, edited by Robert Mayhew, 285–304. Lanham, MD: Lexington Books, 2007.
———. *Viable Values: A Study of Life as the Root and Reward of Morality*. Lanham, MD: Rowman & Littlefield Publishers, 2000.
Smits, Katherine. *Applying Political Theory: Issues and Debates*. New York: Palgrave Macmillan, 2009.
Soper, Barry. "Kiwis Have Themselves to Blame for Obscene Bank Profits." *New Zealand Herald* (6 November 2018).
Sowell, Thomas. *Basic Economics: A Common Sense Guide to the Economy*. 4th ed. New York: Basic Books, 2011.
———. *The Housing Boom and Bust*. Revised ed. New York: Basic Books, 2010.
Spurlock, Morgan. *Super Size Me*. Directed by Morgan Spurlock. Movie. The Con, 2004.
Sternberg, Elaine. *Just Business: Business Ethics in Action*. 2nd ed. Oxford: Oxford University Press, 2000.
———. "The Need for Realism in Business Ethics." *Reason Papers* 31 (Fall 2009): 33–48.
Stone, Oliver, and Stanley Weiser. *Wall Street*. Directed by Oliver Stone. Movie. American Entertainment Partners, 1987.
Stossel, John. *No, They Can't: Why Government Fails—But Individuals Succeed*. New York: Threshold Editions, 2012.
Strouse, Jean. *Morgan: American Financier*. New York: Random House, 1999.
Swanton, Christine. "Virtues of Productivity versus Technicist Rationality." In *Economics and the Virtues: Building a New Moral Foundation*, edited by Jennifer Baker and Mark D. White, 185–201. Oxford: Oxford University Press, 2016.
Szenberg, Michael. "Philosophical Pattern Comparisons among Eminent Economists." *The American Economist* 37, no. 1 (Spring 1993): 10–20.
Tarbell, Ida M. *The History of the Standard Oil Company*. 2 vols. New York: Cosimo Classics, 2009.

Tarr, Robert. "Economic Theory and Conceptions of Value: Rand and Austrians versus the Mainstream." In *Foundations of a Free Society: Reflections on Ayn Rand's Political Philosophy*, edited by Gregory Salmieri and Robert Mayhew, 327–83. Pittsburgh: University of Pittsburgh Press, 2019.

Teays, Wanda. *Business Ethics through Movies: A Case Study Approach*. Chichester, West Sussex: John Wiley & Sons, 2015.

Thompson, C. Bradley. "Americanism and the Spirit of Liberty." In *A New Textbook of Americanism: The Politics of Ayn Rand*, edited by Jonathan Hoenig, 139–50. Chicago: Capitalistpig Publications, 2018.

Twitchell, James. "Two Cheers for Materialism." In *The Consumer Society Reader*, edited by Juliet B. Schor and Douglas B. Holt, 281–90. New York: The New Press, 2000.

Veatch, Henry B. *Human Rights: Fact or Fancy?* Baton Rouge: Louisiana State University Press, 1985.

———. "Might 'Objectivism' Ever Become Academically Respectable?" *Liberty* 5, no. 3 (January 1992): 61–65.

Veatch, Henry B., and Francis H. Parker. *Logic as a Human Instrument*. New York: Harper & Row, 1959.

Vogel, David. "The Ethical Roots of Business Ethics." *Business Ethics Quarterly* 1, no. 1 (January 1991): 101–20.

———. *The Market for Virtue: The Potential and Limits of Corporate Social Responsibility*. Washington, DC: The Brookings Institution, 2006.

von Mises, Ludwig. *Bureaucracy*. Edited by Bettina Bien Greaves. Indianapolis: Liberty Fund, 2007.

Vornholt, John. *Antimatter*. New York: Pocket Books, 1994.

Walsh, George. *The Role of Religion in History*. New Brunswick: Transaction Publishers, 1998.

Walsh, Joan. *What's the Matter with White People? Finding Our Way in the Next America*. New York: Touchstone, 2012.

Ward, James. *The Perfection of the Paper Clip: Curious Tales of Invention, Accidental Genius, and Stationery Obsession*. New York: Touchstone, 2014.

Weber, Jessica Ketcham. "Buy Nothing Day." In *Encyclopedia of Activism and Social Justice*, edited by Gary L. Anderson and Kathryn G. Herr, 285–86. Thousand Oaks, CA: SAGE Publications, 2007.

Weber, Max. "The Spirit of Capitalism." In *Economic Morality: Ancient to Modern Readings*, edited by Henry C. Clark and Eric Allison, 285–89. Lanham, MD: Lexington Books, 2015.

Weir, Alison. *Henry VIII: The King and His Court*. New York: Ballantine Books, 2008.

White, Robert. "Ayn Rand versus Adam Smith." *The Journal of Ayn Rand Studies* 7, no. 1 (Fall 2005): 141–80.

———. "Corporations Are People Too: An Argument for Corporate Moral Personhood." *The Journal of Ayn Rand Studies* 14, no. 2 (December 2014): 97–123.

———. "Egoless Egoists: The Second-Hand Lives of Mad Men." In *Mad Men and Philosophy: Nothing Is as It Seems*, edited by Rod Carveth and James B. South, 79–94. Hoboken, NJ: John Wiley & Sons, 2010.

———. "Profit Maximization Does Not Necessitate Profit Prioritization." *The Journal of Ayn Rand Studies* 17, no. 2 (December 2017): 201–26.

———. "Two Sides of Think Different." In *Steve Jobs and Philosophy: For Those Who Think Different*, edited by Shawn E. Klein, 127–36. Chicago: Open Court, 2015.

Wild, John, and J. L. Coblitz. "On the Distinction between the Analytic and the Synthetic." *Philosophy and Phenomenological Research* 8, no. 4 (June 1948): 651–67.

Windsor, Duane. "Corporate Social Responsibility: Three Key Approaches." *Journal of Management Studies* 43, no. 1 (January 2006): 93–114.

Winter, Terence. *The Wolf of Wall Street*. Directed by Martin Scorsese. Movie. Red Granite Pictures, 2013.

Woiceshyn, Jaana. *How to Be Profitable and Moral: A Rational Egoist Approach to Business*. Lanham, MD: Hamilton Books, 2012.

———. "Lessons from 'Good Minds': How CEOs Use Intuition, Analysis and Guiding Principles to Make Strategic Decisions." *Long Range Planning* 42, no. 3 (2009): 298–319.

Wolff, Richard. *Democracy at Work: A Cure for Capitalism*. Chicago: Haymarket Books, 2012.

Wormald, B. H. G. *Francis Bacon: History, Politics and Science, 1561–1626*. Cambridge: Cambridge University Press, 1993.

Younkins, Edward W. *Exploring Capitalist Fiction: Business through Literature and Film*. Lanham, MD: Lexington Books, 2014.

———. "Preface." In *Capitalism and Commerce in Imaginative Literature: Perspectives on Business from Novels and Plays*, edited by Edward W. Younkins, xi–xii. Lanham, MD: Lexington Books, 2016.

The Z Why. Wellington: Z Energy, 2017.

Index

About the Author

Robert White is dean of faculty and assistant professor of philosophy at the American University in Bulgaria. He chaired the Department of Business for five years before being appointed dean in 2016. He teaches courses on business ethics and the philosophy of capitalism. He holds an honors degree in law from the University of Waikato and a PhD in moral and political theory from the University of Auckland. He has contributed chapters to *Mad Men and Philosophy*, published as part of the Blackwell Philosophy and Pop Culture series, and *Steve Jobs and Philosophy*, published as part of the Open Court Popular Culture and Philosophy series. He has published in *Ethical Perspectives* and *The Journal of Ayn Rand Studies*. He has written on Adam Smith, corporate personhood, the distinction between profit maximization and profit prioritization, and the meaning of "selfishness."

www.ingramcontent.com/pod-product-compliance
Ingram Content Group UK Ltd.
Pitfield, Milton Keynes, MK11 3LW, UK
UKHW040232290926
15471UKWH00002B/155

9 781498 542654